At Work in Paris

AT WORK IN PARIS

Raymond Mason
on Art and Artists

Title-page: Raymond Mason, *The Crowd* (detail), 1969

The majority of these pieces were originally written in French and have been translated
into English by Andrew Doughty in collaboration with the author

This edition of *At Work in Paris: Raymond Mason on Art and Artists*
© 2003 Thames & Hudson Ltd, London
Originally published in French by Edizioni d'Arte Fratelli Pozzo
Art et Artistes © 2000 Raymond Mason
English text and translation © 2003 Raymond Mason

First published in hardback in the United States of America in 2003 by
Thames & Hudson Inc., 500 Fifth Avenue, New York, New York 10110

thamesandhudsonusa.com

Library of Congress Catalog Card Number 2002113177
ISBN 0-500-51114-4

Printed and bound in Italy by Conti Tipocolor

Contents

Raymond Mason drawing rooftops of Paris, 1976. Photograph by Henri Cartier-Bresson

My Early Artistic Life in Birmingham

THE EVENTS OF MY CHILDHOOD IN BIRMINGHAM ARE bathed in what seems to me now as a general flow of happiness. As the only son of two devoted parents, how could it have been otherwise for me? Yet, since I was born in 1922, my childhood followed its course across a troubled period of economic crises. Mind you, I was a working-class boy living in the simplest of working-class areas, and as a taxi driver my father earned so little that a world financial crash could probably have little further effect on us. At least Dad was never out of work, and this was certainly due to the fact that in his early days in Scotland he had been a gifted and noted motor mechanic, driving some of the earliest cars on the road, and, although he had come down in the world, his boss Mr Wheatley was too smart not to know that if they lost 'Andy' they might as well close down the garage.

My mother was a vivacious, dark-haired Birmingham woman from publican stock whose father, Frederick Brown, was quite a force in his trade and in political circles – literally so, since he was reputed capable of throwing unwanted customers from the steps of the various big pubs he handled to the middle of the tram-lines. Luckily for me, he didn't deal out this drastic treatment to the young Andrew Mason who, arriving from his native Stirling, had taken lodgings in Summer Road, off Lee Bank Road, and frequented my grandfather's pub nearby. Because it was here he met the barmaid, the publican's daughter Edith and, as can be guessed, his future wife and my mother.

I never knew my grandfather, but Grannie had delighted my early youth by running first a tea shop opposite Dudley Road Hospital with the morose customers that can be imagined and then, and hence the delight, a sweet-shop in Bell Bank Road. But that big pub on the corner of Lee Bank Road and Ryland Street I knew well, at least by sight. All my background was food and drink since my Scottish side, with whom we had lost touch, were in catering and my Uncle Willie, after running a successful restaurant in Glasgow, built himself a new hotel, the Loch Lomond Hotel, in Balloch at the foot of the loch. After my father died and when I was already well installed in Paris, Mother made many appeals for me to come back home to help her run a pub, saying that it was my natural calling 'to return to the liquid'.

All my life in Birmingham was spent in Wheeleys Lane on the poor edge of stately Edgbaston; and there, where Wheeleys Lane ceased and Wheeleys Road began, was the actual frontier between red-brick terraces and great gardened houses. Our house in that all-brick street was the typical three tiny rooms, one above the other, joined by an almost vertical staircase. At the back, it gave onto the common courtyard and the common lavatories and wash-house. This courtyard was the province, the state, almost the entire world for us youngsters living in the adjoining houses. There we spent our entire time outside school, playing – with bats, too bad for the windows – lighting bonfires on 5 November, celebrating holidays because nobody went away, neither the children nor their parents. Up to my teens, I'd been to the seaside for a day's outing maybe three times. And when I volunteered for the Navy in 1940, it was literally to 'see the sea'.

Looming on the other side of our narrow street was a giant red-brick factory. But it was a peaceful giant and even a secretive one, because I suddenly realize that in twenty years I never even knew what it produced. All the same it was there, an immense presence which must have marked my childhood at least visually, and later on in life I would mention it immodestly as my Mont Saint-Victoire* and felt obscurely that one day my art would have to pass that way. Such a thought, emerging at a time when I was engaged solely in making bronzes, was strange but was subsequently realized in my polychrome sculptures. And many of my large sculptures share a characteristic abrupt climb-up.

At all events I had time to gaze both at the street and its factory, since from infancy I was afflicted by asthma and, because I could not go to school in the morning, would sit in an armchair taking in not only the asthma powder burning on the arm of the chair but also the street's little activity which I

---

* Paul Cézanne's vision was dominated by this mountain. As he always viewed it from his native town of Aix-en-Provence, he saw the conical form of its profile. It is, in fact, a flat-topped mountain many kilometres long.

could see through the parted window curtain. This would be the going to and fro of our neighbours between the two poles of our strip of pavement. At one end was a grocery and sweet-shop, at the other a pub. Up and down the street would roll daily a dozen cars and as many horse-drawn delivery vans. On May Day, heavy cart-horses from Davenport's Brewery, all decorated with coloured papers and ribbons, would be lined up along our very pavement, and I could almost have leant out of the window and stroked their handsome heads. I never did though because the smell of a horse is particularly bad for an asthmatic and I had caught this complaint when taken, a babe in arms, to a circus. As a child I went to a darling of a school, also all red-brick, St Thomas's Church of England. Before it, on the opposite corner of Granville Street, towered the mighty church of St Thomas itself, a fine example of the early nineteenth century's classical revival. Sadly, it was hit by a landmine during the last war and, even more sadly, never repaired. Despite my irregular attendance I was a bright boy at school (thanks to my teacher Mr Nicholls, to whom I here pay tribute) and, because of my sedentary habits, perhaps a bit of a swot. My failure to enter grammar school was due to exam nerves, but I never had reason to regret the excellent George Dixon Secondary School where fate had placed me. I began outstandingly, arriving top of the form the first year, but the little swot was soon replaced by a turbulent youngster who sank rapidly to the depths of most classes. Oddly enough, in the days of my splendour I had received as first prize – on my demand – a Cassell's English–French dictionary; French! The subject in which I was fifty-seventh out of sixty-three at the end of my schooling. This same volume, incredibly battered, is still by my side and has carried me through fifty and more years in France and maybe will come to my assistance – in the reverse direction – in order to record these memories.

I must not forget to mention the George Dixon's school song, nor indeed its colours. Green and red were our blazers and caps. And our song began:

> We will sing of the green and red
> As we march with steady tread…

This is worth mentioning when I explain that my full name is Raymond Greig Mason; that the Greigs of Stirling descend from the great clan of the

MacGregors (Grieg, the marvellous Norwegian composer, too); and that the MacGregor tartan is the most violent contrast of red and green. (I wore a MacGregor tam o'shanter in Paris at one period, much to the joy of the Parisians who love the Scots, until my wife, who couldn't stand its colours, threw it away.) Then, too, my early paintings and my later coloured sculptures played heavily on the duality of red and green – the industrial city, the country outside. The fruit and vegetables of the Paris market, the vineyard gone red of my *Grape-Pickers*, the red brick of *A Tragedy in the North* and my Midi landscapes. I think one could also say that the violent contrast of these colours is symptomatic of how a sculptor will paint. Red and green. There's an explosion and a space is created between the two.

Last of all, George Dixon's played a decisive role in my life in the shape of its art teacher, Mr Kedwards. From my earliest childhood I had drawn, underneath furniture as a crawler and later at the family table, like all children I suppose for family approval, in my case my father's.* But, unlike other children, what I produced were not the flamboyant creations seemingly at the threshold of modern art, but painstaking copies of this and that. My only originality was that afterwards I would glue the watercolours onto wood and then cut them out with a fret-saw to make an object in relief. A miniature form of what, sixty years later, I am still occupied in doing.

During elementary and secondary school I became more adept at drawing recognizably, and my prosaic efforts were often displayed with tickled pleasure by teachers and family friends. I was witnessing for the first time the wondrous awe with which normal folk regard the hand capable of 'catching a likeness'. Since I was good at his subject, Mr Kedwards suggested that I should take the examination for the Birmingham art school. 'But I don't want to be

---

* If my mother had an eye for the finer aspect of objects and decoration which could have flowered in other conditions, it was my father who had the 'artistic streak'. Some of the Scottish side were musical, and in the evenings at table while I drew he would sometimes carve himself a wooden flute and pipe a tune from his youth. Or, and the sheer uselessness of the enterprise enraged my mother, he would write long letters in copperplate handwriting finely twisted in, yes, copper wire and then attached to stiff paper. He could make anything with his hands – which is why he had come to Birmingham.

an artist,' I protested. I wanted to be a research chemist since I was achieving my best marks in years in chemistry simply because 'Piggy' Walker, the chemistry teacher, was the best in the school. However, Kedwards talked me into it, saying that I would get two days off and would meet pretty girls. I took the exam and came out top of the Midlands, with a grant offered into the bargain. I don't know how my enthusiasm for chemistry wilted so immediately in favour of art but, in any case, after the fifth form I left to enter the Birmingham College of Arts and Crafts.

Then my life changed. I did indeed meet pretty girls of whom art schools have an unlimited store, but love in all its forms invaded the callow creature that I was and the girls seemed just like angels fluttering around the great subject itself. Beauty. The beauty of great art, which slowly began to penetrate me through the primitive lantern lectures and the approximative black and white printed reproductions of those days. The beauty of music, because the gramophone was an all-important object in the life class where older or wiser students than me would bring sublime, and for me totally new, recordings of classical music. The beauty of the outer world where we made excursions to draw the great churches and mansions of the Midlands, all standing imperial in the lush, leafy countryside which in those days began as soon as our city stopped. Then, of course, the City Museum and Art Galleries were just opposite the school. How much did I see in their dimly lit and even grimly lit halls, so different from today?

All I can say is that about a dozen years ago, looking through a book on English painting, I realized that some of the paintings I really like belong to my native city, in particular *The Last of England* by Ford Madox Brown. I remember that as a boy I had enjoyed the glamour of the Pre-Raphaelite history paintings, but that as an art student I lost interest in this movement precisely because its paintings were remote in time.* Our art teachers were

---

* Ford Madox Brown was not a Pre-Raphaelite because he was not an idealist. Courbet said that realism is the negation of ideals and Ford Madox Brown was a fine realist. However, he did have the quality of the original Pre-Raphaelites, Masaccio, della Francesca and company: he could compose. And so, to be fair, could Holman Hunt. What, after all, is composition but bringing everything together, including all the emotions from grin to grimace? This we see in

good; looking back, mythically so. Apart from Fleetwood Walker (who, I was happy to read recently, had done his best to promote interest in L.S. Lowry), none were professional artists, but pedagogues they certainly were. We respected them, like Stubbington the life master, and some we even feared, like Smith the composition master. So it was a great moment in my life when one night I was invited to dinner by these two awesome figures who shared a house in Harborne for the days they taught in Birmingham. It was a damp summer night and, after the meal, the french windows open onto their deep garden, they played me a recording of Brahms's violin concerto. I can never hear the first movement of this superb work without instantly reliving that moment of beauty.

I had hardly reached the stage of painting, after a year or two of drawing, when the war broke out. I volunteered for the Royal Navy not only for the reasons I have given but also because I felt capable of finishing off the war with the Germans single-handed – a sentiment fortunately shared with most of the other chaps of my age.

Since I'm talking about Birmingham, I won't follow up my time in the Navy except to say that when I was finally invalided out in 1942 and returned to art school, the Allied war effort seemed to take a turn for the better. I didn't stay much longer at the Birmingham College of Arts and Crafts: just long enough to win a Royal Scholarship for Painting to the Royal College of Art, but I can be modest about this since the art schools of Great Britain were then composed almost entirely of girls.

Before I left I met an artist – a distinguished young man who, with his drooping moustache, looked a little like Marcel Proust, and who attended evening classes. An evening class where, one night, I blew in to ask if anyone could play chess. 'Yes,' said the man, whose name was Harry Blomberg. He could indeed, and over the years he generally beat me. Harry's father was the Swedish consul in Birmingham and he'd been brought to this country

FMB's Manchester murals, which I applaud because early Italian frescoes became a central influence on my work, to the point where I describe my coloured sculpture compositions as three-dimensional frescoes. My interest in composition originated at the Birmingham art school, particularly with regard to the work of Stanley Spencer.

and this town when a babe in arms. He was Swedish by nationality and exempt from military service, so he was working in his father's industry which made tubes, but Harry, who had an office and even a secretary, spent his days reading Dostoyevsky behind his files and his evenings studying art. But he was already painting pictures which made a great effect on me. This super-dilettante, with his cushy home in Solihull (where I first ate asparagus and began at the white end like celery until I noticed the consul and his family eating the green), his interest was the dirty, dipping streets of lower Birmingham, painting their gleaming damp bricks in deep reds with dark skies and the black accents of doors and windows. After an unsuccessful term at the Royal College (which was at that time evacuated to Ambleside in the Lake District and where all I did was to draw the hill opposite), I returned home and shared a flat with Harry. Then we painted night and day for six months, earning our living by painting portraits and doing odd jobs, Harry having renounced his family job. Because of this his father was vastly irate with me, but inwardly I forgave him because he had known Sibelius and had all the rare recordings of the Sibelius Society, which Harry transferred to the flat. I could see the latter turning out his beautiful cityscapes, yet, although charmed and convinced, I did nothing but portraits, still-lifes and an occasional view from the window, as though I felt my inferiority.

Indeed, I was still a student and he was an artist, which is exactly what the critic of the *Birmingham Post* very correctly said when Harry and I put up a little exhibition of our work in our top-floor flat in Pershore Road. The rest of the house was full of drinking, fighting Irish workers. One of a mere handful of visitors was a young man with heavy spectacles who said he was a science student, and he looked it. In his odd, dreamy way he asked us why we continued to paint in oils and not with ultra-violet colours. Seeing that we were astonished and sceptical, he invited us to his laboratory at Birmingham University and there, a night or two later, we painted in the famous colours. But they weren't too good to look at when the room wasn't in darkness, since they all had the same pinky-grey tone which, for Maurice the scientist, was a mere detail, but for us painters was an insurmountable handicap which made this attempt our last. Then we lost touch with our scientist, although we heard that he had been to California to work on the atomic bomb. Later, Harry maintained a friendship with Maurice; they were both older than me, but I believe I hadn't seen the latter in years before coming across him one day in Oxford Street on a brief visit to England. When I said, 'Hello, Maurice, what are you up to?' his reply was so evasive that when we parted I shook my head with regret, sorry that such a remarkable young student should have gone to seed. Later that year I read in Paris that Professor Maurice Wilkins had been awarded the Nobel Prize for his breakthrough with James Watson and Francis Crick on the structure of DNA, and I realized why I hadn't understood a word of that Oxford Street conversation.

My encounter with Harry Blomberg and his painting, his culture too, had come to complete my education in my native city. Up to then I had lived happily among its warm bricks. Our house was very near town, so as a boy I had walked there constantly, returning home from the public library loaded with books, while the deer on Mitchell and Butler's lamp-lit sign on the corner of John Bright Street leapt from right to left, so happy it was to see me. And later, the art school being right in the heart of town, it meant that I had wandered about all these years perfectly satisfied and even proud of what I saw, although, by the time I met Blomberg, I was beginning to realize that the rest of the world considered us, our factories, our slums, as champions of ugliness. Now I could suddenly judge it as an artist would his subject. Why, it was a painter's dream, it was so beautiful.* And there wasn't only the setting, the decor. Its citizens, the actors, were solidly present, performing significant, useful tasks. The whole scene had a graphic density which haunts me still, and a recent visit to the North of England, after so many years abroad, confirmed to me that our industrial cities had the wholeness not of handsome sites and prodigious monuments but of decisively shaped buildings encompassing the human act. With what variety! Yes, I know, the inhuman factories, the crushing mills, yet from it all springs the saga of the working man. What did I learn from my early

---

* I've already repeated this word several times and I do so without a blush. That, in case our contemporary art world has forgotten, is what art is all about.

years in Birmingham? Why, that. What is important is man. Sitting on pavements with a score of other children, living a life of community by the sheer necessity of existence, could only inculcate in me a spirit of fellowship. It did.

When my feelings were beginning to crystallize artistically, my earliest admiration was obviously for Van Gogh, who had lived and portrayed the industrial scene with what seemed like contemporary rigour. The world of Van Gogh is a peopled world. Factories or farm-fields, man is always present. Of course, Van Gogh was also France and its painting, so, progressively, I lifted my eyes from my home town to look abroad. Harry had married a beautiful French painter who talked about Paris. We had begun to frequent the company of one or two modern artists of Birmingham, John Melville and Conroy Maddox, and also John's brother Robert, already a famous art critic as a result of his book on Picasso. I left Birmingham for the Slade School, then to Oxford, and towards the end of the war settled in an empty house in London. From London, as soon as war was over, I left for Paris with Harry and his wife, Mimi.

There, a difficult if exalting life awaited me and the years went by quickly. I made one or two short visits home, and Mother a few trips to France. My first longer stay was, alas, when she died, in 1958. After the funeral I went back to live in Wheeleys Lane, this time to sell the furniture and close up the house. That week was rainy, but I managed to make several very complete watercolours of the street, the factory and its surroundings. It was a necessity. My mother was dead and clearly the city I knew was dying. Around me the bulldozer had cleared away the houses I had known. Looking down Lee Bank Hill, all was waste ground. Gone the pub of my grandfather, gone my past.

I have related elsewhere how the last night before leaving for Paris I returned to look at this scene. All day it had rained but now the clouds rolled away and suddenly a great sunset lit up the red-brick city.* With emotion I realized that when that sun sank, the moon of modern times

* On my return to Paris, I made my last oil painting of this subject entitled *Birmingham in Memoriam 1958*, in memory of my mother and my city.

would rise and all would be white concrete. I was almost right except that high-rises leave room for greenery. My red-brick Wheeleys Lane is now a strip of grass. Green.

Ginette Neveu and Roger Désormière

A S A YOUNG MAN, I OFTEN WENT TO HEAR THE BIRM-
ingham Symphony Orchestra, conducted by Leslie Heward, which in those days played in the Town Hall at the very centre of my native city. In its heyday in the latter part of the nineteenth century, Birmingham, whose harsh, down-to-earth existence as the first manufacturing town in history (the factory was invented there) had curiously long inspired a love of music, commissioned important works from the leading musicians of the day. Felix Mendelssohn composed and conducted his oratorio *Elijah*, and Antonin Dvorak his *Requiem*, for Birmingham and its Town Hall.

As a student at the Central College of Arts and Crafts, I was a mere hundred and fifty yards from the prestigious concert hall, and to earn the pocket money all young men need I would sometimes work there as an attendant, taking tickets and showing people to their seats. On one occasion I was backstage when I heard a strange air coming from the main dressing room. The concert that evening was being given by the celebrated Italian tenor Benjamino Gigli, whose *La Bohème* I would come to know by heart. The door was open, and I saw him fixing his bow-tie, while, to 'fix' his voice, he was quite simply humming 'Roll Out the Barrel', a popular refrain in those early months of the *drôle de guerre* in 1939.

I remember the marvellous conductor Sir Thomas Beecham leading his own orchestra, the Royal Philharmonic, through passages of Berlioz's *The Trojans* (long before Colin Davis) and berating the audience – myself, as it happens, pulling my seat down with its noisy springs slightly too late.

The most moving occasion, however, was when the Orchestre de la Société des Concerts du Conservatoire turned up at the end of the war with the great French conductor Roger Désormière and the violinist Ginette Neveu. She was playing the Beethoven, but between them, of course, they represented France, and the audience was in seventh heaven. The first movement of the concerto was so beautiful and passionate beneath the bow of this great violinist that, against all ethics and aware of the fact, I shouted 'Bravo!' I was sitting a short way back from the orchestra; glancing round, Neveu said 'Merci' before starting on the slow movement. With my French-speaking friends I went to pay homage to these distinguished French musicians, both destined to vanish from the scene a few years later, Ginette Neveu in the plane crash that would cost her her life in 1949, and Désormière, the incomparable conductor of *Pelléas et Mélisande*, as the result of a stroke in 1952 that left him mentally diminished until his death in 1963.

Not long after the concert, I made a little painting of Mademoiselle Neveu. I showed it at my exhibition in London before leaving for France, but had forgotten all about it until twenty years ago, in 1982, when the Assistant Keeper of Modern Pictures at the Tate Gallery in London, Richard Morphet, discovered it in the Swindon Art Gallery and contacted me about it, marking the beginning of our friendship.

The then conductor of the Birmingham Symphony Orchestra was Simon Rattle, already justly famous and well known in France. In 1991, I returned to Birmingham to attend his last concert at the Town Hall before the move to the brand-new Symphony Hall with its awe-inspiring acoustics.

The local council offered me a special seat, champagne during the interval
and a meeting after the concert with Simon Rattle. His female soloist that
evening was French, and I told him of the coincidence that my last concert in
the Town Hall, almost fifty years earlier, had also featured a French woman,
conducted by Roger Désormière. Rattle couldn't possibly have known
Neveu, but he was enthralled to hear the French conductor's name, since he
was preparing his own recording of *Pelléas et Mélisande* and Désormière was
his absolute touchstone. Was he aware at the time that Roger Désormière
was also his precursor in reanimating the baroque music that was soon to
tempt Sir Simon, as he has since become?

Francis Poulenc

IN THE EARLY MONTHS OF 1946, A LARGE COLLECTION
of paintings came up for auction at the Grand Hotel in Birmingham. A
copy of the catalogue fell into our hands, artists from Birmingham.
Stupefying. Announced there were 'paintings' (sic) by Giotto, Fra Angelico,
Raphael, Michelangelo and all the great names of Western painting, including Picasso.

Our presence at the hotel the following day seriously hotted up the auction. From the back of the hall we denounced the succession of daubings that
the auctioneers had the nerve to present. There was a painting signed in a
florid modern hand 'Fra Angelico'! 'The paint isn't dry,' we shouted gleefully
at the sight of these 'Old Masters'. At the end of the day, a maudlin, pitiful
painting appeared, supposedly by Renoir, depicting a young girl looking
round, entitled *Where Are my Glasses?* The next painting was nothing but a
triangle, bearing the signature 'Picasso'.

At that moment, a loud guffaw revealed a man standing behind us in a
camel-hair coat. He was French, however, and in those days I didn't speak the
language. Mimi and Harry engaged him in conversation. It was Francis
Poulenc, who had come to Birmingham to give a recital with the tenor Pierre
Bernac and was staying at the Grand Hotel. He couldn't wait, he said, to tell
his friend Picasso the affront done to his name. Seeing that we fully shared

his views, he handed all three of us tickets for his concert that evening. The concert was way over my head, partly because I couldn't understand French, but also because, as a music lover, I didn't much care for Bernac's voice.

Ten years later, I met Poulenc again at Carmen Baron's salon in Paris, but didn't speak to him. He had a group of friends round him, laughing at his caustic humour. A few years later, at the mansion of Marie-Laure de Noailles, I spoke to the man at last: 'Maître, you are certainly unaware that the back of your apartment on the rue de Médicis overlooks the courtyard where I have my studio. I often have the pleasure of hearing you at the piano.' Poulenc stared at me for a moment, then said in his affected voice: 'My dear sir, that must be my maid.'

Henry Moore

IN MY LAST YEAR IN ENGLAND, ON 7 MARCH 1946 TO BE PRE-cise, I walked up to Hampstead to visit Henry Moore. It was as though I had wanted to pay tribute to the art of my country through its most distinguished representative. In the small studio, I found him on all fours trying unsuccessfully to light a small coal stove. While I waited respectfully, a thought crossed my mind: how was it that Henry Moore, a miner's son, was incapable of lighting a coal fire? I offered to do it for him, which he accepted with relief, and soon the first flames sprang up. At that moment, the phone rang and Moore rushed to get it. He returned with a big smile on his face. The maternity hospital had just announced the birth of a daughter – at last the child he and his wife had longed for all those years. That was why Henry had been unable to light his stove that morning. Almost forty years later, at the cocktail party given for his huge exhibition in Paris, we were sitting on a sofa together. He was getting on in years and his feet, I noticed, didn't touch the floor, but he said to me: 'Raymond, do you remember the first time we met?' 'Oh perfectly, Henry,' I replied.

In 1952, the Musée National d'Art Moderne in Paris had presented a large exhibition of works by Henry Moore, who was already world-famous thanks to the activities of the British Council. I went round the exhibition with Alberto Giacometti, serving as an interpreter between him and Moore, since neither of them spoke the other's language. Moore said straight off that he had seen a marvellous sculpture by Alberto that very morning in the rue de Seine. 'What!' said Giacometti, 'I haven't even begun!' The reply came as a great disappointment to Henry, who thought he was conducting a conversation on the heights between two great artists, but he recovered to ask Giacometti when he would be coming to England. 'Shortly,' replied Alberto with great conviction, which for anyone who knew him meant never. 'When you do,' said Henry Moore, 'you can stay either at my house in town or in the country.' I couldn't think how to translate this last remark for Giacometti, since he was hostile to any form of possessions, happy with his three-by-four-metre studio with a mound of plaster in the middle.

The following day, a cocktail party was held for the exhibition, for which the British Council had bizarrely chosen a luxury hotel, the Plaza Athénée. When I arrived I saw a trail of white footprints running all the way along the red carpet of the hotel, then turning right into the reception room. They were the footprints of Alberto Giacometti, who had called a taxi to his studio then climbed straight in. There were a lot of people at the cocktail party, in addition to Giacometti: Léger, Le Corbusier, Zadkine and a crowd of other important names. Hardly anyone spoke English, however, and Henry, who couldn't speak a word of French, was eager to talk. He pushed me up against a wall for a hearty chat between Englishmen. 'Raymond, when are you moving back to England?' 'It's funny you should ask, I just renewed my French identity card this morning.' Henry tut-tutted. 'What a shame. I'm very fond of Paris, you know, it's great fun here, but to get any serious work done you should come back to England. What's more, we have a fine little team of up-and-coming sculptors.' I felt as though I was listening to the captain of a cricket side announcing the next season's line-up. He was in fact referring to Butler, Chadwick, Armitage, Paolozzi and Turnbull.

A few years later, in 1954, I had my first exhibition in London at the Beaux-Arts Gallery, run by the formidable Helen Lessore. The private view took place on the same day as Henry Moore's at the Leicester Galleries, his first one-man show there since the war. The following day an article appeared in the *New Statesman* by John Berger, a highly regarded critic at the time. He hadn't liked the Moore exhibition and in his usual brisk manner didn't hesitate to say so. And, to my utter astonishment, he concluded with a short sentence urging all those who disliked stones and bones to visit the Raymond Mason exhibition to see sculptures which dealt with human beings!

The day after the article appeared, I received a telephone call at the gallery from the London offices of the Arts Council, informing me that Henry Moore had been very upset by what had been said. 'You're a friend of Henry's, aren't you? In that case, we think it would be a good idea if you apologized to him.' Before describing my astonishment at such a request, I should note that the episode combines two factors which have always accompanied Moore's career: his extreme sensitivity to anything that might undermine his fame, and the corresponding actions undertaken by the official bodies, the Arts Council and the British Council, to promote the national sculptor. I note with amusement that at the very moment I write these lines, 18 June 1992, Queen Elizabeth II is inaugurating an exhibition of giant sculptures by Moore at the Bagatelle, organized by the British Council.

Needless to say, I refused to apologize to the aggrieved sculptor. After all, I had had nothing to do with the article, since I didn't even know John Berger. I was greatly surprised, then, when the following day the same smooth voice informed me that Henry was very touched that I was so 'upset' (sic) and had invited me to visit him at his home in Much Hadham. An Arts Council car would pick me up at the Beaux-Arts Gallery at two o'clock.

It was largely out of curiosity, I think, that Mimi and I decided to go. It was all very comical, after all. Here was this extremely famous man fussing in this way over a total young unknown like myself. Things became even more outlandish when we arrived, since Moore was waiting for us when we stepped down from the car, flanked by a photographer who duly took a photo of Moore and myself shaking hands. This was followed by a visit to the studios to admire his work, which, even at that time, I was already much less interested in.

Another extravagant moment was when Moore patted a large reclining figure, in reality an undulation of pipe-like forms, and declared: 'Because, after all, Raymond, I am the one who invented the hole,' a remark worthy of *Punch*.

It isn't true, of course, that Moore invented the hole, since it had long existed in primitive art and had been taken up at the turn of the century by Archipenko, Zadkine, Brancusi and others. When discussing his style, Moore willingly admits to the influence of Mexican and Aztec sculpture, gleaned from the British Museum, but passes over in silence the crucial influence of the great Picasso nudes of the 1920s, the latest novelty to arrive from Paris when Moore left art school. Nor should we forget to take a look at certain works of de Chirico, particularly *The Disquieting Muses* with the town of Ferrara in the background.

To return to our visit to Moore. With great courteousness, he then showed us round the house. (This was in 1954, it should be remembered, far removed from the years to come when Much Hadham would be invaded by officials and museum directors from all over the globe.) It was a farmhouse that had the changes of levels and unexpected aspects, in a word the charm, found in all dwellings built up out of necessity over the generations. Henry led the way, and I noticed that before entering a room he would bend down to switch on the display cases, where selected items of Aztec and primitive art alternated with small objects and bronzes of his own making. What with the comfort and the drinks trays, you might have been in the home of a country gentleman who owned a fine collection of Henry Moores.

After having tea in the greenhouse and tasting Mrs Moore's home-made cake, Henry suggested we take a stroll round the grounds (with the possibility of admiring more sculptures) while waiting for dinner, but Mimi, making one of those snap decisions to which women are sometimes prone, whispered in my ear: 'Forget the dinner, we're going back to London.' Henry Moore was taken aback by our announcement and I can understand that. Like all artists, he enjoyed that moment in the evening when you sat around a table conversing about art. Yet once we were in the train – the chauffeur wasn't due back until later – I was pleased to have shown a bit of backbone. I also had in mind a remark Henry had made in the studio about Giacometti, since he had seen me with him in Paris: 'Yes, but Alberto has his brother. He's very lucky to have Diego.' As he was saying this I could hear assistants

Henry Moore, *Family Group*, 1948–49

working outside. Later on, he had a good twenty assistants working for him full time. When I repeated the remark to Giacometti he stamped his feet with rage, revealing his violent Italian nature and perhaps his opinion of Henry Moore's sculpture, concealed during our tour of the exhibition two years earlier. It was true that I sided with Giacometti, the starkness of whose life and work appealed to me, and I didn't care for that side of Moore that was always holding forth like the art-school teacher that he was at that time. Nevertheless, I have a high regard for the man's qualities as a sculptor and draughtsman, a fondness even for the early works which had marked my youth and influenced me,* and which are inextricably bound up with my memories of England and of the beauty of that country.

* Notably in the passage from head to shoulder and shoulder to head in the grouped figures of *The Crowd*.

In December 1977, Henry Moore came to Paris to see the Courbet exhibition at the Grand Palais. In the evening, he couldn't get back to England since the planes were grounded by fog. The following day, having spent the night at the hotel, he asked the American art historian James Lord to drive him to the airport in his car. When James arrived at the hotel, he said to Moore that they were in very good time and suggested they go and see my exhibition at the Galerie Claude Bernard, just round the corner. Henry thought this a good idea and they arrived there the moment the gallery opened. Henry made a strong impression, not only by his presence, but by announcing that he had come to see the work of his friend Raymond. It was at this point that the staff of the gallery, who had known me for fifteen years, started calling me 'maître'. For my part, when I heard about the visit I wrote to Henry Moore, for the main work in my exhibition was *A Tragedy in the North*, evoking the aftermath of a mining disaster in the Pas-de-Calais. Moore was himself a miner's son and had been brought up in a world about which I knew next to nothing.

I didn't get a reply to my letter, or not exactly. Just recently, however, James sent me a copy of a letter Henry had written to him shortly after the episode in question, thanking him for motoring him to the airport and also for taking him to my exhibition, and adding that he had just received a 'most interesting' letter from me to which he was going to reply. It was only then, five years after his death, that his message got through to me.

In 1982, I saw a great deal of Michael Peppiatt, an English art critic living in Paris who had been the curator of a retrospective of my work in London under the aegis of the Arts Council. At a party at his home one evening, or at the home of his friend Alice Bellony-Rewald rather, I met Henry Meyric-Hughes, who was delegate for the arts at the British Council in Paris at the time. Though he was perfectly pleasant, I took the opportunity of scolding him for the fact that his administration never invited me to the official exhibitions organized by the Council. An eloquent example was there before us. A major Henry Moore retrospective was shortly to be held at the Orangerie in Paris. Though myself a sculptor, and even as one of the most senior members of the English colony in Paris, I had not been invited to it. I added that this was going a bit far, given that I knew Henry Moore personally. My interlocutor was immediately apologetic and promised to arrange things at once, when in walked Francis Bacon, a close friend of Peppiatt and whom I too had known for a good many years. He was tolerably drunk, which, as everyone knows, in no way diminished his bite, and, having overheard a phrase or two of my conversation with Meyric-Hughes, chipped in with: 'How right you are, Raymond. They do everything for Henry Moore and nothing for us.' The member of the British Council gave a shudder but kept on smiling. After all, it was Bacon speaking, the other great glory of English art. But there was worse to come. 'And when one thinks about it, Raymond, it's so b-a-d. If I ever see his *King and Queen* once more, I'll throw up.' Thereupon Mr Meyric-Hughes said he was expected at home and promptly left. Much later on, Francis and I walked back together, for he wanted to be sure I shared his view.

The private view of the Henry Moore exhibition had almost come round and I still hadn't received an invitation. So I telephoned Mr Meyric-Hughes to remind him of his promise. In a bizarre voice he said to me: 'Are you sure you're a friend of Henry's?' I had completely forgotten about the evening with Francis when I had stood listening to his outrageous remarks with a grin on my face. 'Yes, yes,' I insisted, 'I know him perfectly well.' In the end, he didn't invite me to the private view in the morning along with all the officials, but to the normal private view in the afternoon – and, it is only fair to add, to the cocktail party at his home on the avenue Franklin Roosevelt. On the evening in question, I saw Henry sitting all alone on a sofa in the end room, as I mentioned at the beginning of my account, and it was at this point that we reminisced about our first meeting nearly forty years earlier. Looking up for a moment, I caught the eye of the delegate of the Council staring at us in disbelief from the door. So I did know him after all! Oh yes, and one final note. At the end of a delightfully friendly conversation that evening, I added that I had much admired the drawings of sheep in the last room of the exhibition. Henry had done them as they nuzzled up to the windows of his studio, the work of an aged man who couldn't move about much any more. He stiffened and in a hardened voice interrupted me: 'Raymond, I'd like my name to go down in history for rather more important things.' It was the last time I saw him.

Alexander Calder

MONG THE FEW SCULPTORS' ADDRESSES I HAD IN MY pocket upon arriving in Paris was that of Alexander Calder, given to me by the English painter Julian Trevelyan. Calder was staying in a small hotel huddled up against the old Gare de Montparnasse. The room was very small, and made still more so by the gigantic figure of the American artist it was trying to accommodate. The artist in question was on all fours, wearing a bright red shirt and a pair of jeans, and was busy twisting pieces of wire. What he was actually doing, of course, was preparing his forthcoming exhibition of mobiles at the Galerie Louis Carré, the catalogue of which was to include an important text by Jean-Paul Sartre – at the height of his fame at the time, since this was in 1946 – that would make 'Sandy' Calder's name once and for all. Under the circumstances, he obviously had neither the time nor the desire to chat with a young stranger like myself, as the blue eyes under the white mane of hair made perfectly clear. 'Do you know Katherine Dudley?' On discovering that I knew nobody at all, he assured me that she was a great girl, gave me her address and, opening the door for me, packed me off in her direction.

A quarter of an hour later, I was standing outside her home at 13 rue de Seine, just round the corner from the Institut de France. As for the girl so called, she was a woman of about sixty. Luckily for me, I would know her for a great many years, and for the rest, Sandy was quite right – she was a perfectly wonderful lady. She was American like him, but had been living in Paris since long before the war. She came from a well-to-do Chicago family, was a painter and knew all the interesting artists in Paris. 'What, Sandy sent you? But how marvellous, he's coming to dinner this evening. Care to dine with us?'

Calder's good nature will immediately be apparent when I say that at no point in the course of the evening did he let on that he didn't know a thing about me. We struck up an agreeable friendship which was to last all through the years. We would meet from time to time, but it never occurred to me to visit him at Saché, his studio in the Touraine, for our conceptions of sculpture were too different. No matter: the fact that he had introduced me to

Katherine, who in turn would introduce me to the people crucial to my future life in Paris, had put me for ever in Sandy's debt. When I later came to organize an exhibition by Katherine's niece, Annie Harvey, it was to Sandy that I turned to borrow the superb still-life he had asked her to paint.

Whenever he was in Paris in later years he would put up at the Hôtel Madison behind the statue of Diderot on the boulevard Saint-Germain; opposite the church of Saint-Germain-des-Près, that is to say. His home port, therefore, was the café Les Deux Magots. One day at noon, I happened to be passing that way when I saw Sandy sitting on the terrace. 'Hi, Raymond, come and have a drink.' As soon as I sat down next to him, he began patting my hands affectionately in his own and asking for my news. Then his fat palms dropped into my own one last time and no longer opened. Sandy had fallen asleep. I was tall and strong in those days, but caught between the paws of this gigantic polar bear there was nothing I could do. I had been taken prisoner, and to add to my discomfort, everyone on the café terrace, which was packed with people on this beautiful spring morning, had noticed my strange predicament. This lasted for half an hour. Katherine had often told me about his quite remarkable strength. Once, while lunching with her, he was flicking his olive stones out of the window onto the pavement of the boulevard Saint-Germain. When the proprietor of this classy establishment protested, Sandy stood up and, with one shove, sent the man careering through two rooms. Hostesses excited at the idea of receiving the two great friends Miró and Calder would change their tune when their drawing-room mirrors shattered from their antics. Sandy, moreover, liked to toss beautiful women high into the air – and then forget to catch them.

One memorable evening was when Katherine invited Mimi and myself to dinner with Calder and Giacometti. The drinks before dinner had already been lively, Sandy serene and sure of himself, Alberto rather het-up. They didn't agree on anything. At one point, Sandy said to Alberto: 'You're a gypsy, aren't you?' 'What do you mean, a gypsy! Like hell I am!' 'Well then,' said Calder, 'what's the name of your village?' deliberately pronouncing village as *vie lâche* ('cowardly existence'). Katherine promptly called everyone to table, but hardly had the first dishes been served than Sandy slumped down over his plate and fell asleep. Delighted, Alberto presided over the meal with his remarkable conversation and, once dessert had been dispensed with, whispered under his breath that we would go and have coffee at Le Flore. We took leave of Katherine and had almost reached the door, when Calder looked up and said: 'I'm going to have coffee at Le Flore, too.' Alberto's face fell, and once outside, the four of us set off in the direction of Le Flore as though it was the retreat from Russia. Then, on the pavement outside the church, before arriving at the place Saint-Germain-des-Prés, Alberto, who had walked on ahead, rounded on Calder and said to him in English: 'Go home, you big fat pig.' Sandy turned a deaf ear to this stinging insult, and we all sat gloomily drinking coffee together. But I have never forgotten that resounding phrase. I can still hear it to this day. Yet Diego Giacometti swore it was impossible, that his brother didn't know a word of English. Believe me, those few plain words – and the feeling behind them – he knew them perfectly well.

The last time I witnessed Sandy's strange habit, or extraordinary faculty, of falling asleep in company was at the Villa Medici in Rome, with Balthus. The latter had organized one of those receptions in which he excelled for an exhibition at the Villa. The Roman aristocracy had turned out in large numbers for the occasion. While listening to the official speeches, I found myself next to Sandy, who had come to Rome to put the finishing touches to his stage designs at the Opera. I looked at him a second time. He was asleep on his feet.

Constantin Brancusi

CONSTANTIN BRANCUSI WAS UNIVERSALLY ACKNOWLedged to be the finest sculptor of his day. He had retained the austerity of his Romanian peasant origins, even though his fame had brought him into contact with some of the wealthiest people on the planet. I was astonished therefore, upon arriving in Paris, to see that he was listed in the phone book, along with his address, impasse Ronsin, in the hinterlands of Montparnasse. And still more astonished that he should answer the phone in person, replying 'yes' without difficulty to your request – which you hardly dared pronounce – that you visit him in his studio.

When you rang the bell, a few minutes would pass before he half-opened the door, then a further minute or two while he sized you up. It wasn't long before I found out that if you had a pretty girl in tow you were admitted at once. Once inside, the shock was guaranteed. A dazzling white studio, with white sculptures in plaster or marble; the sculptor himself, with a white skull-cap on his head and a white beard, looked like a miller in a fairy-tale. First he would switch the motors on that set his sculptures slowly revolving, and then pick up what looked like a cocoa tin. In it were boiled sweets and, with the aid of a tool, he prized one out and offered it your lady friend. For yourself, nothing.

There was very little conversation. He showed you his work, and that was all. In the course of my visits, moreover, I noticed that the studio didn't change at all, there was always the same heap of marble dust next to the work in progress. One day, however, he noticed my admiration for a sculpture carved in wood with the utmost simplicity and force. 'I made that for the Maharajah of Indore. But that was in 1927, and you know what happened in 1927.' I was casting about for what might have happened that year, when Brancusi added: 'It was the outbreak of the Great War.' This muddled sense of contemporary history led him, screaming with rage, to throw his great friend Katherine Dudley out of his studio when, after the Second World War, she tried to tell him what she had learned about the concentration camps.

One time I unwisely mentioned Picasso. He looked completely baffled for a moment, then, having found the man, said: 'Ah yes, the film star.' The Clouzot film had just been screened.

Since he did everything himself, this also meant doing his own shopping on the rue de Vaugirard. Waiting in the queue outside L'Oeuf, Beurre et Fromage, he would sing to while away the time. And because he looked such a nice old man, people would give him money, thinking he was a street singer.

Like all old people, he broke one of his legs. At the hospital he got on everyone's nerves by the same business of singing at the top of his voice. And also because he kept burning the sheets with the ash from his pipe. Finally, he was sent home, where he died not long afterwards. For lack of suitable care, perhaps. But still singing, for sure.

Because of this concern to do everything himself, all the furniture and objects of his domestic life were made by his own hand. He had given Katherine two table-lamps, the bases of which were made of plaster, Brancusi-style, the lampshades of parchment. When she died, they were inherited by her niece, the painter Anne Harvey, the author of a superb portrait that Brancusi had posed for; and when Anne died, her brother Jason brought them to me to keep in memory of her. I left one of them in my *basti-don* in Provence, where it lit up magnificently the beams of the kitchen. The other remained beside my bed in Paris.

When they reconstructed Brancusi's studio outside the Pompidou Centre, I thought of giving them my lamps to complete their collection. Then the Centre contacted me to ask whether, as a sculptor, I could remember if the works in plaster in Brancusi's studio had been whitewashed by him. Yes, indeed. I had forgotten this, though it had struck me at the time.

On the day of the opening, I was invited neither as a sculptor, nor as a consultant, nor as a long-standing friend of the organizers. Piqued, I decided to keep the great man's lamps at my home, where they remain to this day.

Jean Cocteau

AFTER ARRIVING IN PARIS AT THE END OF JULY 1946, I spent the month of August on my own in the seemingly deserted city. My first real meeting with the French at the *rentrée* the following September was nonetheless a happy one. It took place in Montparnasse, where I had discovered a very cheap little restaurant called La Soupe Merveilleuse, situated between Le Dôme and La Coupole. It was run by a family from the Auvergne, and the father, Monsieur Alaux, sported a handsome white handlebar moustache. You ate quite well there, but meat was non-existent, it didn't even feature on the menu. (I had already been intrigued to see all kinds of animal hooves and heads hanging up in butcher's shops, but never the piece in between, the body of the animals, which had gone elsewhere, of course.) On what was virtually my very first evening there, I heard two young men, eighteen years old no doubt, loudly ordering dishes in a mad rush. They were two painters, Serge Rezvani and Jacques

Lanzmann, who had sold a painting that day and were enjoying their first square meal for quite some time, since they were completely broke – so much so, in fact, that their only address was a bench on the Ile du Vert Galant where they slept and managed to get through the day with a baguette and an ersatz coffee.* Guessing my nationality, they came over and asked me for English cigarettes, but once they realized I was just as hard-up as they were, they led me off to Jacques's mother's house, where they went each week for a bath and to have their clothes washed. I soon adopted the same ritual myself and, like the other two, would be stripped naked by Paulette, the Jewish mother in all her splendour, my clothes plunged into a basin, myself into a tub, while our beefsteaks were cooking on the stove. On the evening of my first visit, I also met Jacques's elder brother, Claude Lanzmann, a philosophy student. We became very close, and in this way I came to know his friends Gilles Deleuze and Jean Cau, secretary to Jean-Paul Sartre at the time. Claude, intimately linked with Sartre and Simone de Beauvoir, took over the editorship of the review *Les Temps modernes* when the philosopher died. In recent years he has become famous because of his remarkable film *Shoah*, and we resumed our old friendship after I wrote him an admiring letter about this great work.

The house was also made very interesting by the presence of Paulette's second husband, Mony de Boully, an expatriate Yugoslavian poet who had once been very wealthy. His arrival in Paris before the war had been hailed by the Surrealist group, which had turned out in its entirety on the station plat-form to greet him, and he still had ties with André Breton and Paul Eluard. Another friend was Jean Cocteau, and I was afforded a brief glimpse of this enormously talented charmer.

The previous winter Serge and Jacquot had gone to warm their young bones in Nice, and, on the beach there, Serge had engraved a series of entic-ing female figures using the planks of old orange crates. Mony, who had

* It is amusing to think that, in the end, Rezvani, after a successful early career as a painter who exhibited in major galleries in Paris and London, has become a famous writer, without forgetting the music and lyrics he wrote for Jeanne Moreau in *Jules et Jim*, while Lanzmann is a well-known figure of Parisian café society through his annual novels and as writer of lyrics for the rock musician Jacques Dutronc.

doubtless got his genders confused, had decided that these woodcuts would look well in a book of Cocteau's, and to arrange the matter had invited the poet to dinner. We – the artist and his two friends, that is to say – were to turn up later for coffee. On arriving on the evening in question, I realized at once that the dinner had not been a success. Cocteau had been bored. He perked up a little on learning that I was English (I wasn't too bad-looking in those days). 'Ah, England!' he exclaimed, 'the last home of fancy.' I knew perfectly well what he meant, having heard it said countless times before, but in view of my working-class Birmingham background, I chose to contradict him. 'Well then,' retorted Cocteau, 'what do you have to say about this?' He then went on to talk about his English uncle, a well-known ornithologist who lived in England and used all the rooms of his stately home to house his birds, while he himself lived in a tree. Cocteau, seeing that I took the whole thing more like one of his own flights of fancy, protested: 'But I can prove that only the English believe in gnomes, elves and fairies. A great friend of mine, Cecil Beaton, was staying at a seaside resort in England. On the first day there, he spotted a very handsome young boy on the beach, accompanied, alas, by his nanny. Every day of the week he watched this same couple. On the Saturday, Cecil was just getting ready to leave when to his great delight he saw the little boy on his own. Racking his brains as how to approach him, he was taken aback to see the boy walk towards him, to then ask: 'Tell me, Sir, are you really a fairy, because Mummy says you are?'

The company at table was delighted with this proof of English fancy, while Cocteau and I looked at each other, laughing with even greater satisfaction. Thereupon, the doorbell rang. 'Ah,' said Jean Cocteau, 'that must be my own little boy.' And in came the huge, athletic body of Jean Marais. Then off they went.

Aimé Maeght

AIMÉ MAEGHT WAS THE GREATEST PARISIAN ART-DEALER of the third quarter of the twentieth century, and a little beyond too. After starting out as a lithographer's apprentice, during the war he ran a small shop with his wife, Marguerite, on the seafront at Cannes, where they sold reproductions of artworks and household goods such as radios and so forth. The life of Aimé and Marguerite changed the day a rather shy elderly gentleman came in to buy exactly that – a radio. His name was Pierre Bonnard and he lived in Le Cannet in the hills behind Cannes. His wife had died a short while before, and though he still worked, indeed was going from strength to strength as a painter, he was at a loss when dealing with the problems of everyday life, which were now being made even more problematic for him because of the war. The Maeghts were perfectly attuned to ironing out his difficulties for him. Marguerite was a fine cook, while Aimé had a car and could solve any problem. Bonnard was soon sufficiently pleased with the arrangement to mention it to his old friend Henri Matisse on the other side of the hills at Nice. Matisse was equally happy to enjoy the little extras the couple were always able to produce.

I leave it to the biographers of Aimé Maeght and his wife to chart the progress of their ambitions until they moved to Paris with enough money to acquire the superb gallery at the corner of the rue de Téhéran and the avenue Messine. I mention those two famous artists to make an obvious point: it was an excellent start for a couple wanting to launch out into the art trade.

Despite that, the early days of the Galerie Maeght were no great shakes. The reason for this was quite simple: Maeght had no real taste to speak of and knew very little about art – by which I mean art and the reasons for art, not the commercial activity surrounding it. Odd as it might seem, this judgement remained valid right up to the very end of his life.

Jacques Lanzmann, Serge Rezvani and myself had known him from the very beginning, thanks to Jacques' father-in-law, Mony de Boully, who, in the spring of 1947, had brought him to Boulogne-sur-Seine where we were all working together. No doubt Maeght felt his new gallery needed young blood, seeing that he wasn't having much success with his two main painters, Roger Chastel and André Marchand. All the same, his ambition was already making itself felt. He had taken on Jacques Kober as resident poet responsible for preparing the catalogues, and the latter had put together a first exhibition of young artists, 'Les Mains Eblouies'. There were about ten of us budding artists in all, among them Pierre Dmitrienko and Bernard Quentin. I had been chosen to do the invitation card, and the date had been fixed for October 1947. The previous exhibition, the gallery's first real success, had been that of the Surrealist group. I don't know how Aimé had pulled it off, but the installation was very much in the daring spirit of that movement, and when Madame Maeght saw the artifical rain falling from the ceiling she bemoaned their imminent ruin.

Only recently did I realize that the sculptures I presented at this, my first exhibition in Paris, were all painted, foreshadowing my activities as a poly-chrome sculptor from 1970. The largest of these had a form I find it rather difficult to describe; journalists at the time immediately christened it *The Pipe*. The hollow area was lit up slightly by a slit facing outwards. The whole had a Brancusi-like appearance which had pleased Monsieur Maeght when he had seen it in plaster in Boulogne. He had no idea that I intended to paint it, but, bizarrely, had no objections to my spending the night before the pri-vate view doing so in his gallery. I find it hard to believe that this mania for working at night, which later so irritated Pierre Matisse in New York, had declared itself this early on. The following day, when Maeght came down-stairs – he lived above the gallery – he was dismayed to see *The Pipe* painted bright blue. Despite that, he took me upstairs for breakfast and, seeing what a sorry state my clothes were in, opened his wardrobe to choose a suit for me for the private view; and, when it was over, told me it fitted me and that I should keep it!

Our exhibition was given a rough ride by the press. I have forgotten to mention that all the works on show were abstract, but I don't think it was for that reason, since by that time abstraction was already well installed in Paris, largely thanks to the Galerie Denise René. No, it was in fact one of the very positive things about the period that there was a press that devoted a lot of space to artistic controversies, to say nothing of more specialized journals like *Arts*. The attack was nevertheless sufficiently hard-hitting for Monsieur Maeght to decide to make a public reply. For this purpose he rented the famous cabaret Le Boeuf sur le Toit, associated with memories of Cocteau and the Groupe de Six. We, the ten artists, sat on the stage and, somewhat extravagantly, I, the one non-French artist present, who had only been speaking the language for a year, delivered the speech in defence of our work.

It was actually an attack in which I even managed to assault, without meaning to, my fellow artists, since I began by saying that I was not responsible for the works of my co-exhibitors, prompting several of them to walk out on the spot. I ended with the following plea on behalf of abstraction: 'We give back to the dear Lord, whom we do not know, his masterworks, women, fruit and sunsets, which we know only too well.' It was too much for my friends in the room, and Mimi Fogt stood up to heckle. The text of my speech appeared in issue seven of the gallery's review, *Derrière le miroir*.

Sitting next to Monsieur Maeght that evening was a figure new to the gallery, but of crucial importance later on. His name was Louis Clayeux. Up until then, he had been the main salesman at the Galerie Louis Carré, situated a hundred and fifty yards further down the avenue de Messine. Louis Carré was a sturdy and important dealer who had just made a big splash with an exhibition by Picasso, who had not yet returned to Kahnweiler's gallery after the war. The success of the exhibition, to which hordes of people had turned up, had been taken by Aimé Maeght as a personal affront. And a personal affront it was, since that same month the Galerie Maeght was holding its annual exhibition of André Marchand, the ex-companion of Françoise Gilot, who was now installed in Picasso's life. To cock a snook at the unfortunate Marchand, Picasso had knocked up an exhibition the same month, composed solely of portraits of Françoise which laid great emphasis on her marvellous breasts, which under Pablo's brush turned into gigantic spheres. But Aimé Maeght was looking further ahead than this sparring match between painters. If the Galerie Louis Carré was doing so well, it was certainly due to Clayeux; and Maeght, by offering him a much higher salary, convinced him to move up the avenue to his gallery. Here we see Maeght at work. He may have lacked taste, but he did have real flair. He had a feel for people. So did Marguerite, no doubt, though in her case the flair was for money. Louis Clayeux had taste, connections and friends, many of whom were major artists. In the space of a few years, he had built up the great Maeght stable, of whom Braque, Chagall, Miró, Giacometti and Calder were the best known. Maeght didn't have to spend so much time thinking about his young artists. A second 'Les Mains Eblouies' exhibition was held, which was more successful than the first. Serge Rezvani had a room all to himself for his illustrations for a book by Paul Eluard, while my fellow countryman Eduardo Paolozzi exhibited his Paris sculptures. Then an amusing episode occurred which put an end to the adventure. There was a young painter called Dany who was always on the go and whom Maeght set great store by – until the day Dany, writing one letter to his wife and another to his dealer, mixed up the envelopes and the letter with the offensive remarks about Maeght, destined for Dany's wife, was read by Aimé. All we young artists were thrown out together! 'Out you go, ungrateful wretches!' We fell on hard times, and it was fifteen years before I would show my work in a commercial gallery again. True, I had changed lifestyle, and, furthermore, my brief period of abstraction was over. My career in Paris got under way again in 1963, when I joined Claude Bernard, a gallery that was attracting as much attention on the Left Bank as Maeght was on the Right. Here, oddly enough, I would run into Louis Clayeux again, who, though he still occupied his key position in the rue de Téhéran, was a close friend of Claude Bernard Haïm and an important influence in the early years of that splendid gallery. I always enjoyed seeing him, and I think I can say he felt the same about me. I have to confess that a few words of congratulation from Clayeux the day after an exhibition of mine at the gallery seemed the finest of rewards.

My new partner, Mimi, always said she didn't like Maeght. She didn't trust the man. Nevertheless, we never failed to attend the private views at the Galerie Maeght, which were always spectacular and attended by everyone of interest in the art world. Then the autumn of 1956 came round, and it was time for Mimi to go and see her mother and two sisters in New York. On the eve of her departure, Alberto Giacometti came round to the studio to say goodbye and, in the course of the conversation, mentioned in passing that he would himself be going to the Gare Saint-Lazare the following day, with other artists from the Galerie Maeght, since Aimé was leaving on the same boat as Mimi for his first trip to the United States. We were astonished that Giacometti, who usually went to bed at dawn and rose at midday, was capable of getting to the station at nine o'clock in the morning.

The following morning, in the taxi taking us to the Gare Saint-Lazare, I asked all the ritual questions: 'Have you got your passport? Have you got your visa?' (In those days the visa was separate.) With a shriek, Mimi realized she'd left her visa at home. The taxi turned back and was then faced with the impossible task of returning to the Gare Saint-Lazare at top speed in the morning rush hour. By the time we arrived, the boat-train had left. Dismay all round. Mimi's family were coming all the way from Canada to meet her off the boat. Faced with our lamentations, the cab driver told us he could drive us to Le Havre and get there before the train. We looked up: 'Yes, but for how much?' 'Forty thousand francs return.' They were old francs, of course, but still a fortune for us and, needless to say, we didn't have them. Suddenly I had a brainwave. Once the train had pulled out, what would those artists from the Galerie Maeght be doing, where would they be? In the station restaurant, of course. We ran. There they all were, Giacometti, Miró, Calder and Bazaine among them. In a trice we explained our predicament and asked them point blank if they could lend us enough to pay for the taxi journey. As soon as the meaning of what we had said became clear, I distinctly saw Miró (whom I had met at Maeght's) step back and hide behind one of his fellow artists. Giacometti, on the contrary, immediately came forward and gave us the required sum. We thanked him – then set off *en route* for Le Havre. In a pea-souper we raced along in the fifteen horse-power Citroën. The driver, who was wearing a beret and chewing on a Gauloise, looked for all the world like Jean Gabin, whom I recently saw in a film called *Razzia sur la Chnouf*, made in 1954, belting along in a Citroën front-wheel drive in the direction of – Le Havre. Mimi had now decided that this was a truly romantic way of leaving France. (Though we didn't know it at the time, we were parting for ever, and she was never to return.) As promised, we were in time for the boat, and Mimi climbed aboard. Shortly afterwards, I saw her standing on the foot-bridge between Aimé Maeght and Louis Clayeux, laughing her head off. So much for not liking the man. Clayeux told me afterwards that they shared all their meals together. *La donna è mobile!*

While I was waving at the boat pulling away, a young man standing next to me was doing the same. It was Adrien, Aimé's son, accompanied by his young wife. 'How are you getting back to Paris?' he asked. 'I'm going back in a taxi.' 'No kidding! Can we come with you? There are no trains before nightfall.' 'Naturally,' I replied magnanimously. There was nothing at all natural about it, as it turned out. The lousy cab driver, that poor man's Jean Gabin,

had picked some clients up off the boat and left for Paris. Adrien and I thus
had the entire day to make one another's acquaintance.

It was in 1964, at the opening of the Fondation Maeght at Saint-Paul-
de-Vence, that the big falling-out between Louis Clayeux and Aimé Maeght
occurred. In the presence of the Minister for Cultural Affairs, André
Malraux, and of the entire art world, in his speech Aimé Maeght had painted
a broad panorama of his activities, culminating in the crowning glory of the
Fondation, without once mentioning the name of his gallery director. It was
too much for Clayeux, who for years had suffered from the proximity of an
employer who in intellectual terms was so different from himself. Their collaboration had not been negative, far from it, but this last drop in a vase that
was already cracked, the ingratitude of the man, decided Louis Clayeux to
leave the gallery.

He may have thought, he doubtless did think, that he would be taking
with him his artist friends from the early days. But Miró, to whom Maeght
owed large sums of money, had no intention of walking out in this way, and
in the end only one artist followed Clayeux outside, and not the least of them
– Alberto Giacometti. This gesture on the part of someone of his stature, at
the height of his career with this famous gallery, out of sheer loyalty to his
friend, says a lot about the sculptor's moral qualities. He stood to lose everything, though it has been suggested that Clayeux planned to entice Alberto
into joining Claude Bernard, a sculpture gallery par excellence. Diego
Giacometti, who was thoroughly hostile to his brother's leaving Maeght in
this way, gave me another side of the story. According to Diego, who saw a
great deal of the Maeght couple, Aimé Maeght's plan for a foundation – built
as a memorial to his dead son on a plot of land he already owned near Saint-
Paul that was not in the least suitable and that would require major building-
up of the ground, to say nothing of the cost of a prestigious piece of architecture – was not at all to the liking either of Madame Maeght or of Louis
Clayeux. They were opposed to the idea, saying that Aimé was going to make
them lose all the money they had made in Paris. So, said Diego, why would
Maeght have mentioned Louis Clayeux in his speech, who not only had done
nothing for the Fondation but was actually against the idea? In any case,
Alberto still had certain commitments vis-à-vis Maeght and died in 1966

without having settled them. Yves Bonnefoy contacted me to say that there was a seat for me in Monsieur Maeght's car to go to the funeral at Stampa if I wanted. For reasons I can't really explain, I didn't accept.

A few months later, Jacques Dupin, resident poet at the Galerie Maeght, but with more say in matters since the departure of Louis Clayeux, came to see me to inform me that Aimé and Marguerite Maeght had decided that, now that Alberto was dead, I was the figurative sculptor best suited to take his place in the gallery. Jacques told me that Maeght was in Saint-Paul recovering from jaundice, but on his return would come and see me himself. After my first exhibition at Claude Bernard's, Maeght had said to me one day: 'I'm pleased about your success, for I never forget that you started in my gallery.' It was all very flattering, tempting even, since Maeght was notoriously generous with his artists. There was a complication, however. Dupin spoke to me of an exclusive contract, and at that precise moment in 1967 I was on the point of joining the Pierre Matisse Gallery in New York. Matisse, for his part, the moment he was informed of the matter, lost no time sending me a telegram stating succinctly: 'Do nothing with rue de Téhéran.' The two dealers had been sharing artists like Miró, Chagall, Giacometti and Riopelle for some years but didn't much care for one another, and as Matisse said to me later: 'Another would have been too much.' And, in all likelihood, the same was true for Maeght. So nothing came of it all. Nor do I really regret having stayed with Claude Bernard (as Pierre Matisse wanted), since the moment he found out I was joining Matisse, his behaviour towards me changed completely, and I went on to do some good exhibitions in his gallery, in an environment that was perhaps better suited to my work.

In 1969, my large bronze *The Crowd*, along with other works dealing with my favourite theme, formed the core of the exhibition 'The Crowd' at the Arts Club of Chicago, an institution renowned for its discerning choice of exhibitors, among whom was Brancusi in the 1930s. I went over, of course, for the installation of the bronze in the new building designed by Mies van der Rohe. (Van der Rohe died just as I arrived in Chicago, and I was able to attend the memorial service held at the Crown Hall – the masterpiece he had designed for the Pennsylvania School of Technology – in the presence of architects from all over the world.) On the day I was due to fly back to New York, Pierre Matisse phoned to find out what time I would be arriving. 'Nine p.m.' 'Perfect,' and he explained that the day in question was supposed to have seen the consecration of Jean-Paul Riopelle. In the morning, the Governor General of Canada should have been awarding him the Medal of Great Merit. In the afternoon, his big exhibition was opening at the Pierre Matisse Gallery, and Aimé Maeght had flown over from Paris specially to attend. Riopelle, however, had not seen fit (hats off!) to be present at the two events, and everyone, of course, was hopping mad. 'So,' concluded Matisse, 'you will eat the dinner given for Riopelle by Maeght and myself. Come straight to the restaurant, and don't be late.'

That same morning, just as I was leaving the hotel, I saw some gangsters being chased through the streets of Chicago by police cars, their sirens wailing and policemen leaning from the windows, revolvers in hand. And when they screeched to a halt and rushed into a building, an inhabitant of the city had to drag me into a doorway to stop me wandering over out of sheer fascination. All the same, I thought with satisfaction, Chicago has done me proud. But there was more to come.

O'Hare International Airport in Chicago is the busiest in the world, and you wait quite some time before taking off. While I was gazing out of the window at a scene that was new to me, the other travellers were concentrating on their choice of magazines and drinks. After half an hour, I noticed to my surprise that instead of going towards the runway, we had returned to the boarding gate. At that precise moment, the door of the plane slid open and the Federal police came charging in, rushing down to the end of the plane. They dragged out a hefty man who was putting up a hell of a fight. Wearing a havana-brown-coloured suit, he even had a black patch over one eye. A hijacker! Doubtless a bit drunk, he had been deceived by the long wait into thinking we had taken off and, gun in hand, he had announced to an air hostess his intention of hijacking the plane to Cuba. Once he had been led away, the plane remained at a standstill while the captain and flight staff were questioned. Time went by, and I found myself thinking about my dinner in New York, which was looking increasingly unlikely. When the captain arrived at my part of the aisle to tell his story all over again to the passengers, I grumbled: 'If I had a gun, I'd force you to go to New York.'

His smile vanished and his eyes turned to steel: 'What?!'

Needless to say, I arrived much too late to go to the restaurant. I tried to telephone once I had arrived at Kennedy Airport, and at last made out Matisse's voice in a din of music. He couldn't understand a word of what I was saying, but I for my part distinctly heard him say 'Idiot'; whereupon he hung up. Riopelle and Mason in one day: it was more than he could take.

What would have happened had I dined with Maeght and Matisse as planned? In all likelihood, Maeght, always the dominant one, would have brought up the question of my joining his gallery again, to be arranged on a friendly basis. (It may be that the only thing this budding hijacker had succeeded in diverting was my career.) The following day, Pierre Matisse, very excited by my story, completely forgave me for the dinner fiasco. Back in Paris, I received a letter from American Airlines apologizing for the incident in Chicago and assuring me that it would never happen again. In point of fact, it was just the first in what later turned out to be a long string of hijackings, and the same plane has been to Cuba many times since.

Now that Alberto was dead and Clayeux gone, I went less often to exhibitions at the Galerie Maeght. In recent years, I have dined twice with Aimé and Marguerite, each time on the occasion of Diego's birthday. The first time was in a restaurant, where Aimé was busy explaining how Mozart had composed *Don Giovanni*. He was wrong, but he had the gift of the gab and he told the story with great aplomb. The second and last time was at his magnificent home on the Champs de Mars. After dinner Maeght harked back to the early years of the gallery, spurred on by my presence, since it was true to say that, with the exception of his wife, of the twenty people present it was I who had known him the longest. 'Do you remember, Mason, when Juliette Gréco sang for us at the gallery?' In the imagination of Aimé Maeght, everything that was a success at the time had first come to light in his gallery. It wasn't at all what I remembered. It was the man's grandiloquence that wanted it that way.

The same *rêve de grandeur* built his gallery, his Fondation, his publishing houses and his printing studios. We all profited by it. Thank you, Monsieur Maeght.

'L'ami Jean'

IN THE EARLY 1950s, MY GIRLFRIEND'S SISTER, A BEAUTIFUL tall brunette who had perfomed on the stage and had even acted in a film by John Huston, had as a lover – as is often the case – a tiny fellow called Jean Lévy. He was a delightful character and, as a teenager, had shown such a flair for business that he was at the head of the Paris Monoprix supermarket chain although so very young. We knew him at a somewhat later stage in his career, when the ebullience of his ever-active brain, bored with the usual run of business life, had spilled over into more dubious affairs. This led to his serving a short spell in the Paris prison La Santé. When he was released, he was the same sparkling Jeannot as ever and read us a poem he had sent to his judge, asking to be freed and ending:

> 'Cher Monsieur le Juge…
> Gardez votre Santé
> et rendez-moi la mienne.'

Needless to say, it wasn't the small-time hoodlums that fill the prisons that Jean was interested in. His life revolved around expensive restaurants and the racecourses where the bigger clients hung out.

One morning, he came bounding up to my door, wanting to take me somewhere – to the racecourse, in fact, I think. 'It's out of the question, my dear Jean, I have an appointment with the dentist. I'm just on my way out.' He wanted to have things his way, of course, but seeing that my mind was made up, relented: 'All right then, and since I like you, I'll drive you there.' This surprised me, as I knew he didn't have a car. At that time, not everyone had a car, weekends and country houses were not yet *de rigueur*, and for Jean the daily round was limited to the eighth arrondissement and a quick visit to Longchamp… 'I insist, I have a car waiting outside.' So we walked down to the place de la Sorbonne, which was almost deserted apart from the incongruous presence of a huge, white American limousine with tinted windows and a figure at the wheel. Jean bundled me into the back with him, issued instructions to the chauffeur and off we went. At one point, Jean tapped the heavily built fellow on the shoulder and said: 'Joe, I'd like to introduce you to my sculptor friend, Raymond', then to me: 'Raymond, this is my great friend, Joe Renucci.' Joe Renucci!! The man driving me to the dentist was public enemy number one, the prime suspect behind the shoot-out at the Porte de Champerret, an incident that had something to do with cigarette smuggling and that had left a large number of people dead, including several policemen. In the meantime, the good Joe looked round for a second to give me the Renucci version of a smile and a glance betraying not the slightest curiosity. Jean then explained to me that they were just back from a trip to Belgium. They had crossed the border both ways in this car, driven by the man every policeman in Europe was looking for! I simply couldn't understand it. Nor, as it turned out, were they asking me to do so, since by this time we had arrived at the dentist's. I got out. 'Cheerio, Jean, see you soon. Merci, Monsieur.'

A few weeks later, the private view of an exhibition of paintings by my friend Xavier Coll opened in a highly regarded gallery in the rue de Seine, for which I had written the preface to the catalogue. Xavier, a young dandy and the eldest son of the most important businessman in Barcelona, had recently taken up painting, partly at my own bidding, though his talent was obvious. His parents and friends had travelled to France for the show, but were rather lost in this Parisian artistic gathering and huddled together in a group, not saying very much – all the more so as this was the first time Xavier's mother, a fervent Catholic, had seen her son's paintings, among which were one or two highly suggestive nudes. The atmosphere at the private view suffered as a result, despite the best efforts of us and our friends. It was Xavier's first exhibition and he was in despair.

Towards eight o'clock, the door of the gallery flew open and in walked three men. The first of these was our delightful Jean Lévy; the other two had long, camel-hair coats with their collars turned up and felt hats pulled down over their barely visible faces. Without saying good evening to us, Jean asked his two cronies: 'So, what are you having?' They took a quick look at the pictures, then with a few raisings of the chin indicated half a dozen canvases – including, of course, the nudes so skilfully painted by my ladykiller friend. Without a word being spoken, six paintings had been sold and, having assured us of the deal, Jean disappeared with his two hoods.

You might think: what a threat to our modern cities the rise in crime and all these gangsters are. Well, let me tell you, for us artists, there aren't nearly enough of them.

Alberto Giacometti

WHEN I ARRIVED IN PARIS ON THE EVENING OF 26 JULY 1946, there were no taxis outside the Gare Saint-Lazare and my Blomberg friends and I were obliged to take a hackney cab. The smell of the horse, wafted towards me by the warm breeze at the end of a sweltering summer's day, sparked off the worst asthma attack I had ever had in my many years of servitude to this affliction. A poor welcome from the City of Light! But no, for the attack was my very last, signifying, I think, that Paris was destined to be my true home, as it has indeed been for the last fifty-six years.

Stamping with impatience, my friends had to wait forty-eight hours before we could all make the visit together, the pilgrimage, to the Café de Flore, which in that year, 1946, was considered the cultural centre of the universe. Yet, on arriving outside the venerable establishment, we didn't go in, doubtless for fear of spending our all too precious francs. As it was nighttime, however, I made no bones about peering over the curtain and taking a good look inside the famous café. One client in particular caught my eye, since in a literary place like this he could only have been an artist. With his tousled, greying hair, crumpled clothes and gesticulating hands, he was talking ten to the dozen… I understood at once and curled my lips: he was a failed artist who made up for this at night by talking in cafés. Everything I loathed, and one of the main reasons, in fact, why I had put off this trip to Paris, I who had been formed by a hard-working city, Birmingham, where theories and talk were deemed superfluous.

It wasn't until many months later that I realized that the character in Le Flore was the sculptor Alberto Giacometti, then in the process of creating one of the most important bodies of work of the century. Apart from his name, however, I knew very little about him in those days, my interest as a budding sculptor focusing entirely on Constantin Brancusi, whose studio I had visited several times. As a result of this, at the 'Les Mains Eblouies' exhibition at the Galerie Maeght in 1947, I had shown smooth, Brancusi-like forms, my only personal contribution being the polychrome colouring. My friend Eduardo Paolozzi, who arrived in Paris shortly after me, and as always was at the cutting edge of modernity, advised me to forget about Brancusi, saying: 'It's Giacometti the man.' It's true that I had begun to take notice of the pencil drawings by Giacometti I saw stacked in portfolios at the entrance to the Galerie Pierre Loeb. I had also noticed, during my frequent visits to this very attractive gallery that, despite their price – 15,000 old francs – they didn't decrease in quantity, since I recognized the same drawings.

As I have described elsewhere, upon arriving in Paris I had made the acquaintance of an elderly American lady, Katherine Dudley, through Alexander Calder, and I was often invited to her home. One evening in 1948, at a small gathering of her friends, Alberto Giacometti was present. There were some important people there, including a high-ranking member of the Communist Party, all-powerful at that time (Katherine, although American, wasn't in the least sectarian), but Giacometti stood out among them all. His physical appearance, which I was now able to observe at close quarters, was quite simply astounding. His head was disproportionately big in relation to his body, though the latter was of average height. His eyes were large and handsome, his nose big but noble, his mouth a wide gash, all these features being knitted together by skin as deeply furrowed as that of an old Sioux. His head, with its shock of hair, had great expressive beauty. When a smile appeared on those astonishing lips, to the appearance of a noble savage was added an utterly compelling charm that very few people, and no woman, could resist. My new partner, Mimi, was no exception.

I think I can say that the effect he made on Mimi was reciprocated. Giacometti was responsive to her beauty and vivaciousness, as I saw at once before my own two eyes. I am thus in a position to dismiss out of hand the claim made by my friend James Lord that, deep down, Giacometti was an introvert. This was how I made the acquaintance of Alberto Giacometti, and for a year or two if he addressed me it was more out of politeness than from any real interest, and it was alone that Mimi visited his studio.

One of the remarkable things about Giacometti was the perseverance he showed in the role of scrutinizer of young talent. This astonished the young artists in question, since the man who clambered up five flights of stairs to visit their attic rooms had been lame in one foot since before the war. Alberto surpassed himself on a visit to the fourth-floor studio where we were living, Mimi and I, on the place de la Sorbonne. This one room served both as a living space and as a studio for Mimi to paint in – it was quite impossible to sculpt there. On the landing outside was a ladder for climbing up to a storage space, presumably designed to accommodate luggage and the like. For six months, I had been sitting up there, for want of space in which to stand, making a construction in wood, *The House of the Soul*, heavily influenced by Giacometti's *The Palace at Four a.m.* I was unaware at the time that the work had been made in plaster, and that the example in the Museum of Modern Art in New York was a replica in wood made by a cabinetmaker in the fourteenth arrondissement. My sculpture, moreover, though certainly influenced by his work at the beginning, bore very little resemblance to a Giacometti at the end.

Naturally, I was keen to show it to Alberto, and I suppose he must have been equally keen, out of curiosity, to see it, since he did the unthinkable: he clambered up this vertical ladder after me and, while the two of us sat there suffocating in the tiny space, subjected it to some harsh criticism. Or rather, no, his reaction was one of bafflement. 'What is it? A maquette for the theatre?' I was put out, and we were both in a bad mood when we clambered back down. Bizarrely, this was the turning point in our relations, which from that point on were situated on the plane of sculpture.

I had emerged from my brief abstract period thanks to this *House of the Soul*, the atmosphere of which was ever so slightly Surrealist, after my brush with the work of Giacometti (in reality, it was closer to de Chirico). If he had had so little to say about it, this was surely in part because he had put his pre-war formalist period firmly behind him. As I came to spend more time with him, I was gradually won over by his vision of human figures in streets, all the more so as the city had been my principal source of inspiration in England. I thus embarked on a long series of drawings and reliefs of the urban scene.

Left: Alberto Giacometti, *The Palace at Four a.m.*, 1932.
The Museum of Modern Art, New York

Right: Raymond Mason, *The House of the Soul*, 1949

A childhood friend of Mimi's had married an important dealer in London, John Hewett. Hewett specialized in Negro and primitive sculpture, but had extended his activities to painting and was the owner of two superb, oval-shaped pastel drawings by Francis Bacon, pre-war works for which I know of no equivalent. We had struck up a friendship, and from time to time I would cross the Channel with some important object under my arm, collected from one of Hewett's dealer friends in Paris. Wrapped in newspaper so that it didn't attract the eye of the customs, it was nevertheless destined for Peter Wilson, the celebrated chairman of Sotheby's. Hewett was the regular buyer for Robert Sainsbury, the owner of the supermarket chain and an important art collector. Knowing of my relations with Giacometti, Hewett asked me to see if I could buy one or two works directly from the sculptor. I did this and, contrary to all expectations, Giacometti sold me *The Hand* (which is really *The Arm*) in bronze, complete with stand, for a hundred pounds. He also sold me the cube-shaped white marble head for a hundred pounds! I remember clearly his satisfaction at the deal, which must date back to before 1952, since it was in that year that his affairs were taken in hand by the influential art dealer Aimé Maeght. (For my part, I note that the request made by the Art Gallery of Birmingham to various institutions for financial support towards the cost of organizing my retrospective in 1989 met with an immediate negative response only from the Sainsbury Foundation.)

To return to the early 1950s, it is in vain that I seek to fathom the mystery of how we lived, given that, hardly yet started on my oeuvre, I had neither a gallery nor buyers. Mimi was able to cadge something off wealthy friends who came through Paris from time to time, but it was of little help in the ocean of days. On one occasion, faced with the imminent arrival of my mother in Paris and not wanting to worry her by being too conspicuously penniless, I produced a series of drawings of Paris in the hope of selling them to the tourist galleries in Montmartre. They agreed that my works were superior to their usual wares, but also convinced me that, to make money at once, I should sell them myself on the café terraces of Saint-Germain-des-Près. With a heavy heart – I was thirty at the time – I resigned myself to this. After a while on the first evening, I addressed a client sitting on the terrace of Les Deux Magots with his head in a newspaper. When he at last looked up to see what I was selling, I had the shock of recognizing Giacometti. 'What's this, what's this?' he grumbled. I explained my story to him. 'They're pretty bad,' he said, which, I have to admit, struck me as exactly right and, overcome with shame, I started to make my way home. (I saw some of them again in London recently. They're not bad, simply academic; I was eager to please.) I had crossed the place Saint-Germain-des-Près and just reached the other end of the church on the boulevard when I heard someone following me and calling me by my name. It was Alberto, who was limping as he ran, as always. 'Why did you leave like that? You need money. How much though? 20,000, 30,000, 40,000 francs? Tell me!' I was flabbergasted and touched, but my need was indeed too great for me to turn him down. We settled on 40,000 francs. They were old francs of course, but it was a large sum for me, and it took me a month or two to pay him back. Alberto looked at the banknotes I held out with a show of astonishment: 'But you already paid me back two weeks ago.' I protested, of course, but a certain impatience was starting to creep into his voice and I yielded to his kindheartedness.

Alberto Giacometti was a man of abrupt manners and, since he had been raised in the mountains, it would have been surprising had he been otherwise. He was capable of terrible fits of rage, of unfairness even, as I relate here in my text on Balthus. But his curiosity towards others was great, giving them not only money, but something much more precious, his time. Let us not mention such exceptional moments as when his mother's maid in Stampa arrived at the luncheon table with the letter announcing that Alberto had just received one of the most coveted of all American awards, the Carnegie Prize. He made a gift to her of the total amount of the prize to thank her for her kindness towards his mother.

It's possible that his generosity was brought about by his scorn for money and was simply a way of getting rid of the stuff. When his work started selling for large sums at the Maeght gallery, he left the money in the hands of his dealer, and he once comically told my wife, Janine, that when in the past he had had holes in his shoes they would cause him great discomfort, but that now that he had all this money waiting for him at the gallery, he didn't notice those holes at all. It's possible, too, that his visits to the top-floor rooms of young artists were dictated by sheer curiosity, independent of any idea of largesse. I allow myself to stand back somewhat in this way vis-à-vis Giacometti, because I saw him from the outside. I was a follower, an admirer, not a friend, for he was twenty years my senior. One is very finicky about someone one admires. He has to live up to the reputation one invests in him. I was mystified, for example, by Giacometti's open admiration for Matisse, Braque and Derain, artists whose work had very little in common with his own, and which for my part I was not too fond of, Matisse tending to the decorative, Braque the incomprehensible and Derain the plain bad. The fact that Alberto had turned out texts in praise of all three – in catalogues for his own gallery, it's only fair to say – put my mind in a turmoil. The light dawned one summer's evening when I was sitting with Giacometti and several others, including David Sylvester, at Les Deux Magots, on a terrace at some distance from the café itself. 'Alberto, I've understood why you're always praising Matisse, Braque and Derain. It's because you're jealous of Picasso.' Sylvester immediately dragged me off behind a tree and yelled at me: 'How can you talk in that way to the master?' Perhaps I still had fresh in my mind the story told by Katherine Dudley, whom I mentioned at the beginning, of a visit she had made with Giacometti and others to Picasso's flat in the rue de la Boëtie, which Picasso had had to abandon because it was entirely filled with his works. Picasso had shown them four rooms piled all the way up to the ceiling with canvases. In the fifth room, which was given over to drawings, the sight of drawerfuls of splendid works was too much for Giacometti, whose eyes filled with tears. Katherine, who had a pragmatic nature, was incapable of lying or exaggerating even, and I instinctively believed her. Giacometti's fame after the war made him the only artist who could act as a counterbalance to Picasso, and the two men understood this well. Alberto had told me the story of one of their little sparring matches. Sitting at the Royal Saint-Germain, Picasso, who had come up from Vallauris, was telling his friends how unbearable his life had been made by coaches turning up with the destination 'Picasso at Vallauris' plastered over their sides. 'But why don't you move to the Ardèche under a false name?' Giacometti quipped. One day, Alberto turned up at my studio: 'I've come to your place to have a look at your work, because at midday, when I got back from the café, there was a note from Picasso slipped under the door: "Came by. Back in the afternoon." That I don't want, because Picasso when he's in your studio looks at your work not with two eyes but with two cameras, and the next day does the same thing ten times over.'

During the 1950s, I concentrated increasingly on relief scenes inspired by the city life going on all round me, involving large numbers of figures grouped together before an architectural backdrop. As a result of this multiplication in space I gradually moved away from an exclusive interest in Giacometti's way of seeing. I called round, of course, at regular intervals, and I got to know Annette better, Diego too, the silent, hard-working brother who, years later, was to become one of my dearest friends. Nor did I ever miss any of Alberto's exhibitions at the Galerie Maeght that pulled in the big crowds. Alberto never shirked the duty to be present at the private view, an act I always appreciate in an artist. He also made a point of showing his most recent work as well, that is to say the sculpture he had been working on the previous day, or even the night leading up to the private view. These fragile figures were protected by a glass case, and what with the wetness of the plaster and the warmth of the room, the panes would invariably mist over, making Giacometti's praiseworthy intentions invisible.

In 1959, I put my hands on a property adjacent to my studio, and not long after turned it into an art gallery run by my wife and bearing her name, the Galerie Janine Hao. After inaugurating it with an exhibition of my own work, the second exhibition was given over to the work of Katherine Dudley's niece, Anne Harvey, a prodigiously gifted woman known only to a few artists, Matisse, Miró, Calder and Giacometti. Annette had chosen a painting, and Alberto had come to see if he agreed with her choice. All this was dealt with by Janine, and I wasn't present. On the other hand, it was I who went to Giacometti's studio to settle the bill. Annette received me in the little room next to the studio. Above the bed was a shelf on which were several cardboard shoeboxes. Annette jumped onto the bed to knock one down, the lid fell off – the box was filled with banknotes! She took out the relevant sum and hup! the box was back in its place on the shelf. Alberto explained to me the reason for this. His mother, realizing that her son had started to earn a great deal of money, asked him what he did with it. 'I put it in the bank, maman.' 'In the bank! That's out of the question!' replied the old countrywoman. From then on, he left the bulk of it with his dealer, or alternatively kept it at home. He even showed me the barrel in the studio that you might have thought contained clay, but which in fact contained banknotes.

In 1962, I had made a sculpture of three torsos in space, each larger than life – the same torso in three different positions, in fact – called *Falling Man*. Giacometti had come to the studio to see these large plasters. The moment he arrived, he declared from the doorway: 'It's new, it's new.' 'No, Alberto,' I smiled, 'it's old.' I said this because several people had seen in these torsos, fragments of the human body, the influence of Greek pediments. I particularly wanted his opinion on the third torso which I was unable to complete to my satisfaction. 'But it's fine, this torso,' said Alberto with impatience. While I kept on insisting that something wasn't right, he interrupted me to say: 'A spoonful more or less of plaster, what difference does it make?' 'Yes, but Alberto, you who seek a perfect finish…' He gave a howl of rage: 'I, of all people, seek a perfect finish…', and for a few minutes he admired my work, saying 'It's good, it's good,' while at the same time heaping abuse on its author: 'You're a fool'.* But that wasn't enough. Something more damning was needed. He found what he was looking for. Leaving the studio, we arrived in the courtyard of the building where Janine, standing in the doorway of the gallery, looked at us with astonishment, for Alberto was denouncing me in triumph: 'You're just a *mondain.*' *Mondain*, for Alberto, was the supreme insult. Years before, I was on my way home from a fancy-dress party given by Marie-Laure de Noailles – at Balthus's instigation – disguised as Dr Jekyll and Mr Hyde. Walking past Le Flore in the early hours of the morning, there was still one customer left on the terrace, Alberto. 'What's all this about?' I explained. 'That's socializing.' 'Max Ernst was there too.' 'Max Ernst,' said Alberto, horror-stricken, 'you can't be serious.'

Giacometti also came to our gallery to help his old friend, Gaston Louis-Roux, hang his exhibition there in 1963, but that was a poignant moment. He had just been operated on for cancer and had lost a lot of weight. He kept tightening and retightening the belt of his trousers, saying to Janine: 'And yet I eat, I eat, but there's nothing to be done.' You felt like crying. Alberto, who had always made do with a hard-boiled egg and a banana for lunch so that he could rush back to the studio, was now trying to eat! Sadly, this concern for his health was short-lived, and after the operation Alberto went on with his life exactly as before. He worked and went to the café just as he had always done, and I saw him late at night in a bar in Montparnasse, with his cigarette and his cognac, in the company of Beckett. I will note here that I would have seen a lot more of Giacometti had I, like so many of my fellow artists, dined out at night and then gone on to a café, for Giacometti could be found around midnight at La Coupole almost any night of the year. I am a creature of the daytime. My meetings with Alberto were diurnal, and the ground on which we met was that of sculpture.

In those years, I was working towards my first major exhibition, which took place at the Claude Bernard gallery in 1965, at a time when that splendid gallery in the rue des Beaux-Arts was given over entirely to sculpture and works on paper. The centrepiece of the show was a large sculpture, *The*

* A much stronger word, in fact.

Crowd, comprising some hundred figures big and small, in effect, my first important sculpture, demanding two years' work, what with all the preparatory studies. It was the final conclusion to my many reliefs of city life; any form of architecture had gone, the coming together in a group of my fellow citizens had become the true theme and thus was, you might suppose, a multiplication of those early heads of mine in which the influence of Giacometti had been so pronounced. Though the work was above all a search for composition – the science of bringing things together – I intended to dedicate the sculpture to Alberto. The only trouble was that this plaster was enormous – one critic spoke of 'Notre Dame in the middle of a gallery' – and on the day of the private view I lost my nerve. It had already crossed my mind that people might accuse me of wanting to steal a bit of his fame, but I now realized that, worse still, the thing could be seen as poking fun at the smallness of Giacometti's sculptures.

It was the year when Alberto's health was deteriorating because he had resumed, as I say, his gruelling regime of work, cigarettes and alcohol. Annette informed me that, having been unwell the day before, he was staying in bed and could not be present at the private view, but promised me he would come as soon as he was better. I wasn't pleased to hear this, particularly as it meant that Alberto wasn't well.

As promised, he turned up at the gallery a week later. Quite by chance, my friend Mayou Iserantant, a painter with a very sharp eye, was at the exhibition at the same moment and, from the opposite end of the room, saw Alberto being dragged into conversation by César and Claude Bernard the moment he walked in the door. Later on, however, he didn't go round the exhibition with its twenty or so works, perhaps because fatigue was rapidly getting the better of him. Perhaps also because the ninety-nine figures of my *Crowd*, reaching all the way up to the ceiling, seemed just too much for him. The distance separating our two oeuvres did not prevent a leading London critic of the time from describing *The Crowd*, the bronze cast of which featured in my 1982 retrospective at the Serpentine Gallery, as a 'failed Giacometti'! All the same, I thanked Alberto for troubling to come and see the exhibition. All he said in reply was that he had liked my sculpture *The Hand* – the smallest, and the one indeed nearest the door.

At the time, I saw a great deal of the marvellous New Zealand photographer Douglas Glass, whose portraits of a well-known public figure, generally male, appeared each week in the *Sunday Times*. I had helped him out with his portrait of André Malraux, as I relate elsewhere. He had given me two very beautiful large photographs he had taken of Giacometti, one a striking front view that is possibly the best portrait ever taken of this outstanding model, the other showing Alberto in profile, sitting on the bed in his studio, staring down at a book of poetry, with a painting of Annette leaning against the wall. These two documents had indisputable historical interest – because of the model and because of the photographer. I planned to frame them so that they would stay in the family, and for that reason wanted the signature of the sculptor Janine and I had known so well and whom the children had also met on several occasions. Late one afternoon, I went to see Alberto and found him in the café at the corner of the rue Didot and the rue d'Alésia. In those days, there were two cafés facing one another on opposite sides of the rue d'Alésia. Each was a favourite spot for Alberto. (Both have since become banks.) This time he was in the one from which Cartier-Bresson took his famous photo of Giacometti on the zebra crossing with his raincoat pulled over his head because of the rain. Sometime in the late 1960s, when I was working at the Fonderia Bruni in Rome, I was running one winter's night, likewise in the rain, towards a little trattoria near the Colosseum. I cut through a small alley and got the shock of my life – Giacometti was running towards me! Then I realized that it was only a huge poster of that self-same photo by Cartier-Bresson, glazed over by the rain. Balthus had organized an exhibition of Cartier-Bresson's work at the Villa Medici, and had naturally chosen the remarkable picture of his great friend Alberto for the poster, and this I was unaware of.

So anyway, I took my two Douglas Glass photos to Alberto for him to inscribe. He was with the poet André du Bouchet, whom I had known for years and who had written a text for us for the Galerie Janine Hao. With André around, Alberto was sure of an audience, and he profited from this to give one of his implacable lessons in dialectics. This consisted of saying that, since he hadn't made the photos, he couldn't sign them, isn't that so, André? And that, furthermore, they had already been signed by the photographer.

When I explained that I wanted a complete souvenir – his picture, with his signature – he became more and more intransigent. The tone, however, was mocking, with Alberto constantly referring back to André as though André represented common sense and I the cretin. I stood up angrily, and Alberto, to retrieve the situation, said to me: 'Come to the studio. I'll give you a drawing, and I'll sign it because that I will have made.' The logic was pure Giacometti, and for some reason it made me even more furious. Above all, it prevented me from going to see him, since I feared that a visit would mean that I had come for 'my' drawing. This quarrel went on for several months.

One evening, early 1966, driving home from the Fonderie Susse in Arcueil and passing, therefore, virtually in front of Alberto's door, I decided to put an end to the quarrel. There was no-one in the studio, so I knocked on the door of the bedroom. Annette appeared and said, 'Good evening,' though her mind was clearly on other things. From within I could hear Alberto's voice saying, 'Who is it?' 'It's Raymond.' 'Tell him to come in.' I went in and was shocked to see Alberto in bed, visibly quite ill. His handsome head seemed half its size, his face was grey and his eyes yellowish. Nevertheless, the conversation began with his usual 'How are things?', after which he was content to let me do the talking; and, sitting on his bed, I told him about the interesting or amusing things of the moment. It was a little of the life outside which had entered, and Alberto perked up, saying, 'That's wonderful' or 'That's a laugh.' When, an hour later, I stood up to leave he told me that in a couple of days he had to go to Switzerland for a check-up at the clinic at Chers, but that he would be back in a week or ten days. 'Come and see me then to tell me more of your amusing stories.' I left them, himself and Annette, without too much foreboding, but remembering with nostalgia the past years, even before they were married, when he had been strong as a Turk and she happy as a lark.

When he died the following week, I realized that this last evening with Alberto, yes, there had been friendship. We had known each other a long time, I was part of his world, that world of Paris that he thought he would never, never have to leave.

Giacometti: The Outer Man

NOT SO LONG AGO I GAVE AN INFORMAL TALK AT THE Tate Gallery, London, on the artists of the School of Paris I had known personally there since my arrival after the war. I said at the outset to the midday audience that they certainly knew the works and the biographies of the different artists just as well as I did but that I could add the human dimension so often unknown or, worse, distorted.

This is eminently the case with the character of Alberto Giacometti. A man of powerful personality, he had many famous and powerful friends, quite a few of whom were writers and who did indeed write about him and his work. They have left us a picture of the dishevelled existentialist artist pursuing his eternal quest to comprehend the human being at his most denuded. The tragic artist.

Just as many photographers, also personal friends, have fixed his figure in surroundings of equal nudity, the studio, the street, the café late at night. Did he ever smile, could he laugh? Nobody mentions this, nobody catches this with a camera.* The answer must be no. He was a tragic figure and well-nigh exhausted as well.

This has always astonished me. I knew him for twenty years but the others had known him for more and had benefited more than me from that incredibly persuasive smile (if you can imagine an alligator smiling you get somewhere near it), from his raucous laugh and, above all, from his gift to make you laugh, to make you cry with laughter with your head on the café table.

I have said elsewhere that I have often noted that profoundly serious men can also be great humourists. It makes sense in a way – a great man has a great range. Giacometti was capable at will of outclassing any company

---

* The exception being Henri Cartier-Bresson, as is so often the case with this great humanist of the camera. Even so, working in the intimacy of the Giacometti family house in Stampa, Switzerland, he portrays essentially the tender smile of the sculptor in the presence of his mother.

with the perfect amusing word. Then, let us not forget that Giacometti's physical appearance was astonishing.* Because of his game leg, his gait, particularly when he moved fast, consisted in a bobbing up and down which once in the studio I saw him transform into a hop, skip and jump act, his hands drawn up in his sleeves, which perfectly evoked the devastating arrivals on the screen of Chico Marx. It's true, there was a resemblance and he knew it.

When there was great talk about Giacometti the tragic figure last year,[†] I phoned Balthus to ask his opinion on the matter. 'Alberto,' he said firmly, 'was, apart from anything else, one of the most amusing men I have ever known. He was not tragic, he was tonic.' This was the word I had often used to qualify Giacometti, and I was glad to hear it coming from his great contemporary and friend Balthus.

Of course he was tonic. If people clustered around him, if young artists knocked constantly on the door of his studio, it was to get a charge from his dynamism. He was not a lone frequenter of dizzy peaks, he was a leader. In post-war Paris he was a figure to whom a young artist in love with the outer world, yet desirous of real art, could turn.

Giacometti accepted quite naturally the homage of fellow artists – and they included many well-known abstractionists – insofar as it was concerned with his approach to art. I've often heard him say that he couldn't understand why everybody else didn't work in the same way as himself. That is to say, why

---

* Alberto's dress was astonishing, too, for its sobriety – a sports jacket, grey trousers, white shirt and black tie – and for the fact that it was clad in this way that he sculpted and painted. A silk scarf would be added for evening wear. The sports jacket always came from the famous British store in Paris 'Old England', which at the turn of the century also clothed Claude Monet.

† Witness the cover photograph of James Lord's *Giacometti* (Farrar, Strauss, Giroux, New York, 1985). Here we have the rare event, a first biography certainly destined to be the definitive one. No-one can conceivably come to closer grips with the life of Alberto Giacometti, a task to which Lord devoted fifteen years. His analysis of the intimate and sexual life of Giacometti brings a pungent, obsessive tone to the book that is very true to the period, but also, intimate being intimate, conjectures that are cruel to his widow. On the other hand, this short tribute of mine concerns the outer man as he walked among us.

each artist did not sit down in front of the model and try honestly to represent what he saw. The study of the human figure, and above all the human
head, seemed to him the only source of enrichment and, given the difficulty
of the enterprise, the only real challenge. He once told me how this total
involvement with the head had come about. He had been pleased with his
construction of 1932, *The Palace at Four a.m.* He had made it quickly in plaster and now had a similar idea in mind. But whereas the *Palace* contained an
effigy of his mother in skittle-like form, this time he planned to include his
brother, his head on a small base like a piece of a chess set. According to
Alberto, he didn't make this element as easily as he'd intended. So he asked
himself, why should he struggle, since his brother Diego was in the next-door
studio? All he had to do was to come in and pose. Once Diego was sitting on
the chair, Alberto had a sombre revelation. This, he remembered, was precisely the problem he had never succeeded in facing at art school and which
he had shirked by slipping into modern art. He had been trying to solve the
problem ever since.

To favour the cause, not only did he open his door to young artists even
when he was busy, but he scrupulously visited their studios or rooms to look
at their work and comment lengthily on what he saw. However, he drew the
line if the younger man betrayed any sign of hero-worship. Before I knew
him better I had once burst out with 'You're the most important artist of the
period.' 'Poor period, then,' he snarled back. His antagonism towards Picasso
was largely because of the way he basked in a sea of notoriety which Alberto
perceived as being detrimental to work.

The dialectical power of his conversation was no less appealing than his
art. I would be inclined to say that it was truly irresistible, since his testing of
truth by discussion had a Socratic inevitability to gain all hearts, and if you
chose to argue – no matter how improbable Alberto's initial premises – you
were inevitably crushed. I remember him one summer night at Les Deux
Magots maintaining before a sceptical audience that *The Raft of the 'Medusa'*
by Géricault would reach up to the third floor of the houses opposite. Trivial,
indefensible – yet he won.

On another occasion, and on better grounds I admit, it was a question
of Henri Matisse's recent decoration of the Vence chapel, which Alberto had

just seen and greatly admired. I have never been a 'Matissian', preferring to the stripping-down of forms their multiplication, and, having seen photographs of the chapel, I had my doubts. Still, in order to voice them I had to wait until I, too, had made the journey to Vence. My visit there confirmed my fears. The colour of the stained-glass windows, which should have been projected by the Midi sun to fill the simple black outlines of the mural on the tiled wall opposite, fell instead in a puddle on the floor of the chapel. The walls with their white ceramic tiling looked empy.

Again at Les Deux Magots, Giacometti amid his friends listened to my verdict. First of all indignant – 'Rubbish. That simple oval without features of Saint Domenico is the most interesting thing that's been done ever since we've been painting faces *with* features' – he then calmed down. 'So Monsieur Mason doesn't like the chapel of Henri Matisse. Mason doesn't like the chapel of Matisse,' repeated several times. Then, with a winning smile at me, the sledgehammer: 'And what would you wish to see in its place?' I hasten to add that his arguments had notably more important victims than myself. In conversation with Alberto, dauntless talkers like Jean-Paul Sartre and Simone de Beauvoir were more than usually silent.

There again, sitting talking in cafés was an essential part of Alberto's life. He had two small studios. In one he worked, in the other he slept and telephoned. All other activities – eating, drinking and meeting people – took place in the café. I doubt whether he had a cup, a plate or a spoon in the studio. The bottles he often painted were simply old bottles of linseed oil or turpentine. Now, there's a tenacious legend that Parisian artists go to cafés to talk about art, when the truth is, and it's perfectly logical and evident, that they go and they went to cafés in order to escape from art. An artist's life is harrowing, always poised on the brink of success or of failure, but the gaunt mask of battle remains in the studio. Outside, and even more so in the crowded café or restaurant, we witness the exuberance always associated with an artist's character, laughing and talking with friends, talking to unknown girls, ready to talk to anybody about anything.

Giacometti was no exception, except that he would have been driven out of the studio by the sheer pangs of hunger and the obsessive work of the studio would prolong itself for a time in the café. Freshly arrived, solitary but not for long, he could be seen drawing intently on the table-napkin, some-times with no pen or pencil between his fingers. This would stop when the first friends arrived. People were far, far too interesting to Giacometti for them to take second place. Into the lives of his friends, his sitters and his numerous encounters in the late café hours, he plunged generously, some-times even recklessly. The innumerable ball-point drawings he did while listening to others were mere doodles, umpteenth variations on the heads of Annette and Diego. He was listening, not drawing.

He would come to himself when the café or bar closed its doors. Slumping into any taxi, he heard its driver simply say, 'Going home, eh?' since they all knew his address. Once there, he would often return to the studio and create until morning, when Diego arrived and Annette awoke. Then and only then, he would put himself to bed and doze in the studio, without blinds, but with the hammering of Diego next door, until midday when he went to the nearest café for a first coffee.

I knew Alberto and Annette as quite a happy-go-lucky couple. He used to bully her in an affectionate sort of way, but in any case his heavyweight personality and definitive statements were kept at bay by the pert, irrepress-ible remarks of his young wife. Friends knew that Annette could be counted on for a deliberate 'gaffe', a controlled indiscretion, which would reveal Alberto's intimate convictions on this or that. Gallery solidarity could make Alberto swear until blue in the face that such and such exhibition of another Maeght artist, opened the day before, was 'Très, très bien'. Then Annette, with wide-open eyes, would say candidly, 'But last night you told me it was all shit.' 'You shut up!' roared Alberto, secretly content, I always felt, that truth had been honoured. Annette, at all events, clearly adored her Alberto. He, to pre-serve his bohemian dignity, could play the tough man, but he relied on her, and her opinion mattered to him, often making him say like the most dutiful of husbands: 'Yes, but I'll have to ask Annette first.' On one of his last nights in Paris before the final journey to Switzerland and the clinic, I dropped by the studio. Annette opened the door and showed me in. Alberto was lying on the bed, emaciated and grey of complexion. As one always does at a bedside, I told funny stories and we were all laughing, Alberto suggesting that I come back just ten days later on his return to tell some more. Then I left them,

Alberto and Annette, in the little studio where I had seen them together for the first time eighteen years previously. What had changed? What indeed. A few days later, as Annette left his room on the night of his death, he said to her the customary and beautiful French words: 'A demain.' 'See you tomorrow.'

The stereotyped image of the tragic artist is tenacious and often superficial. If an artist is blighted by outer signs of ill health or ill luck it is assumed that the inner man is also attained. It is very often the exact contrary, with the artist not complying with his fate but resisting hard. Yes, Beethoven was stricken with deafness, a malediction for a musician, but to the end he loved his glasses of white wine and a good laugh; his contribution to the symphonic form was the scherzo, a joke, and his final symphony an 'Ode to Joy'. The vivid image of a great man comes precisely from the contrast – and the cohabitation – of light and dark. This span is necessary and probably inevitable.

Giacometti smoked four packets of American cigarettes a day, ate haphazardly but drank cognac, slept far too little and, to keep awake, drank too much coffee. He had disregarded his aches and pains for years. All he was interested in was pursuing his course. With this regimen it could come as no surprise that he developed a cancer. No surprise, that is to say, to anybody except Alberto. When he finally knew, he was surprised and baffled. But this didn't last long – one should say alas – and, once the major operation was over, he pursued his course exactly as before until, three years later, his heart crumpled beneath the strain. He had no foreboding, made no will – once again alas – and finished, without knowing it, in the nick of time, his great book of lithographs *Paris sans fin*. Paris without end!

This shows, and it is important to underline, that Giacometti was not a pessimist but a resolute optimist. The way he conducted his life and captained the shattered health of his doughty body proves this. The way he conducted his art no less so. Who but an incorrigible optimist would destroy remarkable sculptures and paintings simply because he intended to do better the next day? This is not fiction, one witnessed it happening countless times. On the eve of his last exhibition at the Galerie Maeght, I saw the paintings the day they were to leave the studio. An outstanding portrait of Annette laughing seized my admiration and, in the short time that remained, I phoned a few friends so that they would not miss the opening and this painting. They looked at me queerly that night. There was no such work on the walls. Alberto, the perfectionist, had scrapped it.

Yet he had no desire for singularity, and for the second half of his life concentrated with an investigator's zeal on the essential problem, the meeting point of aesthetics and life, each at its most intense. His scale was necessarily small since he was taking in. When the artist gives out, proclaims that he is singular, his scale can be gigantic. And, in American art, it is.

Here was the human dimension of Alberto Giacometti – fundamental integrity and a balanced mind. He achieved the almighty difficult equilibrium of structure and expression for, if his literary friends can exalt his pathetic regard on humanity, artists will always be thrilled by his far-reaching analysis of the human head and figure. The 'subject', so often on his lips, he deepened by his art to a profound realism. His irreducible message reminds us, never more pointedly than today, that the proper study of man is man.

Written in English for the catalogue of the Alberto Giacometti retrospective, Hirshhorn Museum and Sculpture Garden, Washington D.C., 1988. (Not published.)

Pablo Picasso

I MET PABLO PICASSO FOR THE FIRST TIME IN THE SUMMER of 1952. When Mimi and I went to visit him in Vallauris with his nephew, the delightful Xavier Vilato, he was working on ceramics in the studio of the potter Ramié.

There were seven or eight of us in all, and Picasso had decided to show us his studios on the hills overlooking Vallauris. They were giant barns, and when Picasso made to open the largest of the doors I realized for the first time just how small he was, for the key, attached to a chain on his belt, only just reached the key-hole.

What he particularly wanted to show us were the huge surfaces waiting on the walls for the moment he would paint the compositions of *War and Peace*, destined for the disused chapel of Vallauris. 'It's big, isn't it?' he kept asking all round. 'Oh yes, maître,' everyone chorused back, this being the required response at all times. 'It's as big as the Sistine Chapel,' he added. In Paris, to make a bit of money, I had just finished translating a book on the Sistine Chapel into English. I knew perfectly well, therefore, what its dimensions were, and without even thinking about it, a 'No' slipped out of my mouth. It was indeed as though Picasso had never heard the word before, since he asked all round, disbelieving: 'What did he say?' I repeated what I had said, explaining why, but he interrupted me to declare in a loud voice: 'Well, almost,' glaring at me with his dark eyes. 'And that's not all,' he went on. 'I now have to paint them. Matisse, of course, would just lay on a few flowing lines and it would be done. But I, Picasso, will have to work much harder. It's dreadful!' My English sense of humour led me to open my mouth for a second unfortunate time. 'Yes, but console yourself, maître. Once it's finished, it will be even more dreadful.' I intended this as a compliment to the *terribilità* of Picasso; instead, everyone present gave a cry of horror, and Vilato was so alarmed that he dragged me out of the studio, and I didn't even get to hear Picasso's reaction.

Just the same, I caught up again with the procession when it was looking at the ceramics workshop, crammed with daring inventions. (It had all begun with Joan Miró making a few ceramics with his friend, the great Catalan potter Artigas. When Picasso saw them, he decided to try his hand, and in a year had turned out 1,760 works!) We finally came to the studio reserved for works in progress. The room was long and narrow, and while Picasso held forth with the women at one end, I wandered around with Xavier examining things at the other. A matador's sword was hanging on the wall, and taking it to be a collector's item I mumbled to Xavier that it was almost certainly not sharp. In a bound Picasso was at our side, grabbed the sword from the wall and placed its tip against my throat: 'Not sharp, hey? Shall I press down then?' With a roll of the eyes, I didn't utter a word, begged for mercy and the master returned, triumphant, to the women. Xavier separated me once and for all from the assembled company, saying gloomily: 'It's just too bad. He doesn't like you.'

Two years later, recovering from an operation for peritonitis, I was convalescing at Mimi's father's home behind Grasse. I felt very weak. My survival had been a miracle of friendship. I had been rushed into the hospital at Sèvres, where my friend Charles Odic, the mayor of the town, was also head doctor. On the evening of the operation, Odic was dining in Paris, but in the middle of the meal had stood up to drive out to the hospital and see how the operation was getting on. He found the surgeon sewing me back up, saying there was nothing to be done with such a bouillabaisse. Odic begged him to reconsider the case of his young friend…

I felt just strong enough to do, say, a few small reliefs in terracotta, and bizarrely I thought of Picasso at Vallauris, who could open the doors of any studio to me. Mimi was in Spain, and I had taken the big, light-blue Dodge to drive to Golfe Juan. On my way down from Vallauris to the coast, I saw a mother and child waiting at the bus stop with their bathing things under their arms. I offered to take them to the beach, and they got in, delighted. A few moments later, I was overtaken by a Vespa. Recognizing the driver, I muttered under my breath: 'It's that cretin Pignon.' Needless to say, the woman sitting next to me was Madame Ernest Pignon, the writer Hélène Parmelin in other words, and hardly had we arrived at the beach than I saw her explaining to her husband what a pig I was.

It was a beach typical of the Côte d'Azur, with a hundred or so people tanning themselves under a beautiful sun and thinking of nothing. In reality, of course, everyone was thinking of only one thing. They all knew that on the dot of noon Pablo Picasso would arrive at the beach and sink his parasol in the sand like an emperor's standard. The waiter at the restaurant nearby said that Picasso was so punctual that he could set his watch by his arrival each day. And here he was, with most of the bathers already on their feet, walking towards him. Having only just arrived myself, I found myself standing next to him and, since I was among the first, was able to ask him if, later on, he would care to look at a few photos of my work. 'There's nothing I enjoy more than looking at photos. See you later,' and he ran down to the water for a dip. Pleased with the way things were turning out, I went for a swim, then sat down on my towel to take a look at this unusual beach. All of a sudden, Françoise Gilot arrived. The previous year, she had walked out of Picasso's life, declaring with great style that she didn't want to live with a national monument any more. Now she had brought her two children to see their father during the holidays. I knew her well. Before meeting Picasso, she had had a boyfriend, Luc Simon, a young painter the same age as me, and since the break-up had gone back to live with him. Being figurative artists the pair of us, a certain camaraderie had grown up between Luc and myself, and just recently he had settled down with Françoise in the rue du Val de Grâce, not far from my studio in the Latin Quarter. I had been there for dinner several times, to talk about art late into the night, with the children Claude and Paloma tucked up in their cots in a corner. This explains why Françoise made straight for me that morning on the beach to bid me a friendly 'Bonjour'. At that precise moment, I noticed Picasso's piercing gaze fixed on us in the distance, and it became agonizingly clear to me that to engage in conversation with this contentious beauty would be to rule out all chance of speaking to Picasso again and showing him my work. It was a predicament worthy of Corneille, and to wriggle out of it I acted like a coward. I lowered my eyes and remained silent when Françoise said 'Bonjour' for the second time. At that point she understood. Understood above all that I was a miserable creature unworthy of her interest and she turned on her heels. I was upset by this, and when I focused my attentions on the beach once more, it was to see everyone leaving. Picasso himself came rushing out of the water and disappeared with a group of friends into the restaurant on the beach. Soon I was the only one left and, with a heavy heart, started gathering up my affairs. At that moment Picasso came out of the restaurant and said: 'Aren't you coming?' 'But…' 'Come on, come and have lunch, old man.'

I thus found myself seated at table opposite Picasso, together with a number of other artists, among them Pignon and the sculptor Adam, whom I knew slightly. I was astonished to see that none of them uttered a single word, being quite happy just to be eating at the master's table. The master, on the other hand, talked a great deal, and I, therefore, who greatly enjoy a good conversation, turned out to be his only interlocutor. This time, I had my work cut out. Pablo's talk was every bit as inventive as his art and was littered with jokes and booby-traps. 'Where do you live?' (He used the familiar form 'tu' when addressing me, as is *de rigueur* among artists, great or small.) On learning that I lived in the Latin Quarter, he asked me where exactly. 'Not far from Maubert-Mutualité.' He was overjoyed. 'Maubert is all I know. I even have a canvas of the place Maubert-Mutualité. Now, who painted it? You must know him. A curious fellow. I can't remember what he did for a living: a baker, a postman, a station-master? No, I've got it, he was a customs man.' He was referring, of course, to the Douanier Rousseau painting with the place Maubert in the background, *Les Représentants des puissances étrangères viennent saluer la République française en signe de paix*, which formerly belonged to Picasso and is now in the Musée Picasso in Paris. Our conversation continued gaily, then in came some Spanish dancers touring the coast, friends, of course, of Pablo. Before long, the woman in the company, a beauty, had climbed onto the table and broken into a wild dance. The noise was deafening, and I was just saying to myself how marvellous it was to have lunched with Picasso and too bad about the photos, when all of a sudden he clapped his hands and called for silence, saying: 'Yes, but that's not all. We have here a young artist who has come to show us his work.' It was a little glimpse of Picasso's cruel side. All my fellow artists' eyes were now focused unkindly on me, as I laid out the few works I had accomplished to date. There were busts of children, done to make money, that Picasso passed over in silence, a few reliefs and, finally, *Barcelona Tram*, my first, recently completed high relief. It is one of my good works, one on which I can be judged, and Picasso's enthusiasm was immediate. (It's only lately that I have understood Picasso's emotional fixation on that city. Moreover, the scene depicted in my relief was the façade of the Estación di Francia, the station from which Picasso had set out more than once for Paris.) He told me that he liked the work because it was my own, wasn't cosmopolitan or in keeping with the style of the day. Thereupon, he called Adam over to come and look at the *Tram*. Adam, who made bulky abstract forms, looked at it and declared: 'Yeah, it's not bad, but it's not sculpture.' To which Picasso retorted: 'It's precisely because it's not sculpture that I like it. Sculpture that's just sculpture gives me the shits.' Adam, sensing the remark was aimed at him, hurried back to his seat. Picasso continued to sing my praises, before adding: 'You're an English artist.' I deflated at once, but Picasso, seeing my disappointment, hastened to reassure me that he was very fond of English art, and without a moment's hesitation or a single omission rattled off in chronological order all the important English artists from Hogarth down to the turn of the twentieth

century. 'But nowadays there's no English art any more. It's become cosmopolitan' – a word he was fond of – 'like that sculptor, what's his name? You
know the one.' I didn't dare breathe. 'M-M-Moo-Moo,' he went on, tapping
me on the chest. 'Moore,' I timidly suggested. 'That's it, Moore. He's the same
thing.' I could hardly believe it. Moore, who had had the honour of seeing
Picasso painting *Guernica*, being talked about in this way. I should add that
in 1954 there was little chance of Picasso knowing much, or even anything
at all, about Francis Bacon. By way of conclusion, Picasso told me to go and
see Kahnweiler in Paris and to tell him he had sent me, a spectacular recommendation. Only on the road back, still glowing with pleasure from my
afternoon with Picasso, did I remember that I hadn't asked him a thing about
the potters in Vallauris!

As it happens, I didn't go to Kahnweiler's, I didn't take advantage of the
recommendation that thousands of artists would have envied me, and here is
why. Roughly one year earlier, there had been a big private view of Picasso's
work at Kahnweiler's old gallery in the rue d'Astorg. At the time, I was desperately searching for somewhere I could use as a studio, and it occurred to
me that since everyone who was anyone in the Paris art world would be present at this event, it would be an excellent moment to hand out a leaflet at the
entrance to the gallery saying that I would accept anything, anywhere, that I
might use as a studio. That is exactly what happened. I spent two uncomfort-
able hours standing outside the gallery pestering people, and when I had
nothing left to hand out I went inside to see the exhibition. In those days I
saw a good deal of the fine arts delegate for the British Council in Paris, Frank
McEwen, and I found him there with his friends, among whom was Georges
Charensol from Radiodiffusion Française. Charensol was rounding people
up to talk about the exhibition, and instead of doing it in the rooms of the
gallery, he was taking his group down to the radio studios. Frank, who was
taking part, suggested it would be interesting to have the views of a young
artist, myself it just so happened, and Charensol said fine, good idea.

There were some important figures at the studio. Kahnweiler himself,
Michel Leiris, André Fraigneau and three or four others. While these leading
lights were singing the great man's praises, the rest of us were asked to make
sounds as though we were in the midst of a private view. For the same

purposes of reconstruction, Charensol said at the end: 'Ah, but I can see above the heads of the crowd a young English artist. This way, laddy, don't be nervous. Tell us what you think of Picasso.' I cleared my throat: 'Picasso is the king.' 'Bravo, bravo,' said Kahnweiler and his company. 'Provided,' I added, 'we understand that today *le roi s'amuse*.' Bam! that was the end of the live broadcast. Kahnweiler started screaming: 'Who let that little cretin in?' With everyone furious and Frank none too pleased, I scurried off home. Some time after this, with all the nonchalance of youth, I returned to the Kahnweiler gallery to see an André Masson exhibition. Kahnweiler must have seen me from his glass-fronted office. A secretary came to show me the door. How could I possibly return there, even with a word from Picasso on my behalf? I had my pride.

To the five hundred leaflets I had handed out, I received only one reply, proposing literally any old thing. Four walls in the middle of a field on the outskirts of Paris...

I met Picasso once or twice after that. I introduced my mother to him the following year, and he very graciously shook hands with her and did a little pirouette to show that, though he didn't know a word of English, he did know how to dance. My mother's reaction was equally amusing. The moment we were in the car I asked her how she felt after meeting the man everyone was talking about. 'Very clean. He's very clean.' 'For God's sake, is that all you have to say?' But it was true, he was always very clean, impeccably turned out.

Another time, I was with my two English friends, Ralph and Pauline Daubeny, who had driven all the way to the hotel at Eden Roc in a small Austin that Ralph had painted by hand on the eve of their departure. It wasn't until they parked their car among the Cadillacs and Rolls-Royces that they noticed in the strong sunlight that the brushmarks didn't even reach all the way down the bodywork, the bottom of which was of a different colour. They wanted to take a photo of Picasso and myself, so we stood there with our arms round each other's waist waiting for Ralph to fire the camera. There was nothing to be done. The camera, like the car, wasn't made for the Côte d'Azur. Impatient, Picasso, though photographed a million times over, didn't want to miss this one either. On all fours in the sand, he tinkered with the machine and, by golly, got it working again. We resumed our pose. We then said our farewells, everyone was very pleased, and there were the usual promises to send the photos on. A few weeks later, Ralph wrote to me from England to inform me that the photos were fantastic, and that he would be 'sending them on'. Nothing arrived, and a few months later I learned that my two charming friends had decided to divorce. They then did precisely that, and in the upheavals my photos with Picasso were lost.

Marcel Duchamp

BEFORE TALKING ABOUT MARCEL DUCHAMP, I MUST first of all say a few words about an astonishing character, Henri-Pierre Roché, since it was through him that Mimi and I came to know the great man.

Roché is a perfect example of what in French is called an *éminence grise*. His importance in his day was real and helped change the face of modern art. At the same time, hardly anyone had heard of him, and it was only very late in life that he acquired his celebrity, which looks set to last. His function was to act as a go-between between artists and their potential patrons, and it was he, if you please, who introduced Picasso to Gertrude and Leonard Stein, and Brancusi to his maharajahs. He told me that he had slept for ten years with the Douanier Rousseau's famous painting, *La Bohémienne endormie*, rolled up under his bed, before selling it to the American collector John Quinn, who later donated it to the Museum of Modern Art in New York. Roché was an old friend of Marcel Duchamp, and when I visited him in the early 1950s in his apartment at Denfert-Rochereau, his drawing room was filled with Duchamp's works. Two books written towards the end of his life – *Jules et Jim* and *Deux Anglaises sur le continent*, which I saw him writing in bed, this time at Sèvres – made him famous, particularly the first. François Truffaut's film adaptation of *Jules et Jim* turned it into a cult book, an effect further reinforced by the publication of Roché's private journals, in which we discover that the story of *Jules et Jim* was indeed his own.

Henri-Pierre Roché had a long-limbed silhouette and was a great womanizer. The moment I found out he was interested in Mimi's painting, I hadn't the slightest doubt he was equally interested in her person. The nobility of her face struck him as the very incarnation of the French republic, and with this idea in mind he even wrote to his friend the statesman Edouard Herriot to propose she be elected president of the republic, so that stamps could bear her profile! Then he decided that Mimi would do Marcel Duchamp's portrait on his forthcoming trip to France, and it's true that she excelled in male portraits. Roché was also interested in my own work and, in the last letter he addressed me, regretted that his physical condition did not permit him to be present at my private view in London in 1954.

Duchamp's return was announced with great feverishness in intellectual newspapers like *Combat*, because he had remained elusively in New York since the war. He was accompanied by his new wife, Teeny. The day after they arrived, the Duchamps were extricated, by what force of persuasion on Roché's part I can hardly imagine, from the swarm of their admirers, André Breton and the Surrealist group at their head, and diverted to our humble little fourth-floor studio, with no lift, on the place de la Sorbonne.

It was there that I found them after the portrait session. Night had fallen, and our table, hardly ever cleaned, was lit up by our only lightbulb. Teeny Duchamp, *grande dame* of New York, visibly felt she was not in her place. As for Marcel, it took a lot to astonish him, but still… The four of us were standing there staring at each other, when a knock came at the door. I opened it to find our good friend Clive Hubbard, the Woolworths heir, holding a huge silver platter on which was everything he had prepared that day in his course at the Cordon Bleu – a lobster and plenty else besides. Behind him was a ravishing young Swedish girl carrying bottles of champagne. The ice was broken. Teeny Duchamp knew what to do with a lobster, and accepted our proposal that they dine with us in a flash. The dinner was extremely merry, despite the fact that Clive, needless to say, had never heard of Marcel Duchamp. As for the Swedish girl…

When the meal was finished, Mimi whispered to me that I should show my work to Marcel. I resisted as best I could, but finally had to take out photos of a few works, since our four-metre-by-four-metre studio contained nothing. It was pretty much what I had shown Picasso shortly before – a few busts of children, a relief or two, followed by the high relief of the *Barcelona Tram*. Duchamp complimented me on the latter work, but I didn't believe him. He was so polite.

Many years went by. With my second wife, Janine, I had set up an art gallery in the courtyard of the building in the rue Monsieur-le-Prince where I had my studio, and in 1960 we inaugurated the gallery with an exhibition of my work. Four months had passed with only a single work being sold when, on the very last day, the writer on art Patrick Waldberg, an old friend of mine whom I had run into at Carmen's flat the previous evening, walked in accompanied by two painter friends, Jacques Hérold and William Copley. All three bought something.

What I didn't know was that William Copley came from a very rich family from Chicago, and that in the city he had a foundation: the William and Noma Copley Foundation. The names of its advisors were Man Ray, Max Ernst, Darius Milhaud, Sir Herbert Read, Hans Arp, Alfred Barr Jr and, as a director – Marcel Duchamp. Each year, the Foundation awarded a prize for the arts, and in 1961 William Copley was busy describing the works of interest he had found during his recent trip to Europe. Among the names on his list was my own, and when he pronounced it Duchamp said: 'He's the one.' Thus I received the $2,000 Foundation Award, which thirty years ago was quite good going.

The only other occasion on which I saw Marcel was five or six years later, at the exhibition of his friend Richard Lindner at the Galerie Claude Bernard. When I arrived at the private view, it was to find Marcel and Teeny Duchamp sitting with the artist on a bench in the middle of the room and the entire gathering lined up along the walls in silence, staring at them. When he saw me arrive, Marcel sprang to his feet in his ever youthful way – he was nearly eighty – and said to me: 'Good evening, Raymond, how are things?' It was not in itself a remarkable phrase, but it made a powerful impression on the staff of the gallery, and a no less powerful one on Claude Bernard.

Balthus: A Testimony from the 1950s

I MET BALTHUS IN 1955 AT THE HOME OF THE MARVELLOUS Carmen. It is important to state this at the beginning, and Balthus will certainly share my view. Carmen's salon on the rue de Varenne was the last at which major artists of all kinds could get together to come and go as they pleased, certain of their welcome. There were still the unrivalled receptions of Marie-Laure de Noailles, of course, but you couldn't just turn up there when you felt like it. The Noailles didn't leave their key under the mat. Carmen did.

Ordinarily, however, Carmen assembled her circle by telephone, telling you who would be there on the evening in question. The line-up was irresistible. Among those I saw gathered about the mistress of the house and her husband, François,* and on more than one occasion all together, were Balthus, Cassandre, Man Ray, Max Ernst, Poulenc, Sauguet, Auric, Jacques Prévert, Jeff Kessel and Maurice Druon, Patrick Waldberg, Jacques Lacan and Boris Kochno; Giacometti, for the space of a dinner, and Dora Maar; Marie-Laure herself, but in her capacity as an artist; César at his most entertaining and already well known; Carmen's old chum Gaston Palewski, and another great friend, Christian Dior, whom Carmen had known since before the war, when he had been the business associate of Pierre Colle.

I am not straying from my subject, since Balthus was the darling of that household. After all, I cannot hope to compete in these few brief lines with specialists of his work, and, before I touch on that subject, I would like to situate the painter in his milieu, in that warm soil of friendship and affection which, until very recently, has enabled him to remain secret and self-reliant. Nourished in this way, he had no need of a public life, let alone publicity,

---

* Of Mexican origin, Carmen was by her first marriage the wife of Pierre Colle, Balthus's dealer in Paris before and during the war. Their three daughters, Marie-Pierre, Béatrice and Sylvia, make an appearance in the history of art as Balthus's *The Three Sisters* (1960). After the death of Pierre Colle, who died prematurely in 1948, Carmen married François Baron, with whom she has a son, Jean-Marie.

and I think he will hold out to the very end against any form of interview or photo session.* Today, it is his work that has dragged him into the limelight.

My own recollection of that moment in the 1950s amounts to a delicious, sweet fragrance of happiness. I was on intimate terms with several important families, and for some time was penetrated by the beauty, still more the grace, of a society which ten years later had ceased to exist. I was less tormented by my artistic ambitions, since art seemed to be firmly in the hands of these lords and masters of my profession, whom I had met at last. I wasn't envious of them. I admired them. I was, in the strict sense of the term, their 'protégé'.

In Carmen's drawing room, then, the walls of which Cassandre had painted in an astonishing orange-coloured *frottis*, we tasted of the pure delights of art and friendship. That the figures gathered together in this way spoke neither of career nor money added, of course, to the dignity of these top-floor rooms, from which we gazed down on the elegant and peaceful city surrounding us, so remote from the mercenary years of today.

Whisky, on the other hand, was firmly established as the drink indispensable to conversation, and everyone smoked Gauloises, having never heard it said how harmful, even deadly, those little marvels were. In fact, while art brought us together and politics at times divided us, the atmosphere was largely dominated by laughter, and of this company of brilliant and witty men – and women, of course – the most amusing was without contest Balthus. I have often remarked that men of the first water who are extremely serious in their lives can be great comedians. Like Giacometti, Balthus could describe his preoccupations, which were very pessimistic at times, with a mordant irony and a sense of phrasing that immediately provoked laughter all round.

In those days, he would arrive in Paris from his retreat in the Morvan,

* A few years ago, I was caught up in a curious ballet in which Henri Cartier-Bresson, whom Balthus admires, had with his usual extreme reticence asked me to tell Balthus that, in the course of an artistic journey through Italy, he would like to go to the Villa Medici to do the portrait of the artist whom he profoundly esteemed. It's true that after zigzagging for a long time in Umbria and Tuscany, Cartier-Bresson arrived at the Villa. By what common accord the photo was then not taken I do not know.

the château of Chassy, furnished, I later found out, with little more than his own magnetic personality. If he needed to stop over for a few days, he would stay at Carmen's. He was, as I have said, at home there. The first time I saw him, I was wearing tartan trousers. Balthus immediately bowled me over. 'Are you Scottish?' he asked. 'Yes,' I replied (I'm only half-Scottish). 'Me too,' he said, telling me that he was a Gordon like his ancestor, Lord Byron. The odds were that he would not have come forward in this way had he known that the man wearing the trousers was an artist, being little inclined, it seemed – I noticed this later – to talk about art and, by the same token, perfectly willing to speak about a whole host of other interests which he pored over with infinite tenderness and attention. These make up the Balthusian weave. Certain countries, certain places where he likes to meet with a few dear friends. In his own home, certain objects carefully chosen by himself. Also, at the time, English literature. And Mozart always.

The city with its multitudes was hardly suited to someone of Balthus' exquisite taste. At the same time, if he left Paris it was not, I think, because he no longer liked the city, certain aspects of which he knew and painted better than anyone. True, I had often heard him speak with disgust of Paris drowning in a sea of 'lousy cars', but at the moment of his own withdrawal, it was still possible to cross the boulevard Montparnasse twice in order to say goodbye to a friend. His departure was doubtless motivated by a desire to find a large space to live in and the solitude and quiet in which to work. It was no less certainly a way of distancing himself from the artistic centre. That this was not out of any reclusiveness on his part is clear from the importance he attached to friendship and to the company of others. No, it was a sacrifice, a deliberate withdrawal – one that was premonitory even, coming as it did so soon after the war – before an art world that he judged to be unstable. Balthus represented the great attempt at permanence in a neurotic avant-garde climate committed to perpetual change.* In the years that followed, when

---

* I try to give its full value to this departure. His elder and friend Alberto Giacometti was the town-dweller *par excellence*, and his art bears in it the feverishness of the city and the tensions of modern art. The closest contemporary to Balthus is Francis Bacon (born in 1909). I see them as the duality of the classical and the romantic encountered elsewhere within a single generation.

painters would alter the rules a thousand times in order to succeed more quickly, Balthus would take up the challenge of equalling the great painters of the past. To find a new solution to the problem, you have to keep the problem intact.

No clearer indication could be given of the gulf separating the paintings Balthus made at Chassy from the career race under way in the galleries of Paris than the slowness with which they were produced. I say 'produced' rather than 'executed', since Balthus was perfectly capable of covering a canvas in a single session – then of working over it for months, years even. He was equally capable of painting out a major work due to have been carried off the following day in the hands of the shipper.

Fundamentally, however, I don't go along with this idea that Balthus belongs to the past or owes everything to the past. To my eyes, the actual painting, which is indeed very skilful as regards technique, is merely a beautiful gown which barely manages to contain a content of great boldness – of great severity even. His canvases, long in the making, are ultimately *objets chargés*. Their burden of significance far outweighs any question of technique or outward appearance – and I am not referring, of course, to the erotic subjects alone, for his landscapes, still-lifes and portraits display the same disturbing density. A few years ago, when James Thrall Soby died, a selection of major works from his fine collection was hung in the foyer of the Museum of Modern Art in New York, where he had been an extremely important curator. Among the Picassos, Mirós, etc, all of the first quality, Balthus's *The Street* shone out, dominated even, with remarkable ferocity. Nor was there any doubt as to its modernity.

In conjuring up the man I came to know at Carmen's in this way, I should also note how precious, how utterly delicious that meeting was. This recluse from the water-logged fields of the Morvan was a legendary figure and all but invisible. And though I now knew the man, I knew virtually nothing of the artist, his works being as hard to come by as the man himself. I rarely left Paris, not owning a car, so Chassy in those days seemed remote. Later in the year, as though in fulfilment of my wishes, 'Birnam wood [did] come to Dunsinane'. I once more saw Balthus in the evening in the rue de Varenne, and I discovered that, during the day, he was installed with all his paintings from Chassy in Francis Gruber's old studio in the Villa d'Alésia. He was preparing an exhibition of the paintings he had done over the last few years, organized by Henriette Gomès in what had formerly been the Galerie Wildenstein in the rue du Faubourg-Saint-Honoré. Some preparation! He intended to touch up each of his canvases in the light of Paris, and no doubt he did.

My first real meeting with Balthus, then, was my visit to this studio where, all at once, I saw a profusion of works by this singular artist. It changed my life. That day, faced with the calm mastery of these huge canvases, I recognized in Balthus the second pillar, with Giacometti, on which a new art of the figure and of the figurative world could be built. At the same time, these two artists were so dissimilar that they had to be regarded as opposite poles. I passionately admired Giacometti's work, with the despair of knowing that I could never follow him in his quest for the absolute. His gaze grew daily more concentrated, his drawing scanned the object at hand like a laser. Loosening my grip, I had committed the sin of allowing myself to make a few high reliefs in which I had placed my figures side by side in a simple frontality. Balthus's painting immediately struck me as the epitome of breadth, with, from one edge of the canvas to the other, form rolling about form, cheeks well-rounded, eyes wide-set, the gesture monumental and ample. With, transcending that space, the artifice of composition, that sublime intellectual activity which I consider to be the *ne plus ultra* of art.

This plenitude, which was the first thing to captivate me in his work, and which captivates me to this day, is that of the *theatrum mundi*. The stage in his work is large. To begin with, the canvas itself is often very large. Against the backdrop of an entire street, of a mountain landscape, of a large room with all its fixtures – all so many still-lifes – a human comedy unfolds in which the *dramatis personae* perform public roles but at the same time reveal their private lives, and where the powerfully allegorical descriptions of the figures go hand in hand with the most subtle portraiture. The sublime and the grotesque sit side by side, as in any work of vast dimensions and superior ambition. Here, precisely, is the most astonishing detail in this lofty body of work: from the enraptured adolescents to the little old people bent in two, his world remains that of humble, simple folk, sometimes innocent, sometimes

Balthus, *The Passage du Commerce-Saint-André*, 1952–54. Private collection

not. This has not been sufficiently remarked upon, and it goes to show that the very life of a painter at work is secret and fundamentally different from the one he displays in public.

It is in the painting of sentiment that the true originality of Balthus lies; the much-vaunted painterly qualities associated with his name are of secondary importance. Without him, I think, sentiment would have died. Because the 'what' has the edge over the 'how', people think him somehow not modern. The manner today must be perfect, and in many artists' work it is. But the temptation of the great and the complex, even if this means failing, would be far more salutary in an age which oversimplifies everything. I allow myself to venture an opinion. In that minimalist art, so admired by the aesthetes, in which everything is stripped bare, it is actually the public that is fleeced. In an age ruled by purists, Balthus has done his work. Bravo!

Picasso, a great one for pacing the stage, admired Balthus (and vice versa, let us note). They were two sides of the same coin, he said. There is his customary genius in that remark. They do curiously have the same histrionic gift. Two men of the theatre – dramatic, poetic, no matter. The theatre presupposes an audience, it is intended for others.

We are that audience. If we are present in large numbers today, that is only just. The exhibition Balthus was working on in the Villa d'Alésia that winter of 1955–56 finally opened its doors; by the time they closed, it had received only a few sardonic lines in the press. This silence provoked a splendid article by Georges Hilaire, 'Complot contre Balthus'. Since then, of course, he has become famous, but I was reminded of that exhibition, and of the time needed to build up an *oeuvre* and have it accepted by the public, when I saw *The Room* again, painted in that same period (1952–54), now given pride of place here in the Pompidou Centre exhibition 'Réalismes' in 1981.

Yes, bravo Balthus. Thank you, Carmen. Greetings, dear Cassandre, your presence was enchanting. *Larchant* hung beside your bed. Thank you also to Marie-Laure, who loved Balthus dearly. As did Pierre Jean Jouve, though in his case he seldom set foot in Carmen's home, nor outside his own doorstep even, other than to visit Sils-Maria each summer in a Paris taxi.

What links these people together? I'll tell you: fantastic class.

Published in Balthus, *exhibition catalogue, Centre Georges Pompidou, Musée National d'Art Moderne, Paris, November 1983.*

Marie Bell and *Phèdre*

MARIE BELL WAS THE MOST FAMOUS FRENCH TRAGEdian of her day. I met her in 1958 thanks to a rich and generous artist friend called Diana Esmond. It was Diana, no doubt, who persuaded her to think of me for the stage sets and costumes for Racine's *Phèdre*, a series of gala performances of which Marie Bell wanted to stage – Phèdre was her greatest role – on the days when she wasn't acting alongside

Jeanne Moreau in Félicien Marceau's *La Bonne Soupe* at the Théâtre du Gymnase. The actors she had engaged were all three well known and very handsome: Jacques Dacqmine in the role of Thésée, Paul Guers as Hippolyte and her own husband, Jean Chevrier, as Théomène. The director had not yet been appointed. When she first contacted me, Marie was hoping for Jean Cocteau, but as this situation dragged on for a good six months I was able to engage in a lengthy *tête-à-tête* with Jean Racine, a period I consider to be one of the most fascinating and fruitful of my life as an artist. The choice of an Englishman born in the same county as Shakespeare for a work so rigorously classical and French as *Phèdre* might seem surprising. In fact, Racine's taut, chiselled alexandrines were ideally suited to a sculptor, and I am certain that I came very close to the true feeling of the play. I immediately situated the action in its distant mythological setting, which is conjured up for us, in artistic terms, by Greek sculpture alone, with its statues and low reliefs. There was also a restriction in terms of stage machinery that worked to my advantage. Since a moving walkway installed for *La Bonne Soupe* could not be changed, the only area in which the actors could withdraw was at the centre of the stage, making a side passage obligatory; to my way of seeing, however, this fitted in perfectly with the low reliefs and pediments of ancient Greece. The arrival in the rusticated stone palace at the forefront of the stage, which drew the spectator's gaze into a spiral labyrinth, I reserved for Phèdre alone. When Phèdre entered from the back of the stage, the red light pursuing her

made the spiral revolve into the full fire of the sun 'qui l'éblouit'. To the right was an alcove of the same palace, to the left a footpath beside a raging sea. Over the entrance to the central passageway, I placed a bull's-eye window of rough stone, the intersections of which formed a kind of black sun – a reminder *a contrario* of the radiance of the Sun King and the century of Racine. The men's costumes were modelled on the musculature of a naked man, gold for Thésée and silver for Hippolyte. Their hair was curled, a further reminder of the seventeenth century.

When Raymond Gérôme, an accomplished professional, was named director, I presented him with a series of drawings describing the movements of all the protagonists in each scene of the play! Never having worked in the theatre before, I was unaware that the stage designer came last in terms of importance. This soon became clear to me from the anger of Gérôme. My stage set was assembled in the famous workshops of Monsieur Laverdet, this being his last piece of work before retirement, but the painting was done entirely by my own hand. I had also decided to do the stage curtain, which flabbergasted the studio painters, who were accustomed to scaling up and executing the projects of the most famous painters from a small painting done on paper. As a result, they lined up to see how this bizarre Englishman was going to solve the problem. I began to realize the folly of my undertaking when I saw the canvas for the curtain, which was the size of a tennis court. Adding to this, there was a small detail I had overlooked: I could only stand back from the canvas, which was stretched out on the floor of the workshop, by the length of my own body. The subject of my stage curtain was a foreshortened version of the giant figure of Venus extending diagonally across the entire canvas – 'Vénus toute entière à sa proie attachée' – with an enormous hand that would remain visible once the curtain had gone up so as to underline that all the characters in the play were manipulated by her. I would have liked to have made a very forceful image using large, furious brush strokes. Alas, the only way of doing this would have been to have the thing scaled up by these professionals who stood around poking fun at me as I worked. Nevertheless, I battled on with the brooms placed at my disposal; not brushes, brooms. I was young and healthy, and after two heroic days of work, had succeeded in placing my lovely pink goddess on the black canvas. I later found out that Chagall, after asking for *Daphnis et Cloé* to be played on the gramophone, had made do with projecting vivid colours from the edge to brighten up the surface scaled up by the studio painters. Balthus, on the other hand, had stretched out across the finished curtain to touch it up with watercolours!

My honeymoon with Marie Bell started to sour when she turned down the costume I had designed for her. All my costumes incorporated pieces of black fabric so that they would blend with the stage set, which was based on black to suggest a distance in space and time. Marie destroyed this idea by pulling from one of her clothes-trunks the autumn-gold robe that she wore for her performance as Phèdre at the Comédie Française. I later realized that *monstres sacrés* like Marie are also *sacrés monstres*. But though I didn't like her conception of the play, which was too much like a Parisian *ménage à trois* for my taste, I admired her force and diction, which was a touch *faubourg*, it's true, but projected Racine's verse with absolute clarity into the furthermost reaches of the theatre.

The first gala performance was a huge success in terms of audience, with everyone who was anyone in Paris present, including the entire Rothschild family and, in the *loge d'honneur*, André Malraux, the new Minister for Cultural Affairs since De Gaulle had returned to power. My stage set was warmly applauded, and dressed in my costumes the actors really did look like gods of Greek mythology, with a touch of the astronaut as well. Marie and her troupe, of course, had a thoroughly deserved triumph, and the crush when everyone crowded backstage after the show to greet the actors was monumental.

It just so happened that my wife and I, while heading in the direction of our friend Jacques Dacqmine, found ourselves blocked in the crowd back to back with Marie Bell, who was leading André Malraux off to her dressing room. 'And the stage set?' asked the minister. 'Oh, a lad I know,' said Marie off-handedly. 'Well, he certainly knows how to pull something out of a box,' concluded Malraux. A remark which astounded me, since I had just finished my first high reliefs – sculptures in boxes, in other words – and since they had not yet been shown anywhere, nobody could have known about them. Malraux the visionary existed true enough.

I was paid very little for all these months of work, but had been given to understand that in the event that the play were performed other than on these few gala evenings I would receive an additional sum of money. I later learned that my stage sets had travelled to England and Greece without the slightest gesture on the part of Marie Bell. This marked our falling-out. I addressed a letter to the director of the Théâtre du Gymnase ('For love of Racine, and out of friendship for Marie Bell, I undertook...') in which I stated my contempt for this milieu in which great actresses call you 'chéri' and stage hands 'maître'. It was all bogus, like an oriental bazaar that the true artist must flee at the risk of ruining his integrity for ever. Needless to say, Marie Bell had ceased to exist for me. Five years went by.

Shortly after this, I had opened a small art gallery with my wife as a means of subsistence. In the course of our exhibitions we received visits from a Rothschild widow, who was getting on in years and was very humble in appearance. We were friendly with her in a kindhearted sort of way. One day an invitation arrived for a 'chez-elle' at six o'clock. Thinking it was a tea, and thinking that she was probably a bit lonely, I persuaded Janine to go. All the same, to my usual sports attire I added a white shirt and dark tie. To my great surprise, she lived in a huge mansion on the avenue Foch. The Baronne Edouard de Rothschild, as she was called, was receiving the best of her circle, with all the men wearing dark dinner jackets or evening dress, before dinner. Among them were at least twenty people I knew perfectly well. On that particular evening, however, no-one knew me, the country hick who had turned up in casual dress. When I sat down at my table, everyone else stood up. 'Let's go,' said Janine. Of course we were going to leave, but before doing so I wanted to look at the artworks – a further surprise – I could see all round me: Goya, Fragonard, Gainsborough and, among a hundred other things, a Vermeer now in the Louvre.

Just as I was tearing myself away to leave, Marie Bell and Jean Chevrier were announced. Like ordinary everyday fans, everyone stood up to applaud. Marie, long accustomed to such things, looked calmly round at the room, since she was also a bit short-sighted. 'What! You here, you pig-headed thing! Come and explain yourself,' and she marched the four of us off to a small table in a corner, so that I could speak to her while Janine talked with Jean

Chevrier (and she was certainly pretty enough for that). The other guests immediately queued up to pay their respects to Marie. 'Ah, good evening, my dear Viscount, do you know my great friend the sculptor Mason?' 'But of course, comment allez-vous, cher ami?' said one after the other, the very same men who had been snubbing me all evening. Good old Marie. With that, we were quits, in my view.

Ten years went by, then I ran into her again on the death of our mutual friend Diana, at the crematorium in Pantin. It had come as a great blow to us both, and Marie was sitting not far from me during those long, painful moments while you wait for the body to burn. She was very elegantly dressed in a Chanel suit. She rolled an eye in my direction and whispered 'How sad it is' in her superb stage voice. Always the joker, I replied: 'Yes, but for a tragedian like yourself...' Completely forgetting where she was, she exploded into booming laughter! She wanted to take me to Diana's house for the funeral meal, but, I don't know why, I felt I was needed at the studio.

More years went by, then one day the phone rang. She assumed I would recognize her 'Comment vas-tu, mon chéri?' I didn't. 'Ah, that surprises you, hey? Chéri, I need a beautiful black marble statue for my hall.' Given that I had spent the last twenty years making polychrome resins, I flared up: 'Black marble! That proves you haven't kept up with my career, Marie.' The tone got heavier. 'You don't have a black statue for me?' 'I'm sorry, Marie.'

Bang! She had hung up. A week later she was dead.

The Rothschilds

IN THE EARLY 1950s, DORA MAAR INTRODUCED ME TO Antoinette de Gunzbourg, who lived in a splendid mansion on the Esplanade des Invalides and for whom I made a bust of her little daughter, Alix. It was through Antoinette that I came to know Baron Alain de Rothschild and his wife Mary, as well as, for a few brief years, the exclusive world of Parisian high society. Alain and Mary had a daughter, Béatrice, who was strikingly beautiful, half-Nefertiti, half-gypsy, with a slender neck and jet-black eyes and hair. I attended the great coming-out ball given for her on the avenue de Marigny, where, on a gorgeous summer's night, the happy few danced beneath the beautiful pavilion put up by Jacques Frank in the gardens of the Rothschild home opposite the Elysée palace. This modern-style country fair, with silk dresses rustling among the floodlit groves and shadows, I rendered in a low relief with, in the foreground, the baroness Mary, as beautiful and statuesque as Ingrid Bergman, and more beautiful still on account of her natural distinction. The Baron came to the studio to purchase the work and, little by little, a friendship was formed which was further strengthened when Alain met my new wife, Janine, whose piquant, semi-Asian beauty pleased him greatly. Hitherto, he had assumed I was everything he imagined an artist to be. He had astonished me one day by telling me that he envied me, for while he was stuck in the bank all day (this was, in fact, true and I soon came to appreciate the Rothschilds for their devotion to work), I, in his imagination, rose in the middle of the morning and, having performed my ablutions, went out to lunch with a group of friends and easy-going young women, one of whom I then chose to take back to the studio with me. After making love, I would, of course, do a drawing or a quick sketch in clay, before going out again for the traditional dinner with my fellow artists. Wine, women and song!

In those days, to make a bit of money while pursuing my true calling, I specialized in executing highly detailed watercolours of the interiors of rich families, with all their paintings and *objets d'art*, the entire family, cats and dogs, etc – what in English we call a 'conversation piece'. The first one I did, of Carmen Baron's house at Garches, was particularly successful, since I was inspired by the beauty of her works of art and the warmth of her hospitality, and while those that followed were not of quite the same quality, they were well executed and the buyer got his money's worth. The Baron de Rothschild asked me to do the drawing room of their country house at Chamant, near Senlis. My arrival was fixed for Boxing Day 1956.

I had to be up early to catch the train to Senlis, where Mary would be picking me up by car, but just as I was putting my shoes on, while Janine was still sleeping, I realized to my annoyance that my thick winter socks, which I hardly ever wear in the city, had large holes in them. It was too late to do anything about it. In any case, who would ever see them? *En route.* Two hours later, Mary de Rothschild was waiting for me at the station at Senlis. 'Raymond, there's been a change of plan. We're going to join the men, who are out on a shoot, and have lunch with them.' A short while later, we arrived in front of a huge ploughed field, in the middle of which the small group of gentlemen could be seen leaning on their guns and chatting together and, sinking our heels in, we went over to meet them. 'Ah, there you are,' said Alain. 'I remembered you would be joining us, so I brought along a pair of Wellingtons for you.' Did this mean I would have to take my shoes off in front of this select company, revealing that my socks had holes? It did, and with the most extravagant contortions, I performed the operation as best I could while they stood by politely, watching; I may even have succeeded in hiding the holes, but at the price of convincing them that I was a particularly agitated artist.

The rest of the afternoon was hardly more restful. To stand next to some of the finest marksmen in France is to risk receiving from one moment to the next a dead bird on your head, for they rain down from the sky. My only distraction was the boar that suddenly came charging out of the tall grass in my direction, but, phew! he was stopped dead in his tracks by the village mayor. Despite everything, I kept sketching away at this busy scene, which was new to me. As was the tally at the end of the day, an impressive mound of birds and beasts, given in royal fashion to the people of the village before we made our way back to the old mill, Alain and Mary's country retreat. Here a last and unexpected ordeal awaited me: a manservant, his hands stretched out to help me off with my boots! My mind had been quickened by the open air, and the moment the holes appeared I cried out: 'What did I say? I told the Baron those boots were too big for me. And now I have holes!' The socks were whipped away on the spot, to return an hour later washed, darned and folded.

Normally, a Rothschild drawing room is heavily furnished, and even corners are not overlooked but receive a hanging, a genuine still-life or, more often than not, a sculpture on a pedestal. It's what is known as the Rothschild style. The drawing room at Chamont would pose me a further problem, since hordes of Christmas cards were scattered about the tables or strung out across the room on a washing-line. I knuckled down to the task, of course, sealing off the entrance at night with a large pile of weapons that I had taken down from the walls in the corridor to discourage the domestic staff from entering. The latter belonged to a hyper-motivated race that is likewise peculiar to the Rothschilds, I imagine, and, on leaving, I assumed, perhaps mistakenly, that I was supposed to tip these superior beings accordingly.

My watercolour was well received, but was to be my one-before-last. Shortly after this, Claude Serreulles, one of the Rothschilds' banking friends, asked me to make a watercolour of his drawing room in the avenue Montaigne. The room was prettily decorated, and at lunchtime I added monsieur and his wife, the beautiful Marie-Hélène, along with their two children and the household pets. On my very first day there, Claude Serreulles had warned me I would need to leave a blank space on my paper above the commode for a large yellow Chinese vase that he was having turned into a lamp. A week was not too long to do each of the family portraits, along with all the little knick-knacks, before the lamp arrived in Claude's arms and, after being much admired, took up its future place on top of the commode. After lunch, when everyone had left, I was about to put on a record as usual to keep me company me in my work, but as I was walking over to the machine something caught my ankle and tripped me up. As I fell, I managed to look round and see the Chinese vase following me in my fall and smashing into pieces. The new addition to the familiar geography of the room had been fatal to me. Claude Serreulles was very gentlemanly about the loss of this priceless vase, paying me for the watercolour – which, when I saw it again later, I found of good quality. But people probably started saying about me: 'Mason, it's true, what talent! But watch out, he breaks everything,' since I never received a commission again. We remained friends, however, and later on they often came to my private views. It was only recently, glancing through a weekly magazine at the dentist's (where else?), that I discovered that Claude Serreulles had quite simply been the man who had taken over the leadership of the French Resistance on the death of Jean Moulin. This handsome and distinguished man could put up with the breaking of a Chinese vase.

To return to the time when Béatrice was still living at her parent's home but, like every member of the younger generation, was eager to shake up the family way of life, Janine and I were very close in those days to Tony Saulnier, a top photographer at *Paris-Match* who lived with his mother in an apartment of great historic interest in the rue Jacob, surrounded by their staggering collection of primitive art. Tony, through his work with the magazine, had met a young flamenco dancer known as La Chunga, who was very sexy *à la* Brigitte Bardot and just starting to make a name for herself. He was looking for somewhere to hold a large party in Paris that would launch her career. Béatrice, who had met Tony through us, had offered them the Rothschild mansion! For the photographer and reporter from *Paris-Match* it was a gift from heaven: gypsies at the Rothschilds' (since La Chunga always travelled with a large family in tow)! It should be said that the Baron, who was very young at heart, was not unduly put out by his daughter's bold behaviour, and decided to assemble his own family for the occasion, who were equally numerous. The project, swelling in proportions, resulted in a great party in the gardens of the Rothschild mansion attended by a good slice of the 'Tout-Paris', the lawn turned over to accommodating a giant barbecue with an entire animal on the spit. It was a beautiful summer's night. Naturally, Janine and I were there surrounded by our friends, among them my dear friend Jacques Dacqmine with his sparkling Simone. Everything was perfect, absolutely perfect, until the moment La Chunga, to thunderous applause, climbed onto the rostrum to dance. Dance? The poor girl, apart from wriggling about, hadn't the faintest idea. It wasn't long before this particularly demanding audience was poking fun at her, and had it not been for her younger sister, aged ten, who came striding up to the rostrum to show what a gypsy could do, the whole thing would have ended in disaster. Tony, the instigator of it all, was in any case in no fit state to observe the damage, for his wife, who had arrived back from the country that very morning, had discovered another woman's hair in their bath and given her husband a solid boxing. He didn't take a single photo all night (Baron Alain, disgusted, went upstairs to get his Kodak), and the great article in *Paris-Match* never appeared. As Georges Mazouyer, the journalist who had been lined up for the job, remarked to me later that night in a bar: 'We really hit the bottom of the cesspool tonight.'

My studio on the rue Monsieur-le-Prince was no more than a glass-covered courtyard overlooked by three windows belonging to the property next door, and, though the latter had wire mesh placed over them, one of them was partly open. Inside the place (which had been lying empty, I later found out, for fifty years) I could see busts and old leather-backed furniture, all buried under the dust of the past and that, more recent, of my plaster. It had once been home to the oldest insurance firm in Paris, Les Sauveteurs de la Seine. Balzac had been a member and, as I write these lines, I can see from my window the stepping stone in the yard which they used to mount their horses in those days.

At the end of 1959, I had the nasty surprise of hearing voices next door and discovered that there were plans to turn the place into a youth club. In heaven's name, the tranquillity of my work-place would be done for, so it was clearly urgent that I acquire the place myself. Since the key money was a million old francs and I didn't have anything remotely approaching such a sum, I finally got my courage up to go and ask Alain de Rothschild for a loan. As I waited in the corridor of the old family bank on the rue Lafitte, I was greatly impressed by the documents on the walls, among which, for example, was a cheque for a million thalers to the order of the German state. Once I had been admitted to the no less impressive office of the Baron, the latter listened to me and then informed me that he never lent money to a friend (it's not hard to see why). On the other hand, he would gladly commission from me for the aforementioned sum a bust of his wife or his daughter, leaving it to me to choose. I opted for Béatrice, who had more pronounced features than Mary, who was too beautiful. It was the beginning of a long story.

As is often the case in a story that endures, things got off to a terrific start. In a few sittings I had put together a good bust of Béatrice, and we were able to phone her father at the office to say that the thing was finished and was a great success. 'Fine,' said Alain, 'come and pick up the money.' This we then did, and afterwards Béatrice and I went to celebrate in a bar nearby. Needless to say, her face was now more relaxed, she held her head more proudly than when she had been sitting for me on a makeshift dais in the studio, and I said to myself that a small touch here and there to the clay would make it even livelier still. With two or three beers inside me – and the million francs in my pocket – I returned to the studio, my mind set on doing exactly that.

By midnight, the bust was a ruin and I was fully sober once more. No matter, I would sort it all out the following day. But no, neither the following day nor on any other day of the month did I sort it out. The money, on the other hand, I had used immediately to secure the property next door. This wasn't right. I should have taken it back to the rue Lafitte. But what on earth was I talking about, since I was sure to complete the bust the following day? Yet a year went by, and my friend, Baron Alain, became extremely annoyed about the whole business, all the more so as people were now talking about me in parties as the person who had swindled the Rothschilds!

In the meantime, Janine and I had decided to turn our empty property into an art gallery, since I wasn't making a living from my art. I knew some talented young artists, I knew how to present their work, how to ensure the proper lighting, could write meaningfully about their work – yes, all this I knew, but not how to sell them. My wife, on the other hand, had a gift for human contact and business, and knew everything about accounting and quite a lot about the legal side, too. We put our two skills together and, all in all, it worked, and after three or four years the Galerie Janine Hao had made a name for itself. But not straightaway, for the four months of the opening exhibition – my own – went by virtually without a sale.

During all this time, though it's hard to believe, I was working on the bust. I always lunch alone at the studio and one day, after intending to eat a steak, had placed a knob of butter to melt in the frying pan, and then gone out to get the bread. In the street I ran into a friend, we chatted for a while and, on my return, the studio was filled with blue smoke from the burned frying pan. As I was standing in the doorway, puzzled and annoyed, I heard the doorbell to the gallery ring, Janine being at home feeding the girls. Walking round to answer it, I discovered Mary de Rothschild radiant in a pale rasberry-coloured twinset and matching turban – it was spring – and with half a dozen rows of pearls around her neck. 'Raymond, I've come to see the bust.' 'Quite impossible,' I replied, 'come and see for yourself.' Mary plunged fearlessly in. Needless to say, she couldn't see a thing, not that I would have shown her anything anyway, but one thing is sure: everything the Baronne de Rothschild was wearing that day would have to be thrown into the dustbin when she got home.

A more serious incident occurred a few weeks later. I had returned to the studio one evening to struggle with the bust once again, being troubled by its non-success, when all of a sudden there was a knock on the door. Since I wasn't expecting anyone at that late hour, I said: 'Who's there?' 'Alain,' replied a voice I didn't recognize except that, yes, I thought it might be a visit from a delightful friend, the Scottish architect Alan Colquhoun, in Paris at the time. I opened the door and, like a tiger, Baron Alain leapt into the studio in evening dress. 'The bust,' he said, walking towards the work in the middle of the room that I had covered before opening, since I showed it to no-one. 'Out of the question,' I shouted, snatching the cloth from his hand. A short struggle ensued which I found extremely unpleasant, being obliged in this way to offend a man I sincerely liked. Then Alain de Rothschild left, seriously angry.

I no longer remember at what moment Béatrice telephoned to say that her father demanded the immediate arrival of the bust at the Rothschild mansion. Faced with this diktat, Béatrice put forward a temporary solution to the problem, for, she argued, I had an extremely important exhibition coming up at the Galerie Claude Bernard and, while the Baron had lost patience with me, I for my part was wasting my time and perhaps losing the chance of my career. (This makes it easier to determine the moment when she called, since the exhibition was scheduled for May 1965 – and the bust had been begun in 1960!) Her idea was that I should bring the bust, wrapped in canvas and tied up with string, round to their house, where it would be placed in the attic until, once my exhibition was out of the way, I could start work on it again, calmly and with a whole new eye. Naturally, I had to agree. I went back to the bust to make one last great effort – I should add that I had moulded it in plaster months before, thinking I would be able to sculpt the hard surfaces better – and, at the end of the day, wrapped it in canvas with a strong piece of cord, which I knotted as I still remembered how to do from my days in the Royal Navy. Then I climbed into a taxi and set off for the avenue de Marigny.

The bust, which went down to the waist and was slightly larger than life, plus the square plinth, was heavy and I was carrying it slowly up the steps of the Rothschild mansion when I heard the Baron striding briskly up behind me, his day at the bank over. 'To what do we owe the pleasure of a visit, Raymond?' I quickly explained the situation to him, that I was taking the bust up to the attic and… 'What, I at last have this wretched sculpture in my home and I'm not allowed to see it? Take it straight into the drawing room!' I had no choice but to obey, though I was instantly filled with the blackest despair at the idea of having to show him my aborted bust after working on it in vain for all these years. Alain pointed to a commode and, to make room for me – this gives you an idea of the tension in the air – with a sweep of his hand flung a small painting by Alberto Giacometti onto the floor – a head of Béatrice!

With clenched teeth, I undid the covering of the bust. There it was at last before our eyes. The astonishment was all mine. Shining in its white plaster, the sculpture was good. The pose of the head, the likeness – it was all there. Taken out of the harsh light of the studio, set off to its advantage by the flattering lights of the luxurious drawing room, there was an unhoped-for gentleness about it. Alain exploded with joy and, before I could stop him, grabbed the sculpture, covering his dark grey suit with plaster dust, and started walking out of the room, explaining to me on the way that he wanted to show it to his wife, who was in bed with lumbago. Béatrice having joined us in the meantime, we all found ourselves together in the end, lying on Mary's bed, clinking our glasses of champagne to the bust's success!

Success or relief? Béatrice told me that when Balthus saw it he spent a long time pondering it. Her husband by her second marriage, Pierre Rosenberg, the director of the Louvre, has no hesitation introducing me to people as 'the sculptor who made my wife's bust'. Above all, my friendship with the Baron was repaired, he and his wife holding a party for me at the Rothschild mansion to celebrate my exhibition at the Galerie Claude Bernard.

Claude Bernard

CLAUDE BERNARD HAÏM, OWNER AND DIRECTOR OF the Galerie Claude Bernard in the rue des Beaux-Arts in the sixth arrondissement of Paris, was my dealer for twenty years. My opinion of him is in the main positive, which is saying a lot of a relationship as difficult as that between an artist and his dealer.

He once told me that when his father found out he wanted to open an art gallery he agreed to help him. He collected paintings himself. He was only anxious to know if Claude intended to work hard, in which case it would have to be the Right Bank, or just enjoy himself, in which case it would be the Left Bank. For once in his life, Claude Bernard opted for the Left. At the beginning, in 1957, he tried to enjoy himself with a piano in the basement of the gallery and concerts to go with it. It may not sound very serious, but Claude Bernard is a musician at heart and had originally thought of making a career of it. To really enjoy himself, however, is not in his nature. Throughout all the years he gave dinners, parties and entertainments for his large circle of friends, I never once saw him other than with a slightly furrowed brow. He wasn't enjoying himself because he wasn't really present, his thoughts already running on ahead to his plans for the following day.

In the late 1950s and 1960s, his gallery exhibited only sculptures and related works on paper, a fact remarkable in itself and, indeed, unique. His reputation was already considerable thanks to his stars, César, Ipoustéguy and Roël d'Haese, all of them relatively young at the time, and to his fine exhibitions of modern sculpture. Exceptionally among dealers who have a large gallery to run, he had launched all his artists himself. He didn't take them on with their reputations already made, as was the case with the Galerie Maeght, for example. Let us add to the names already cited Szafran, Botero, López-Garcia, Claudio Bravo, Segui, Barthélemy and myself. All of us, in the first fifteen years of the gallery, began our real careers with him. Later, he took on celebrities like Balthus, Bacon and Dubuffet and a good twenty others, and though, of course, his reputation didn't flag, far from it, his early period as an inventor was over.

At the end of the 1950s, I still didn't have a dealer interested in my work and, through a series of coincidences, had set up to the best of my abilities, and with the skills of my wife, an art gallery in the property adjoining my studio in the rue Monsieur-le-Prince. We inaugurated the gallery with an exhibition of my sculptures in plaster and accompanying drawings. César, whom I knew through Carmen Baron, came to the private view. He mentioned it to Claude Bernard, telling him to go and have a look. This the dealer did, but since Janine ran the gallery, which bore her name, I was not present at the time. In any case, he didn't say a word, as is customary among dealers on such occasions. Nothing came of the visit, which didn't in the least surprise me, since my work, being resolutely figurative, had nothing in common with the sculptures exhibited in his gallery.

Three years went by. A few small breaches were slowly being made in the abstract movement (Giacometti and Balthus were figures apart). I went to see Claude Bernard to suggest that the time had perhaps come for him to reconsider my sculpture. With perfect readiness, he confessed that he had reached the same conclusion and that he would come to my studio. A date was fixed, and one morning Claude Bernard turned up with a severe-looking woman whom I took to be a business associate. I was expecting him to offer me a contract, no doubt modest, César having warned me that I would have to enter by the *petite porte*. Instead, the dealer, after inspecting everything, asked me quickly how much it would cost to make six copies of this, ten of that, and so on. The impressive-looking woman was quite simply his secretary, pulling out her pad to note down the ridiculously low prices which fell from my lips. In this way I sold off my entire studio, with multiple copies of good sculptures, for next to nothing.

A date was fixed for an exhibition, and the sum due to me would tide me over till then. However, I was no longer thinking of money, but of the exhilarating opportunity to show my art in this important gallery to the Parisian public. I was slightly over forty. The time had come.

The result of all this, one of the best periods of work in my entire life, was the large *Crowd*, which was to be the centrepiece of the exhibition. At the same time, I was leaving for the Fonderia Bruni in Rome to have *The Barcelona Tram* and the *Carrefour de l'Odéon* cast in bronze. A magnificent foundry with magnificent craftsmen, to say nothing of the absolute beauty of the city, where I met up with Balthus once again, now director of the Académie de France at the Villa Medici. The preparations for the exhibition were going ahead under happy auspices. I made the acquaintance of Jacques Bornibus, an old friend of Claude's who ran the Musée de Roanne and wrote the preface to my catalogue. I liked the text, which was subtle like Bornibus himself, and the catalogue, printing and photo-engravings were first-class.

Another piece of good news was that Baron Alain de Rothschild and his wife, Mary, had offered to hold a large party for me at their mansion on the avenue de Marigny on the night of the private view, to which I could invite any friends I wished. I made a point of inviting the staff of the gallery, including the carpenter, Michel, who had worked so patiently on my behalf.

The party was called off due to a perverse streak in Claude Bernard's character. Arturo Bruni, the eighty-year-old doyen of Italian art foundries, had asked that the payment for the work be made in Rome in one particular form, while Claude felt that it should be made in another. My two bronzes remained stuck at the foundry. Since the exhibition was unthinkable without these two important items, the date of the private view was pushed back. Too late for the Rothschilds, who had already left for Davos.

As soon as the exhibition was in place, I went south to recover. There were a lot of reviews, for the most part favourable. '*The Crowd*, Notre-Dame in the middle of an art gallery,' wrote Jean Bouret, while Claude Roger-Marx in *Le Figaro* spoke of Rodin. Annick, the secretary whom I had wrongly thought dour, told me how surprised visitors were to see figurative art at Claude's. I was the first of that trend, which he was later to adopt so thoroughly that his gallery has acquired something of an anti-avant-garde complexion in recent years. The exhibition was a success. I let a few weeks go by before going to see Claude Bernard to find out on what footing we would be continuing our collaboration – in short, how much money he was going to give me in order to work. He opened his wide, charming eyes, as though taken aback by my request: 'Alas, I can do nothing for you.' The works not sold, including, of course, *The Crowd*, returned to the studio, and I no longer had a centime to my name. In the meantime, people who thought I was over the worst would stop me in the street to shake hands with me and, knowing how long I had struggled in the wilderness, would say: 'At last! But you deserve it.'

With five of us to support – Janine had three splendid daughters – we had to concentrate all our energies on the gallery. Our programme was organized largely around unknown artists, since we had no money to give them, but the friendships I had struck up with a number of important artists and writers resulted in a certain esteem in artistic circles and some striking exhibitions which enabled us to survive, though always modestly after the cost of invitations, catalogues and advertising had been absorbed. When the eighty-year-old Léopold-Lévy walked into the gallery for the first time, he said: 'I'm very fond of this street, mon petit. When I came here with Verlaine…' (His English teacher at the Lycée Rollin had been Stéphane Mallarmé. 'He looked at his watch every five minutes.') Gaston-Louis Roux sold his paintings himself by telephone in the evening in the gallery. After a marvellous show consisting of all the original gouaches for Cassandre's posters and stage sets, we made a big splash with the first ever exhibition of Balthus's drawings and watercolours.

Collectors and dealers came pouring in from all sides. Bizarrely, Claude Bernard, who would later become Balthus's dealer and was already showing an interest in his work, didn't take the trouble to walk the few hundred yards separating us. Others, like Erica Brausen from the famous Hanover Gallery in London, didn't regret their visit. Just as she walked into the gallery there was a power-cut in the neighbourhood. No electricity, and we were at the back of the courtyard without daylight. Not in the least put out, Erica, who was Francis Bacon's first dealer, went and bought herself a pocket lamp, then came back and purchased the two best drawings. It was the caller the following day, however, who really interested us. Janine had received a visit from Jan Krugier, whose gallery in Geneva was already well known at that time. A Balthus specialist, he bought two or three works and was just settling up with Janine when he added in a low voice: 'My dear madame, would there be any way of buying something of your husband's?' Janine was astonished. Sell? Nothing could have pleased us more. 'Oh I see,' Krugier went on, 'I thought that, what with his contract with Claude Bernard…' 'Contract? What contract?' said Janine ironically. Krugier dropped his confidential tone: 'What!

That man! After seeing Mason's exhibition at his gallery, I went and told him that I was very interested in the show and wanted to share the artist with him. He replied that he was sorry, but that he had exclusive world rights with Mason. He lied to me. Where's Mason?'

Into the studio in this way came Jan Krugier, dressed all in white, walking stick in hand, very Central European (he is of Polish origin, which in part explains his attachment to Balthus). 'Mason, it's the greatest day of our lives!' He said that he and I were going to do business together and that the two of us would have to go and make Claude Bernard eat his words. I agreed to accompany him to begin with, then later in the evening called him to tell him to go on his own. We arranged to have lunch together afterwards. The following day, chez Maître Paul at the bottom of my street, a jubilant Krugier arrived, telling me that Claude had tried to scare him off by saying that I was horribly difficult. To which he had replied that if they started counting up all the artists who were difficult, a lifetime would not suffice. 'No, Mason, let us forget this monsieur and think of ourselves. The Galerie Jan Krugier offers and guarantees you a thousand francs a month, and slightly more when you have an exhibition.' Astounded by so insulting a proposition, I got up from table, excusing myself on the grounds that it was time I returned to the studio. (Thirty years later, in the summer of 1997, Zoran Music informed me that Krugier would certainly have been talking in Swiss francs, distinctly more advantageous!)

Pierre Matisse, Balthus's dealer in New York, also came to the exhibition. While he was there, he also acquainted himself with my own work and, to my great pleasure, decided to take me into his gallery in New York. A few weeks later, I went to Claude Bernard's to show him a batch of drawings. He paid me very little for them, but I knew that he bought Roël d'Haese's for the same price – 20,000 old francs. I told him that they would be going up, now that I had joined a new gallery. 'Ah yes,' he said in a mocking tone of voice, 'Monsieur Mason has entered Monsieur Krugier's gallery.' 'No, not at all.' 'Ah, no? Whose then?' 'Pierre Matisse's.' Seldom have I have seen a man look so astonished. He only opened his mouth to tell Annick to go and buy him some cigarettes, and he waited until he had lit one before saying, 'My congratulations, Mason.'

Claude Bernard treated me very differently after that. We conversed in a friendly way and took pleasure in discussing our mutual love of music. Claude's years of luxury had begun, with the addition of a concert hall and a magnificent organ to his already sizeable property of La Besnardière, north of Tours, and the numerous parties he gave there. In Paris, guests invited to his palatial residence at l'Etoile, one of the *maisons de maréchaux* built around the Arc de Triomphe, would almost invariably be treated to a magnificent concert as well, featuring Jean Guillou at the organ – yes, there was even an organ there – or Sviatoslav Richter at the piano.

Needless to say, Claude and I didn't always see eye to eye, and his nature made him inclined to sulk for quite some time on such occasions. Speaking of Richter, I remember an argument with Claude that dragged on and on. He must have felt he had been the one in the wrong and, to soften me up, made a gesture that must have cost him dearly – he gave me his seat next to Richter for a Maurizio Pollini concert at the Grange de Meslay. Richter adored his Claude Bernard. He always stayed with him in Paris and would have liked him to drop his gallery and become his impresario, so the thing must have been equally painful for him.

I can't resist telling the story of that Schubert concert, a strange choice of composer for an athletic pianist like Pollini who excels in firework displays but doesn't seem to know how to internalize. The first part left me so cold that I didn't want to leave my seat during the interval and have to hear ecstatic praise being showered on him by this audience of snobs. Schubert's sublime slow movements were not 'inhabited', Pollini contenting himself with playing the notes more slowly but putting nothing between them. I had noticed Richter shaking his head disapprovingly during this first part, though, as the musical director of the festival, it was he who had programmed his Italian colleague.

Hardly were the audience back in their seats after the interval than the hall was plunged into darkness. After a few moments, the owner appeared, his face lit up by a pocket-lamp, to inform us that the mishap was not the festival's responsibility but was due to a power-cut. As we had come together to hear the great final sonata, I stood up and said: 'Schubert probably wrote his sonata by the light of a single candle.' The audience applauded, and Richter was in seventh heaven. 'Yes, it would be better by candlelight,' he declared in a loud voice, using the word *chandelle* rather than the customary *bougie*, thus proving that he had a much better command of French than people thought. A few minutes later, someone came in with a candelabrum with at least ten lighted candles, and an instant later a second one. Maurizio Pollini sat down at the piano again and had just launched into the sonata when the lights came back on. Our poor virtuoso had to struggle right to the very end of this long sonata under the appalling heat from the projectors and the candles.

A few months after this, Richter himself honoured us with a private concert, likewise devoted to Schubert, at Claude's home at l'Etoile. But with what subtlety and profundity! I made two drawings of him on that occasion, one of which Claude gave to Richter and the other kept for himself. At the same time, it was Claude's lifelong dream to have a similar concert at his home by the great Horowitz. From one month to the next, over a period of several years, he would announce mysteriously or triumphantly that the thing was imminent, however improbable this seemed, given that the master showed no signs of wanting to leave Manhattan at his age. He did, in fact, give a last concert in Paris; Claude will certainly have been present, but by that time I had left the gallery and was not sitting next to him.

My second exhibition at the gallery once again demonstrated Claude Bernard's dogged perfectionism. Each artist had the right to demand a complete remodelling of the gallery space, and each time the walls were painted afresh. This was in the early days of the gallery, at 7 rue des Beaux-Arts, when it consisted of a long, low-ceilinged room broken up by two partitions. It wasn't much, but it exercised a powerful attraction on visitors, and it was here that Claude gained his public. On several occasions he later spread out to buildings to either side, without ever re-creating the impact and compression of that initial place.

In the meantime, it was a question of installing my new sculpture of the departure of the central fruit and vegetable market from the heart of Paris, my first polychrome sculpture. It was large and made larger still by the black frame in which its vivid colours were enclosed – like the country produce by night at Les Halles. It clearly couldn't fit into the gallery. Claude Bernard decided to have the frame removed and the back of the room painted entirely black. It still wouldn't fit in. The spire of the church of Saint-Eustache which features in the work was too tall. No matter! Claude, in kingly fashion, ordered a hole to be made in the ceiling!

The following weekend, a big party was held at La Besnardière to celebrate my exhibition of *The Departure of Fruits and Vegetables from the Heart of Paris, 28 February 1969*. All the tables placed outside were decorated with fruit and vegetables, and my memory of that day remains as fresh as those lovely fruits of the earth. It was a beautiful day, as it always was with Claude, who had a special arrangement with the heavens: whenever he gave a party, it might rain the day before or bucket down the day after, but on the day in question the weather was always perfect. During a walk with Sam Szafran, a favourite friend among the artists of the gallery, we gazed down from high ground on the party spread out below, with its hundred and fifty guests and the many buildings of this extraordinary country estate making it look more like a satellite town. Squeezing my arm, Sam said to me: 'You see, all that is ours.'

For this exhibition organized around my large sculpture, Claude also had the benefit of the eight original ink drawings I had made at Les Halles. When the main work left for an exhibition at the Pierre Matisse Gallery in New York, I decided to do a series of watercolours of fruit and vegetables to accompany it, and this kept me busy during the summer of 1971. They were the first watercolours of mine to be shown in public. I later found myself doing quite a number of them, for since my sculptures were now polychrome and no longer cast in bronze, they were preceded not by ink drawings but by colour studies. Claude turned out to be very jealous of these little works and started a small watercolour war with Matisse, until I agreed to furnish him with an exhibition made up exclusively of watercolours.

The fact that my health required a dry climate, along with the appeal of colour, made me choose Marrakech to do these watercolours. It was the month of February (I would be painting outdoors), with the snow-capped mountains of the Atlas still visible in the background of this enchanting city. On the very afternoon of my arrival I was already outside painting. In the native quarter I found an old hotel somewhat the worse for wear but with typical Arab furnishings. I later found out that it had previously been a brothel for the French army. Absorbed daily as I was in my work, everything interested me. I was very surprised to see Claude Bernard turn up, though I knew how fond he was of the country. He invited me to some magnificent restaurants to enjoy the excellent Moroccan cuisine, but also positioned himself behind me during the day to watch the watercolours progressing. This irritated me somewhat at the time, but thinking about it now, I find it rather touching. One day at noon we were lunching in a restaurant where the surroundings really were very beautiful: a closed patio with a few tables and, in each of the four corners, an orange tree. 'There you have it,' said Claude, 'it's all there. The rigour.' And he told me of his plans to do something similar at La Besnardière in the Touraine.

My exhibition of watercolours was variously received. For some, like Henri Cartier-Besson – this was the globe-trotter speaking – they were the best things I'd ever done. For my main American collector, Louis-Dreyfus, the worst.

Claude's plans for an Arab patio were put into operation – and how! He quite simply hired the tilers and mosaic workers of the King of Morocco, and they came and lived at La Besnardière with their families while they carried out the work. The result was a closed courtyard that was a masterpiece of subtlety, sobriety and rigour. After which, with his taste for luxury, Claude filled it first with sofas, cushions, rugs, ornaments and lamps, then with shrubs and flowers, turning it into something exotic with no sign of rigour anywhere. The main body of the building next door comprised a Nordic living room with a huge fireplace – plus organs, of course – and bearskins that were not only spread over the floor but also hung in front of the windows as curtains. Now when you parted them, you saw outside – Arabia! Elsewhere, you had to cross a pond – which often proved fatal to visitors who'd had too much to drink – to reach a greenhouse that in density and size resembled a Brazilian rainforest. Not far from there was the barn used for concerts that I mentioned earlier, its roof-beams carved by the finest carpenters in the Touraine, and home to a magnificent old organ, restored by Claude's great friend the master-organist Jean Guillou. For several years running, Claude staged a large number of concerts there, as well as two Handel operas, lodging on the premises entire opera companies from England and Sweden. Such was his largesse, in fact, that his sister Nadine feared that the gallery in Paris would be ruined by the extravagant lifestyle of the provinces. But no, Claude understood his public perfectly, and his affairs in Paris only flourished. It was the high point of Claude Bernard's career. Balthus and Francis Bacon exhibited in his gallery, and the company assembled at La Besnardière was of the smartest: famous singers and musicians, all the big names of television and radio, and many sculptors – the lawns were littered with their works – and painters of quality. Roberte, a local countrywoman and very fine cook, ran the house during these glorious years.

We were setting off one day for a weekend party at La Besnardière. At our usual meeting point in the hall of the Gare d'Austerlitz, Claude seemed more than ever to be lost in the folds of his large cloak. He was, in fact, clutching a she-monkey in his arms. A present from a woman friend, he was going to leave her in the country, he explained. 'She doesn't look stupid,' I said.

The country dining room awaited us two hours later. Set with plates and glasses, the dinner table glowed in the light from the big lamp and the great wood fire in the hearth at the end of the room. All the guests knew the house well and also knew that Roberte was worthy of the first-class cuisine in this region of the Touraine so dear to Rabelais. The dinner was sure to be a feast.

And a feast it was. Claude had placed the she-monkey next to his plate, from where, undaunted, she watched us tucking into Roberte's celebrated pâtés and terrines. The main dish arrived. It must have been good, it must have been excellent, for, overcome with excitement, the little monkey dived into it. Having grabbed the best piece, she then took off vertically and clung to the ceiling lamp. The latter swung in great circles round the table, while the monkey, hanging by her tail, stretched her fiendish claws in all directions. Claude's glass of claret was downed in one. My, that's good! She drank a second glass, knocking over more glasses while we looked on dumbfounded.

The festival might have continued in this way until the table had been totally destroyed (there was already a dish of rice strewn about and sauce flowing everywhere). Claude, as though emerging from a dream, put an end to our collective stupor. 'The housekeeper. Go and fetch the housekeeper. Put this animal outside!' The greedy young lady was caught, the wine having had its effect. I never saw her again. Someone told me she had gone back to her donor and had died shortly afterwards. Of indigestion, perhaps.

Private views at Claude Bernard's were the most successful in Paris. I say Claude Bernard's, rather than his gallery, deliberately. One Saturday morning I called by to find Claude standing near the door, looking very pleased with himself. 'You see, Raymond, in all the other galleries in the neighbourhood there's no-one, and here it's packed. What do you put this down to?' 'Your artists,' I replied. His astonishment confirmed what I had suspected for quite some time. Claude sincerely believed that the public came for him, attracted by his aura, eager to catch a glimpse of him. It's true that the unaffected elegance of his person, his beauty one might even say, had undeniable appeal and gave an extra something to the quality of his exhibitions. A private view at his gallery pulled in not only the art world but the smart set as well, and between them they made up a considerable crowd. In the great years, the rue des Beaux-Arts would be sealed off by police cordons at both ends, serving as waiting rooms for those hoping to get into the gallery. At the door, two employees were busy driving people back. By the end of the evening, the street had turned into a lake from all the water thrown by local residents wanting some peace and quiet. When the artist exhibiting was called César or, later, David Hockney or Francis Bacon, the number of visitors doubled. The Hockney exhibition brought in beautiful young men from California, bare-chested with sometimes a young leopard on a leash, while for Bacon a contingent of heavy drinkers from England would turn up who, at midnight, could be found on all fours or lying on their backs under the influence of alcohol. I myself had nothing to complain about at the private view of my last exhibition at Claude's in 1977. I occupied the two galleries of the time, and in the evening Claude invited a hundred and twenty-five people for a sit-down dinner at his home at l'Etoile. The exhibition also received a visitor of distinction in the person of François Mitterrand, leader of the French Socialist party at the time. No doubt a friend similarly inclined had suggested he go and see my big sculpture *A Tragedy in the North. Winter, Rain, Tears*, inspired by the mining disaster at Liévin, but he stopped for a long time in the room before this, where my polychrome relief landscapes of the valley of the Luberon were hung. Though I didn't know it at the time, François Mitterrand's sister owned a house at Gordes, and he told Claude that, while he knew I worked on the other side of the hill, this was the first time he had actually seen my work. He spent quite a long time in the gallery, before going on in the afternoon to give a much-awaited speech on national defence to the Chambre des Députés. The eternal *sang-froid* of the politician.

For several years, Claude let it be known that he was to be made Chevalier de la Légion d'Honneur at the forthcoming nominations. Time went by, none of us saw any sign of this. One fine day, walking into the gallery, Annick rushed up to me and whispered in my ear: 'It's done, the boss has been decorated.' And here indeed was Claude, striding out of his office with his chest thrust out with the rosette pinned to it. He made just a little tour round the gallery and, without saying a word to us, went back into his office. A few minutes later, he came out again, manifestly to satisfy our gaping eyes. Then a third tour. I stuck the pin in a second time by observing in a loud voice: 'Obviously, a red spot has never done any harm to an art dealer.' Everyone laughed. With an annoyed glance in my direction, Claude disappeared for good.

In general, at moments like this, Claude would furrow his brow, purse his lips and make his customary remark: 'English humour!' It is indeed the habit of my countrymen always to find something to laugh about. In any case, the general atmosphere was one of bonhomie. After years of working together, there was a genuine bond of friendship among the artists, as there was with the gallery staff who danced attendance upon us and were proud to work for an employer they adored.

The exhibitions, the moments when you dropped by at the gallery, were our recreation. We were still young. We laughed together, for artists, when they're not working, like to laugh. Work is another matter. The months and years between each exhibition, with the pressure to do as well as one's gifted fellow artists, to be worthy of so distinguished a gallery – that was no laughing matter.

The Crowd

I T BEGINS THE MOMENT I STEP OUTSIDE. IMMEDIATELY I'M bathed in light. Has anyone ever spoken about this astonishing moment? I straighten up, I forget myself and wrap myself in this mantle of light. Outside, more than anything, we are part of the celestial.

We feel ourselves to be lighter, moreover, and it is with a sense of a weight falling from our shoulders that we plunge into the bustling street.

The 'spectacle' of the street. That's putting it mildly. I'm gripped by the dazzling beauty – an explosion, a rending and merging. This crowd of people, growing larger as you approach, smaller as you withdraw, fragmented and altered by being superimposed, concealed then looming up out of sudden gashes in the mass, transformed by sex, age, height, dress, animated by gesture and expression. This inexhaustible whirling, captured and measured by the orderly gridwork of windows and doors, the spaces between which are likewise set in motion as I pass – opening ranks when I stand facing them, closing ranks like stigmata in the side-streets. Where else in the world could you find such a vision of continual metamorphosis? Fascinating like the procession of clouds, the waves of the sea, the diabolical dancing of fire, through its human significance it far surpasses them all and attains to drama.

Man multiplied. My own self no different from the rest, infinitely repeating itself, part of this movement which has to pass through me like a flame through a forest. The dark crowd bearing this flame. This for me is the great subject. If one could only capture this tremor which runs through life, this powerful surge of energy you meet with in the street. The complexity of the theme, the proliferation of images, the multiple articulations make it a phenomenal source for drawing and a sculptural medium *par excellence*, extending from broad daylight to the shadows present everywhere, gouging out an eye, a mouth, a hundred nostrils, running beneath the bosoms and skirts of women, hollowing out gashes in the crowd, in the doorways to buildings, in the spaces under cars. The power of the unknown in everyday reality. I would like to be able to set it all down accurately and lovingly, for its fecundity is on a par with that of nature itself.

If an artist's work were to take as its origin and foundation this everday reality of so wide a base, there would be no limit, in my view, to the heights to which it could attain. Symbolic forms and images can emerge, fruits of a mind hungry for grandeur and humanism. For something greater still.

A work can contain the All.

But, first of all, you must step outside…

Raymond Mason and the minister André Malraux before *The Crowd*, 1968.
Photograph by Martine Franck

André Malraux

IN WRITING ABOUT MARIE BELL, I HAVE ALREADY SAID how astonished I was to hear André Malraux, backstage at the Théâtre du Gymnase, giving a perfectly accurate summary of my work, which he had discovered for the first time two hours earlier: 'He knows how to pull something out of a box.' That was in 1959.

I read each volume of *Le Musée imaginaire* as it came out. The art world was sceptical, but, for my part, the obscurity and abstruseness of so many passages served to bring out the splendour of the original thoughts. I was extremely pleased, therefore, when chance allowed me to make his acquaintance.

Thanks to Jean Hélion, I had recently met the New Zealand photographer Douglas Glass. With his aggressive beard and manners to fit, you might have mistaken him for a savage from the outback, but he was in fact an extremely refined man who for many years was the star photographer of the *Sunday Times* in London, famous for his weekly portrait of an important, generally male, public figure. He went to a castle in Yorkshire for Winston Churchill, to Venice for Stravinsky, to Helsinki for Sibelius, and so on. He had come to see me because the Nobel Prize-winner Albert Schweitzer was staying incognito at a hotel in the rue de Vaugirard just round the corner from my studio. Glass desperately wanted to photograph him, but, having been turned down point blank by Schweitzer's entourage, had rented the room above and was busy making a hole in the floorboard. Then he thought of me, and I was able to step in before matters got too serious.

The second time we met was for a photo of Malraux. This time round, Douglas had an appointment with the man, but because of his shaky French had begged me to accompany him. André Malraux still rented a huge first-floor studio at the home of Monsieur Renard in Boulogne, on the outskirts of Paris. When we rang the doorbell, Malraux opened the door in person. 'Ah, you've arrived at the right time. Last night, I finished my book. Tonight, I'm leaving for Venice. Let's talk.' Douglas Glass plunged his nose into his bag of cameras, so it was I who had to take up single-handedly the terrifying Malraux invitation 'Let's talk'. The talk in question was, in reality, a mono-logue conducted at high speed by a man whose face was distorted every instant by a devastating tic. As Malraux stood almost nose to nose with you to converse, the effect on his listener was devastating. It would have been all right had he been content merely to speak, but no, behind your back he had opened a drawer and suddenly pulled out an object, or a minute sculpture, and said to you: 'You know, of course, what this is.' Since the world of objects is not unfamiliar to me, I came out of this full-scale cross-examination more or less in one piece, albeit reeling. I glanced round the huge studio, which was made even larger by the fact that all the furniture had been pushed against the walls, leaving the floor completely bare. I later found out that Malraux did this so that he could spread out all the reproductions intended for his art books on the floor. Noting the pale beige colour of the carpet, I joked: 'It's to remind you of the Sahara?' Without a muscle of his face moving this time, he said: 'English humour. Let's drink.' And he thrust a bottle of whisky at me.

After that, I walked round the apartment. On the walls were lifesize black and white reproductions of museum masterpieces in gilt frames. It had been one of his first ideas as Minister of Culture to disseminate the masterpieces of art through every school in France. Bravo. When I came across a small Braque, an artist who was a friend of his, hanging above his bed, I noticed that it was also a reproduction. Only one work was real: a large naive painting of Persian origin representing an avenue lined with trees. As the painting was primitive, the avenue didn't recede but rose up towards the top of the canvas like a triangle on its base. Behind my back, Malraux whispered: 'The first avenue in the world.' 'Ah', I said, astonished, 'I thought it was the Cour-la-Reine in Paris.' 'Cours-la-Reine, fourth,' said Malraux, and then rattled off at lightning speed the ten finest avenues in the world in order of longevity! After that, he posed for us with great seriousness and we parted. I took with me the impression of a man consumed by his unfortunate tic, by his work, and by God knows what else besides.

The Centre National d'Art Contemporain was inaugurated at the end of April 1968 with an exhibition entitled 'Three Sculptures'. Three sculptors,

Etienne-Martin, James Brown and myself, had been invited to present a monumental sculpture along with works relating to it. My contribution was the original plaster of my large sculpture *The Crowd*. This official institution was due to have been inaugurated by Malraux in his capacity as Minister of Culture, but shortly before it was due to open, Etienne-Martin had to be operated on for appendicitis and the ceremony was put back until he had recovered. When it finally opened in May, Paris was in the middle of the student uprising in the Latin Quarter. 'Everything's been put to fire and the sword,' whispered Bernard Anthonioz, Malraux's private secretary, whose sons were manning the barricades. But the Right Bank stylishly ignored what was happening on the Left Bank, and the ceremony went ahead in the utmost calm.

Exactly like the André Malraux who entered the room devoted to my work. Holding himself bolt upright in a dark-coloured suit of a very fine cut, his face impassive, his gestures as orderly as those of an automaton, he was the exact opposite of the man I had left in the studio at Boulogne. The doctors and their drugs had done their job. To examine my work he stood facing the wall and, to make his way along, he moved his left leg to the left, followed by his right leg and seemed surprised to find himself brought up short by the corner of the room. Halfway along the third wall, he walked bang into the large sculpture and had to step back to see it properly. At that point, he started talking and, to my surprise, he told me why and how I had made *The Crowd*. I was even more surprised to hear something that made sense, backed up by a knowledge of, even a complicity with, a work that he had in front of him for the first time! I later expressed my astonishment at this to Anthonioz. 'Ah, but he has seen photos of that sculpture, and when he has seen a photo he never forgets it.'

When he had finished his exposé I felt sufficiently spurred on by everything he had said in my favour to tell him how moved I had been when I came across the following sentence in his book *Des bas-reliefs aux grottes sacrées*: 'The low relief and the high relief make it possible to represent people who don't know each other or are not in contact with each other, by comparison with the *rond-bosse*, which requires protagonists who touch and know each other.' At the time I read this, I was working on my first reliefs of streets filled with passers-by. Before I had even finished what I was saying, I saw that I had made the fatal error of introducing a digression with a minister. Malraux was tapping his feet with impatience. The moment my intervention was over, he turned on his heels and left the room.

Pierre Matisse

PIERRE MATISSE WAS A MAJOR FIGURE OF TWENTIETH-century art. As the owner of the New York gallery that bore his name, his contribution to the art of his time can be said to have been decisive, since it was to him that Miró, Balthus and Giacometti owed their careers.

He was the second son of Henri Matisse, and in his youth had shown an obvious gift for painting. I can remember mistaking a series of copies of paintings in the Louvre for early Matisses, before learning that they were Pierre's handiwork. The father had declared peremptorily that one painter in the family was quite enough. His first marriage having failed, his son crossed the Atlantic and, after working in a small gallery in New York for a time, installed himself in the Fuller Building in 1932, where he still had his gallery at the time of his death in 1989. Being the son of a famous father was of no help to him in his early days as a dealer. In a conversation about 'easy money' in the 1970s, Pierre Matisse told me he had had to wait a year before making his first real sale. Nevertheless, he had inherited from his father's studio a remarkable aesthetic sense, made keener still by his own thwarted artistic ambitions, and by the 1930s had made his mark thanks to his unerring choice of artists: Miró under contract by 1932, followed by Calder in 1934 and Balthus in 1938. The hostilities in Europe subsequently brought a wave of major artists to North America, and the Pierre Matisse Gallery became their spiritual home. Chagall joined the gallery; then, after the war, Jean Dubuffet, and in 1952 the first epoch-making exhibition of Alberto Giacometti opened. In his glorious years, Pierre Matisse was president of the Association of Art Dealers of the United States, and in every respect the lord of his profession.

As I have related elsewhere, I first made his acquaintance when he came to Paris to find out how our humble gallery had managed to outmanoeuvre him by organizing an exhibition of drawings and watercolours by Balthus, an artist under contract to him for twenty-five years who had never presented him with works on paper. He had been disarmed on entering the gallery by coming face-to-face with my wife, his love of beauty making him extremely susceptible to a pretty woman, and all the more so since Janine raised no objection to his returning the following day to photograph the works. Just as he was about to leave the gallery, he asked the price of the watercolours hanging on the back wall and, on learning the sum – certainly not much in the ears of a big New York dealer – feigned a nasty shock, crying: 'Well, you've got a nerve.' We have proof that, on his way back to the hotel, he must have said to himself: 'Poor girl. I'll go back tomorrow and buy the lot,' since a quarter of an hour after he had left, Jan Krugier, the shrewd art dealer from Geneva and a great lover of Balthus's work, walked into our gallery and bought the entire line of watercolours on the spot. When Pierre Matisse found this out the next day, he was visibly piqued. That is our man to a tee. The Matisse family comes from Picardie, and Picards are cautious. (Pierre used to recount that, whenever his grandmother asked her husband what he wanted to eat that day, he would invariably reply: 'Butter beans'.) Pierre Matisse had a keen eye when it came to judging a work, and if he found it good, he also had the money to buy it. But he was incapable of acting at once, replacing this by nods of the head and 'hmm, hmms' that left his artists deeply perplexed. Balthus finally mentioned these 'hmm, hmms' that he had been hearing for so many years to his friend Giacometti. 'What, he goes "hmm, hmm" with you too?' guffawed Alberto. It could only be the outward torments of an utter masochist, because sometimes an artist would then sell the work in question to a European associate of Pierre Matisse, whose sufferings were thereby ensured.

For our first contact, he acted in a hasty fashion that was totally out of character. Having noticed one of my plaster reliefs hanging in the storeroom and on being told by my wife that I was working on the other side of the wall, he turned up at the door to my studio and, without coming in, pointed his finger at my large sculpture of *The Crowd*: 'If that sculpture was for sale, would you sell it to me?'

I liked the man right from the word go, from this very first day when I saw him standing in my doorway. Of handsome stature, impeccably dressed, with the rosy complexion of the *bon vivant*, he had a gravity about his person which denoted – as I would later see for myself – the monolithic character of an upright man. His hesitations as a dealer made you smile, but no-one would dare describe him as tight-fisted, so obvious was his authority to all –

even to Giacometti, who was the same age as he. When I arrived in New York for my first exhibition in 1968, he put me up at his home and, as we were going up together in the lift, suggested we *tutoie* one another. I couldn't do it then, and I never did.

The works that had come back from the exhibition at Claude Bernard's had sufficiently impressed Pierre Matisse for him to decide to take me into his gallery. The enormous effort I had made for the rue des Beaux-Arts had twice borne fruit. (Matisse thought very highly of Claude Bernard's work, and when, around this time, I was contacted by the Galerie Maeght, Pierre was anxious I remain with Claude.) At the same time, Pierre Matisse was astonished, he said, by his decision to add me to his gallery, having decided long ago not to take on anyone else. Having done so, however, he went full-steam ahead, insisting that all my sculptures be cast in bronze. On the advice of my sculptor friend Joseph Erhardy, who had worked a lot in Italy, I chose for this colossal undertaking the Fonderia Bruni in Rome, on the south side of the city near the Appia Antica. Signor Arturo Bruni was the doyen of Italian founders, the work was first-class and the prices were a third of those customary in France. Since *The Crowd* was going to be immortalized in bronze, I felt called upon to perfect the crest of the work with a last group of figures falling in the form of a wave, to underscore the oceanic side of the crowd as 'a sea of people'. Weeks, and soon months, went by. Pierre Matisse was extremely put out, beseeching me in letter after letter to dispatch my works forthwith to Rome. For all their threats, I liked these letters; Pierre was a gifted correspondent, spoke readily of his private life and of what he thought about people in the art world, most of his letters being written by hand with amusing 'PSs' and 'PPSs'.

Pierre Matisse came to Rome the moment the works arrived and I was all set to embark on this great adventure. The presence of the famous American dealer was felt to be an event by the Italian founders, with fortune certainly at the end of the line. The atmosphere was euphoric, and Bruni's son, a gourmet, pointed out all the good restaurants in Rome to us. The best, he said, was at Tivoli. One lunchtime, he drove us there. Tivoli, alas, is not just round the corner, the traffic was simply appalling, as depicted in Fellini's *Roma*, and, to boot, when we arrived there the restaurant turned out to be on its weekly closing. Our guide persuaded his friend the proprietor to give us something to eat, and then left us there. The room was very gloomy without clients, the window overlooked a factory of which all we could see was the chimney-stack, it was winter and it was raining. The meal was poor, having been improvised, and Matisse grew more and more furious with me since I had boasted to him beforehand of how beautiful Tivoli was. When the meal was finished, he dragged me outside and, with his customary gesture each evening on Madison Avenue, hailed a taxi. By some miracle, in the small deserted street with the rain pouring down, a car came along and pulled up in front of us. A taxi! Later on, I often heard him telling people about this horrible place I had taken him to. A few years later, after visiting Tivoli, with its gardens and fountains, in the summer season with his wife Patricia, he sent me a postcard, apologizing.

Patricia Matisse came back from a trip the day after I arrived at their home. Small, she came from a very good American family, the essence of which, her Irish roots, is revealed by its name: O'Connell. She was fiery and full of punch (in the case of her male compatriots, this meant a straight fight), and had an incisive way of tackling any problem. Without forgetting that other Irish characteristic, the habit of raising the elbow. An evening at the Matisses' home under the reign of Patricia was a succession of drinks which pushed dinner back to eleven o'clock, despite the French cry of Matisse, on arriving home from the gallery at seven: 'What's for dinner?' My wife and I finally got into the habit of going to bed and getting up for dinner. Pierre thought this a fine idea and tried to do likewise. Patricia had once been known as the Queen of New York nightlife and was sufficiently irresistible for Pierre Matisse to end his marriage with Teeny, the mother of his three children. Pierre must have been extremely pleased with his conquest, though it will have stuck in his throat slightly when Teeny got her own back by marrying Marcel Duchamp.

Patricia was not exactly beautiful, but she was lively and full of spice and I had ample opportunity to see her goading her husband on. It was perfect, however: she was exactly the kind of woman this block of a man needed to be set in motion, stimulated into taking a decision. Patricia, moreover, had another quality that was important for Pierre: she knew the art world inside out and was a better judge of an artist's character than he, keeping a keen watch on Pierre when he took out his wallet. If the artist was young – in point of fact, I was the only one in that category – she would pull out a few extra bank-notes for him. She had previously been married to Matta, the last Surrealist artist to be recognized as such by André Breton, and, in those days, their best friend had been Alberto Giacometti (I have photos, probably taken by her, of Alberto swooning in her arms, cheek to cheek). In short, Patricia Matisse was someone who counted. Once my wife Janine had joined us, a strong sympathy was established between the four of us. The Matisses lived in a three-storey house a stone's throw from Fifth Avenue, with a terrace overlooking Central Park. The walls of the drawing room were given over to various outstanding works by Henri Matisse, and all kinds of important paintings, sculptures and drawings were scattered about the rest of the house. The walls of our bedroom were entirely covered with caustic male portraits by Jean Dubuffet. One day, while tidying out his desk drawers, Pierre called out to us to come and see what he had discovered: a small painting by Seurat.

The other great passion of Pierre Matisse was, of course, his gallery in the Fuller Building, on the corner of Madison Avenue and Fifty-Seventh Street. To enter this old New York skyscraper, with its mosaic floors and its lift doors soberly embossed Art Deco-style, was like stepping back into the 1920s. It was an atmosphere perfectly suited to the great dealer, a further layer added to his already massive dignity. He was far from stout, but the sober cut of his tweed suit and the motionless and vaguely hostile gaze behind the tortoise-shell-rimmed glasses made him look misleadingly like a well-to-do business-man from an era when the business of earning money was taken very seriously indeed. I've always imagined that certain major clients of the Pierre Matisse Gallery made their fortunes as do the characters in James Cagney films. To draw a discreet veil over the fact, they bought Mirós and Giacomettis, in the same way that warlords in the Middle Ages, after wiping out entire populations, had chapels built for the salvation of their souls. The somewhat stifling odour of this old building preserved time intact, as though no-one had ever opened a window.

Pierre Matisse was on the fourth floor, and his gallery overlooked one of

the busiest crossroads of Midtown New York. From my thirteen years with
him, I can still feel myself standing in those rooms of sober elegance, with the
noise of sirens and car horns from the traffic below, and the sensation of
being at the epicentre of that fabulous city. Pierre walks through the gallery
to get some water for his whisky from the water-fountain, and he'll be back
again later. (Patricia was not the only one in that couple to be an impressively
steady drinker.) Little by little, and because Matisse was installed there,
the Fuller Building filled with other art galleries, the Marlborough Gallery
occupying the floor directly overhead. Over the years, the building ended up
forming a sort of vertical rue de Seine.

Because of the numerous additions and finishing touches I had made to
the original plaster at the foundry in Rome, the bronze cast of *The Crowd* was
not ready in time for the exhibition, and it was the plaster that made the journey from Rome to New York, then back again for the completion of the work.
The same plaster figured in the inaugural exhibition of the Centre National
d'Art Contemporain in May 1968, and the front frieze of the bronze at the
opening of the Institute of Contemporary Art in London that same summer.
Yet I cannot remember Pierre ever making a fuss about these additional ship-
ping expenses, nor about others in the years to come, his only regret being
that the bronze was not ready in time to compete for the Carnegie Prize.

Hardly had this gigantic work been installed at the centre of the gallery
than I went on with the little changes I was making, having brought along a
sack of plaster for this purpose. On the eve of the private view, I even insisted
on working through the night, all alone in this gallery filled with works by the
masters of modern art, without giving a moment's thought to the distress I
was causing Pierre, and without my understanding to this day how he could
have consented to it. Janine, who had stayed behind at the house, witnessed
Matisse springing up from table several times during dinner to contain his
rage. The following morning, he could contain it no longer, for there was a
detail I didn't know about and which made matters even worse. Shortly after
my arrival, Pierre had had carpeting put down that I now inaugurated with
traces of plaster! The words we exchanged ended with Matisse losing his tem-
per: 'Okay, it's your sculpture, but it's *my* gallery.' I had just opened my mouth
to reply when I saw Janine, standing behind Pierre's shoulder, signalling to

me with her fingers to shut up. I was worn out with fatigue, but I only left the gallery to go and get changed at the house late in the afternoon. When I returned, the few guests who had troubled to turn up for the private view, my name being totally unknown in New York at that time, had already dispersed. The only people left were my friend the poet Yves Bonnefoy, the author of the fine text of the catalogue, his wife, Lucy, and, of course, Pierre and Patricia. We went to have dinner, the three couples, then Patricia, the expert, took us to a nightclub or two, but I didn't take anything in, my head dropping on the tables before me.

My collaboration with Pierre had got off to a flying start the previous year when he had shown some of my work for the first time in his summer exhibition; the big collector Joseph Hirshhorn had bought my three large torsos in bronze. The current exhibition was important, with twenty-four bronzes of city scenes and landscapes, a selection of ink drawings and the plaster sculpture of *The Crowd*, dramatically lit and rich in shadows. It was to suffer a very different fate, however, on account of an article by Hilton Kramer, in those days the leading art critic of the *New York Times*. Pop art was just starting to break out, and Kramer denounced my fine group of sculptures as 'nineteenth-century European art. The proof, it's all in bronze.' The result of such a verdict coming from such a source was that Matisse sold nothing in an exhibition that had cost him a small fortune.*

Any normal dealer would have sent me packing, but Pierre Matisse was no ordinary dealer. The monolithic man didn't flinch. Fortunately, my subsequent exhibitions were better received.

Matisse was pained when I abandoned bronze for resin, the latter not being a noble medium in his view and little better than pre-war Bakelite (except that it was then painted by hand, which changes everything it seems to me). Nevertheless, he continued to finance my works in this new medium. There was another aspect of his loyalty towards me. Resin enabled me to work on increasingly large compositions, with working life as their constant subject: market gardeners at Les Halles, miners in the North, peasants in the

* Hilton Kramer's final article, before resigning his post at the end of the 1980s, was entitled 'Bronze Is Back. How Happy We Are'…

South, the activity of humble folk. Nothing could have interested Pierre Matisse's wealthy clientele less, all of whom were enamoured of fine art as exemplified by Miró, Chagall and Giacometti. In this, too, Matisse did not waver in his opinion of my work, and at no moment did he recommend I try and do something more saleable. Especially now that the *New York Times*, in a review by John Canaday, had gone so far as to write of my second exhibition: 'Guernica had its Picasso and now Les Halles in Paris have their Mason.' Nevertheless, the article by Hilton Kramer, while it hadn't shaken the confidence of Matisse, didn't encourage him to order further editions in bronze from the Italian foundry, after he had failed to sell the first. This created a tragic situation. In response to Matisse's plans to have several bronze casts made of each of my many sculptures, Signor Bruni had invested heavily, adding an extra floor to his foundry to accommodate my original plasters and their numerous moulds. To make matters worse, the prices had been calculated on the promise of multiple copies, and the Italians were entitled to feel swindled. When Arturo Bruni, a man I sincerely liked and who treated me like a member of the family, died, this was the conclusion his son Bruno came to, and he destroyed my originals – including the most precious of them all, that of *The Crowd*, the number of copies of which was abruptly limited to two. I had begged Pierre to have these original works shipped over from Rome, but given the compensation he would have to pay and his intention, no doubt, despite everything, to have further copies made, he never did. So thank you, Hilton Kramer.

In the days when I was working in Rome, I would sometimes make the journey from Paris in my Alfa Romeo and, on one occasion, stopped off on my way back at Saint-Jean-Cap-Ferrat, where Matisse had a seaside villa and a beautiful black yacht. Having driven straight from Rome to the Côte d'Azur, I was exhausted, but Pierre was keen to take advantage of having a car outside his door to drive over to his father's old apartment in Nice. After a hundred twists and turns, and feeling even more exhausted, we finally arrived, whereupon Pierre promptly disappeared into the attractive-looking house, leaving me outside in the sun. Half an hour later he emerged. Back we went to the villa. He hadn't allowed me to see Henri Matisse's studio, today his museum. It was his cautious side again, a certain affectation of mystery even.

Along with our girls, Janine and I had stayed several times with Pierre and Patricia at their Villa la Punta and admired Pierre at the helm of his boat. One of Patricia's birthday parties will be remembered by all who were present for the occasion. We had heard good things said about a restaurant situated a little way up the coast beyond Beaulieu. It was called La Pirate, and there was something in that name, no doubt, that should have given us pause for thought. Patricia went off in their splendid yacht to place the order for the evening. She wanted something good, and since she forgot to ask the prices, that meant *carte blanche*. The result was magnificent. The waiters, dressed as pirates with swords and torches in hand, staged a mock naval battle against those who had arrived by yacht. Drinks began with champagne punch all round, except that a giant of a man, a big Californian art collector, declared that he wanted some ordinary red wine to make him feel at home in France. Having hit it off with him, I went along with this piece of folly and switched drinks. Hardly had the dinner begun – we already had our costume hats on – than I had to leave this entertaining company and my interesting neighbour, Tériade, to go to the toilets, which were perched on a rock. By the time I got back to the party it was the early hours of the morning and I, who had come by car, was too weak to drive. My daughter-in-law, Lysiane, took us back in the Alfa that she was driving for the first time, on the middle corniche, one of the most dangerous coastal roads in the country. All I had of the fabulous dinner were photos and some rough idea on seeing Pierre return, his teeth clenched, the next day, after settling the bill. Twelve cases of Dom Pérignon and *tutti quanti*…

The Matisses returned to New York that summer to move into their new home, closer to the gallery. It was also to discover a catastrophe. The removals firm, the best in New York, which had been transporting their affairs from their old home on Ninety-First Street to that on Sixty-Fourth, had thought it simpler to leave everything in the lorry over the summer. Lighting a cigarette next to the fuel tank in the middle of the heat wave, someone had blown up Pierre Matisse's lorry with all his inscribed books and drawings, including the original drawing for Giacometti's *The Palace at Four a.m.* Patricia, who was so full of life, hardly had time to put their new home in order and live there for a few months before being carried off by cancer.

My exhibition in 1975 consisted of a large group of Provençal landscapes – sculptures and gouaches on paper – which Pierre was very pleased with. He came to see me in my *bastidon* overlooking the Luberon and did us the honour of introducing us to his new companion, shortly to be his wife: Maria-Gaetana von Spreti, whose father was the Austrian ambassador to America but who had long been involved in the arts. They were travelling together, Pierre told us, for the first time. I had painted a first gouache with a view to proposing a full exhibition in exchange for a certain sum of money, since a beautiful ruin had just been acquired near my house, and I realized too late that it would have made a perfect studio. I intended to make a higher offer to the new proprietors. Pierre liked the gouache, the idea of the exhibition as well, making the atmosphere during the lunch Janine had prepared for us very pleasant. It was only when I saw the big Jaguar driving off that I realized I'd forgotten to ask about the money. The ruin, soon a superb villa, was never to be mine.

I worked flat out that summer in order to finish the work in time for the exhibition, painting the same gouache all day and placing the shadow I saw in the afternoon on the opposite side of the tree to accord it with the light of morning. When I arrived in New York for the exhibition, I still had my last gouache to finish and I was given the use of a studio that Matisse had set up in the attic for artists staying with him, but which I would be the only one to use.

My fourth exhibition, in 1980, was to be my last with Matisse, being also the moment when our relations began to jar. A friend had behaved badly, but the real reason for our falling-out was this. Pierre Matisse's appearance as a solid businessman was misleading. He was a man guided by his passions, the most important of which, for all his love of music, were for art and his gallery. Exhibitions he dealt with more or less single-handed. A charming black chap, Walter, carried out day-to-day jobs, but the hanging and lighting of works were exclusively Pierre's doing, and I would see him, at almost eighty years of age, perched on a step-ladder adjusting this or that. This exclusive passion, this hand-tailored touch, was the cause of countless arguments as to the placing of my works, which I claim to know better than anyone. An artist is always on edge before an exhibition, and I am no exception. In this case, however, I had another artist facing me, and our battles were terrible. Over the years, since I was his guest, we always dined together afterwards at his home, the pleasure of the meal and the fine wine would normally prompt him to forgive me and, sitting after dinner in his library, cognac in hand, in front of Balthus's gigantic painting *The Mountain*, he would perhaps tell me about being taken as a boy by his father to see Renoir. This time there was nothing of that kind to iron out our difficulties, since we were staying with our friends the Louis-Dreyfuses. Perhaps it was the exhibition itself, with its works *A Tragedy in the North* and *The Aggression*, that had cast an evil spell over our relations. But I know perfectly well that the real reason for our arguments was my foolhardiness in contradicting the wishes of this man who was all of a piece. He cut my splendid exhibition down to ten days to prove that he was master in his own gallery. For all that, he had prepared it well, seeking more favourable coverage on the part of Hilton Kramer and the *New York Times*. To arrange this, he had passed on a message through our friend James Lord, who was close to Kramer. The latter came to the exhibition and made a tour of the rooms with Pierre, who sent me a letter in Paris to tell me that all was going well and that Kramer had asked for photos for his page. A short review appeared, with no photo. 'Mr. Mason's *A Tragedy in the North* is itself an artistic catastrophe…' I was very shocked, to a degree I have never been either before or since. A few weeks later, I fell seriously ill with hepatitis. Jaundiced!

By temperament, Pierre Matisse was as much a collector as a dealer, and he admitted to me that he didn't like haggling over prices with clients. After all, loving a work that much, once his infallible eye had made its choice, was already reason enough not to sell. I am perhaps the only artist to have visited his warehouse in Hundredth Street. I couldn't believe my eyes. Silhouetted at the end of the long room were major sculptures by Rodin, then – one artist after another, with all their best works – a staggering quantity of Dubuffets, Mirós, Chagalls and Giacomettis. And there at my feet, my own works.

Pierre Matisse put an end to our collaboration shortly after this last exhibition. He nevertheless congratulated me on my retrospectives at the Serpentine Gallery in London in 1982 and at the Pompidou Centre in Paris in 1985. With Tana, he visited my first exhibition at the Marlborough Gallery in New York, saying to me in a letter: 'It is the right choice of gallery for your large works.'

The first *Crowd* was sold by Pierre Matisse to the French state in André Malraux's last years as Minister of Culture. Pierre had written to me in 1969: 'Despite the arduous and costly undertaking of bringing *The Crowd* to fruition, plus the French devaluation, I am pleased that the first copy went to the French state. Despite all the trials and tribulations that this work had to endure, I still think, as I did when I saw it for the first time in plaster in your studio, that it is one of the major realizations of contemporary sculpture.' After it was installed in the garden of the Tuileries in 1986, I received this, his last letter to me: 'On returning from Barcelona this afternoon, I find your letter and the photographs of the installation of *The Crowd* in the Tuileries, and I thank you for thinking of sending me them. I find the setting ideal, and on my return to Paris in a few days time I shall not fail to go and see this *Crowd* close-up.'

The finest tribute I can pay to Pierre Matisse is that when people say the 'Pierre Matisse Gallery', or even the 'Matisse Gallery', nobody thinks of the painter.

The Departure of Fruits and Vegetables from the Heart of Paris, 28 February 1969

THE MARKET FOR FRUIT AND VEGETABLES, WONDERS OF nature, which opened at night under the stars in the historic centre of the most beautiful city in the world, far transcended the mere question of commerce.

It was a place of joy. Powerful and vast since it made an endless number of people happy, and many tears would flow at the thought that it would cease to be. The work there was hard. The cold and rain to be endured were also hard. There were some very hard and tough men and women to be found in the place. However, its magic was such that this hardness transformed itself into a strange gentleness, and the most fearsome character became peaceable. Of course, it was the pleasure of working together, but it was subtly ennobled by the fresh beauty of that country produce. In truth, the Halles Centrales market was the last image of the Natural in the city. It is now a Paradise Lost.

I have tried, with this present sculpture, to reconstruct to the best of my abilities its dazzling vision. My work, obviously, will be a poor substitute for the emotion I felt before the superb displays. I hope at least that it will speak clearly enough to the spectator who reads its title, *The Departure of Fruits and Vegetables from the Heart of Paris, 28 February 1969*, to announce that other departure, no less definitive, of the men and women symbolized in my procession, whom I spoke about above. A moment of silence. It is the man of the Middle Ages who is leaving. The 'little vegetable' of our own species, he came from the earth and assumed a form as best he could. But he was a natural man and he always grew. We will never again see his kind.

And then there is the church, one of the most remarkable in existence, sole witness of the centuries now passed. Witness? Actor itself, and no doubt the leading actor. From its great height it summoned those thousands of activities and products, lending them a grand scale, their essential and spiritual dimension – felt, however dimly, by each member of the jumbled congregation swarming at its feet.

If you do not believe me, there is still one fruit and vegetable vendor left nestled against the wall at Pointe Saint-Eustache. Ask her if she would have wished to lean against anything but those huge stones during all her years of cold nights. At Les Halles, named 'Le Ventre de Paris' by Zola, we were much closer to the 'Notre-Dame de Paris' of Victor Hugo.

Such a long association of ideas and things had produced an interpenetration of forms and habits which I discovered little by little in elaborating my sculpture. The cabbage leaf that I had hung at the centre of my composition was supposed to raise its main stem following the serpentine line of beauty so dear to Hogarth. But soon the leaf itself recalled with all its veins the Late Gothic of the church. The bristling of the stone pinnacles was rediscovered in the artichokes being carried away. That prolix architecture multiplied the characteristic banks of fruits and vegetables; in its stained-glass windows, filling the triangular tympanums with round shapes, in its tiers rising to the sky like so many stone crates held in balance for ever.

The certainty I had acquired that a great web had held together the

Raymond Mason, *The Departure of Fruits and Vegetables from the Heart of Paris, 28 February 1969*, 1971

subject I wanted to bring to life again had made me decide to sculpt and paint not only the heart of Paris but also all the things that were to be found there – to their very heart. I would separate each cauliflower cluster, each artichoke leaf, as I would count each window on the streets of Montmartre and Montorgueil. Like a reservoir of ink, night would have to spread out everywhere, defining the drawing…

Then there were the moments when I would say to myself at the end of the day: 'Look! a potato nose.' There were even better ones, the colour of eggplants. The cauliflower would return to haunt me, this time in the shape of an ear, even the Adam's apple (it is behind the cabbage leaf). I was even more delighted when I put a couple embracing in the middle distance and could say to myself: 'Now that suggests forbidden fruits.' A benevolent spectator would be able to untangle more threads of thought – I venture to hope more serious ones – which seems normal to me, since this work preoccupied me constantly for two whole years.

A work of art. Does one always know what one can put into it? In these days of simplification, the answer seems to be – the least possible. For me, the answer has always been more perplexing – everything. People explain to me in a friendly way that I am going against the current. Well yes, I am against the current. Endlessly I hear talk about the movements, the trends in art, of those who are making painting and sculpture move forward, of the avant-garde who have already reached the year 2000. The perpetual movement which artists must follow.

But for me, art, on the contrary, should be the means of intercepting thought in its flight, of merging it with matter, giving it weight and body precisely in order to stop time, to hold out against the centuries.

I wish that my little procession from Les Halles did not ever have to leave for good.

Exhibition catalogue, Galerie Claude Bernard, 1971.

Henri Cartier-Bresson

I MET HENRI CARTIER-BRESSON IN 1973 THANKS TO SAM Szafran, who frequents the upper crust of Parisian society and is very generous in introducing his friends. The period of his great photos, or of his great reportages rather, was over, and he was returning to his first love, art. He had painted before the war, but now, having spent a lot of time with Alberto Giacometti, his only aim was to master drawing with the aid of an HB pencil and a few sheets of paper. He would, of course, pick up his famous Leica from time to time, and the result would be as extraordinary as ever; but, as I have said, there just wasn't the same interest any more.

He lives in a fifth-floor duplex in the rue de Rivoli, overlooking the Tuileries gardens and above the apartment formerly inhabited by Victor Choquet, the friend and collector of the Impressionists. This means that Cézanne and Monet had often looked at the same view, and many of Cartier-Bresson's drawings take up the same landscape scenes first painted by Monet, Renoir and Pissarro. In this low-ceilinged apartment full of charm, Henri hangs works by his artist friends and receives a steady flow of interesting company, in general involved in the arts and literature. The food and drink served by his wife, the photographer Martine Franck, are, of course, first-class, and at table Cartier-Bresson gives free rein to his youthful enthusiasm for an endless array of subjects. Occasionally, this turns into equally spontaneous rage if something doesn't suit him – for example, the day he saw me putting water in my wine: 'What, you're putting water in my lovely wine! Stupid Englishman. Get out!' I had got as far as the lift-cage when Henri caught up with me. I mention this to show that even today at his great age there isn't a trace of decrepitude in the man.

One day he showed me some drawings he had made of the panorama of Paris from the roof above his flat. An excellent draughtsman, his love of Giacometti's work had, in my view, made him overemphasize the lines of structure, disembodying his subject, and I told him that it wouldn't do. 'Well, then, I'm going to take you up onto the roof and watch you do it,' said Henri firmly. We had arranged to do this a few days after, but the great heat wave of the summer of 1976 had started and I wanted to put off the experiment until later. Cartier-Bresson, however, once he gets an idea into his head, won't let it drop. Out we went, then, onto the sea of white-hot zinc of the roofs of the rue de Rivoli, only to see before us a young girl lying naked on her back, sunbathing. With apologetic smiles, we were preparing to step across her body when Henri, deciding the situation merited better, disappeared down the hatch and came back with a bottle of champagne. The young lady accepted a glass with good grace, while rolling over slightly onto her front.

Once this interlude was over, we advanced as far as the chimney that was to be my vantage-point. And, from there, we saw in a window further down a slender young girl with a pink turban on her head, the spitting image of one of the famous photos Cartier-Bresson had brought back from India or Bali. It wasn't that, of course, simply a young woman who'd just washed her hair, and the turban was merely a coloured towel. Hardly had I recovered than, looking up in the direction of the great view towards the Sacré Coeur and Montmartre, I saw a zeppelin like a white cigar circling the white dome. In thirty years of living in Paris, I had never seen such a thing. Astonishing. Then Henri left me on my own while I got set up and, looking around me, I discovered that the zeppelin had vanished, the girl in the turban as well. Nor was there any sign of the naked woman. The whole thing had been the charms that life put on show for him wherever Henri the magician passes. For luck and fate go with him always. During a stay in India, he was received by Gandhi in his tent. When he came out, the man going in was none other than Gandhi's assassin, and Cartier-Bresson found himself a witness to the most incredible scenes, standing with his camera just below Nehru when he leaned over the wall of the palace to announce the mahatma's death to the people.

On the chimney, I showed Henri that to make a drawing of that particular view you had to begin at the top and finish at the bottom. As moreover I was drawing, as is my wont, directly in ink, Henri gave a nod of the head and did not stay long. On his way down, from the window below, he fired off once with his Leica, and, while my drawing is good, his photo is extraordinary. There are two figures on a roof, myself cap on head (because

of the heat) and the chimney with its own hat, and, starting from my profile, a whole zigzag of chimneys and asperities likewise profiled against the
sky all the way down to the bottom right-hand corner of the photo. On the
left, behind my back, is the bare horizontal of the roof, and below, filling the
left-hand corner, the perfect black square of an open window. Like all
Cartier-Bresson's photos, it is framed by a thin black band. This indicates
that there has been no recropping, that it is simply what the camera saw. At
the same time, Cartier-Bresson's photographs are of a complexity and precision of composition which almost defy understanding.

Henri Cartier-Bresson is essentially an artist. He has lived all his life in
Paris, a city of art and artists. The Louvre is right outside his door, and you
can still see him there today, sitting on his shooting-stick drawing the Old
Masters. It is his eye, perfectly formed by study of the masterpieces of paint-
ing, which enables him to confront the tumultuous disorder of the outside
world and place it instantaneously in a formal order of beauty. The poet Yves
Bonnefoy has told me that when he was Henri's neighbour in the Alps of
Haute Provence, he had to meet him at the coach stop at Simiane one day.
They were crossing the sunlit and rather sleepy village square together when
Yves saw Henri make a movement with his hand while talking. We later saw
what he had captured by firing from the hip like the hero in a Western: an
arcaded vantage-point with some young people and a few animals, all
distributed in significant poses, and, above all, with all the pillars of the
building perfectly vertical despite the offhand manner in which he had taken
the photo. There's no doubt about it, Henri shoots faster than Lucky Luke –
with this notable difference, that a single shot from the latter left people
dead whereas Henri makes them live for ever.

In those days, I had a house in Provence, at Ménerbes opposite the
Luberon, and Henri and Martine were installed in an old farmhouse near
Reillanne on the Grand Luberon. Our two houses were equidistant, twenty
kilometres to either side of Apt. It is at Apt that the Luberon mountain chain
is divided into the Grand and the Petit Luberon by the valley leading down
to Lourmarin on the south slope. Though close to one another, our two
landscapes were very different. While I looked straight out onto the Petit
Luberon, abrupt and spectacular, across a cheerful valley rich in vineyards

and fruit trees, Henri was perched on the side of a mountain much like any other in the Alpine forelands, but with a splendid panorama of wheat fields and pasture-land before him. We shared the same pure climate and the same beautiful sun, which is extremely important for artists like ourselves who like to *see*. Alas, between us ran a wicked, typically Provençal road lined with plane trees whose roots made bumps in the surface all the way to Forcalquier, where there was an arts centre in an old building run by a mutual friend of ours, Lucien Henry. It was here, moreover, that Henri held one of his first exhibitions of drawings. Since then, exhibitions of his drawings have been held pretty much all over the world, but I would be very surprised if any of them equalled that at the Ecole Nationale Supérieure des Beaux-Arts in Paris in 1989, prodigiously well hung by his publisher, Robert Delpire.

Here is another side of Henri Cartier-Bresson. In 1984, I had just finished my monument for Montreal and needed a photo of the entire sculpture. I had to have it, moreover, that weekend, for the work would be leaving the moulder's studio the coming Monday. I thought of a young disciple of Henri's, Marc, who had the plate camera essential for art photos. I called Henri to get Marc's phone number. He asked me why I wanted it and, when I explained, said in an annoyed tone: 'But I can't do the photo for you, I don't have the time.' I assured him that Marc was the only one who could do it, and grudgingly he gave me the number. Five minutes later, he phoned back to say he would do the photo himself, and that I would have to go and pick him up in the car to drive the thirty kilometres to Brie-Comte-Robert. Knowing that he didn't have the right instrument with time exposure for the job, I was put out by his announcement, but, since this great friend of mine was also a great man, there was nothing further to be said. While I was rolling pleasantly along towards our destination, Henri suddenly said: 'If you continue driving at this speed, I'll throw myself out of the car.' We were off to a good start and, sure enough, the moment we entered the Haligon studio in Brie, Cartier-Bresson, seeing how enormous the monument was, cried out: 'What! I can't photograph a thing like that!' (He always told me his interest was exclusively for small sculptures, Giacometti's or those of his brother-in-law, Pierre Josse.) It was my turn now to shout: 'You're the one who insisted on coming. I wanted Marc. But I have to have the photo at all costs.' We both stood there sulking. At that moment, the moulder Olivier Haligon pointed out a problem to me at one spot on the sculpture, and while I was giving it my attention, someone called out my name. I turned round in the direction of the call and was astounded to see Cartier-Bresson at the top of a tall, metal ladder that he hadn't even bothered to pull away from the wall. The photo was done. It was not the documentary photo I wanted, but a marvellous image of an artist lost in his great work. It served as the frontispiece for my catalogue at the Pompidou Centre, and Cartier-Bresson included it in his album. I have related this anecdote to illustrate the sprightliness of the man, who was 76 at the time. In the Midi, he photographed me on some land near Ménerbes which dropped sheer down to the valley. To get the angle he wanted, I saw him run up the embankment backwards. Try doing it.

He took many portraits of me, none of which quite came off. Though he has taken some great portraits, the best are always those taken *in situ* and not the head alone. I have in mind the portrait of William Faulkner and his dog, or that of Colette with her maid standing behind her. Everything he has done of me in a context is very good. He was present outside the Jeu de Paume in the Tuileries – he only had to come down from his apartment, of course – on the day of Arctic cold in January 1986 when the installation of *The Crowd* in bronze was inaugurated. He and Martine took the usual photos of me and the officials standing in front of the work, but the one that is always used is yet again an oblique view from behind, with me alone looking round – in response to a call – into Henri's Leica.

Afterwards, we all beat a retreat to the nearest café on the rue de Rivoli for a hot grog. The people from the ministry were delighted to be sharing a table with Henri Cartier-Bresson, a living legend, but the business of the Pyramid of the Louvre was still fresh (Henri and I were against this monstrosity), and Cartier-Bresson seized the opportunity of having these gentlemen in front of him to tell them yet again what he thought of it all. Since more than a grog was needed to warm up the atmosphere, we soon parted. Good old Henri!

Clearly, the fact that he's nice-looking and not remotely threatening has made it easier for him to slip into all kinds of situations, record them on film then leave without being spotted. This is also the place to note that most photographers confine themselves to the dramatic and the tragic, and even a photographer out to amuse, like Robert Doisneau, has his subjects pose for him, thereby killing off any vivacity. Henri Cartier-Bresson gives us life in its entirety, the spectacular and the dramatic but also the moments of unruffled happiness or unbridled mirth, as a result of which at an exhibition of his photos we always hear people laughing. The mixture of the serious and the comical is always very potent in a creator and gives his work an added dimension.

This ability to feel optimistic about life is a rare gift in this brilliant man. Not long ago, he was about to undergo an operation of some gravity for a man of his age. He told me about it in a little casual note which he signed 'En-rit' – laughing about it.

Henri, just back from a voyage, phones to tell me that, during a stop-over in East Berlin, he visited a museum where he noticed in the rooms a man of imposing presence. He was introduced to him. It was 'your ambassador', the British ambassador. 'Ah, Monsieur Cartier-Bresson, you've taken a lot of photographs in our country. I hope you never had any difficulties doing so,' said the latter politely. 'On the contrary,' replied Henri, 'every time I pointed my camera at one of your fellow countrymen he would duck and say "sorry", because in his modesty he thought I was photographing something behind him.'

St Mark's Place, East Village, NY

I T IS A SOBERING THOUGHT THAT ALMOST EVERY PERSON who sees my sculpture of St Mark's Place, East Village, in the Pierre Matisse Gallery, must know that district a hundred times better than I do. At least. I saw this particular scene once, for two hours, in November 1971.

It was quite by accident. I went to visit my old friend Jason Harvey, who lives on Cooper Square, and coaxed him into making me a drawing board to fit the piece of paper I'd bought downtown for that purpose. I was waiting for the showing of my Paris market sculpture in this same gallery, and in the meantime I hoped to draw some of the skyscrapers in central New York, particularly the curved one then just nearing completion on Fifty-Seventh Street. With this intention in mind I was re-entering the subway in the same Cooper Square when I realized that it was lunchtime and that I'd more easily find food where I was than uptown on a Saturday midday. I went into the first eating-house I saw, on a corner of Third Avenue. It was Tony Provenzano's Village East Coffee Shop.

I sat down by the window, which on that side looks out onto the first four buildings of St Mark's Place. During the meal, I greedily ate up the spectacle outside where an extravagant populace trouped the sidewalks in sharp noon sunlight. All travellers enjoy sitting watching a foreign world pass by. I felt particularly fortunate because I soon noticed that some of the more curious faces in that street outside passed by my window again and again, as though incapable of breaking through an invisible barrier at the end of the block. Maybe, too, my heart was being warmed by the sight of the brick fronts opposite. I was born in Birmingham in England, and had spent a sickly childhood looking through curtains at a brick-lined street – except that my bricks had been red, to be sure, while these were painted black or white. In any case, I forgot that I had intended to draw buildings which scrape the sky. Here were people very much down to earth, some perhaps barely risen from it, judging by their strange outfits that suggested a bivouac way of life. And here, too, at my side was my brand-new drawing board with its fresh sheet of paper. Not having drawn in days – and feeling hungry in that way, too – I took out my pen and ink. The coffee-shop proprietor had no objections. On the contrary, he stood behind me and told me all he knew about each face or feature as it appeared on the paper. It takes an Italian to recognize things that fast. (If St Mark's Place is part of East Village mythology, Tony Provenzano was my Homer. If it is Hell, as some say, then he was my Dante.)

From then on I can't honestly say whether this or that detail of the scene struck me at the time or only seemed to grow significant when looking at the drawing a month or two afterwards in Paris, or at an even later date when I had begun the sculpture and things were becoming more defined. When did I first give importance to the word 'Pazza', which is situated in the exact centre of the composition and which in Italian means 'mad'? Was it before or after my coming to the very conclusion that a certain streak of folly ran through my little group of characters – the drunkard mad from drink, and his neighbour from smoking God knows what, the girl mad for her man who, with cycling helmet on his head and some sort of palm-branch in his hand, hardly appears an embodiment of reason. As for the man wandering around dressed as a soldier of the War of Independence... Of course, I'd better mention that I saw these individual people exactly as I attempt to show them here, and they all appear in the original drawing.

Two moments do come to my mind which made a mark at the time and, as it were, a move in my direction. I had begun by drawing the police car stationed just outside the window because it had a sculptural silhouette with its siren and its flashing light on the roof. The policemen seemed to have the same battlemented fixity, so I was surprised when I realized that they had left the car and were sitting drinking on my side of the glass in the coffee house. Less large than life they looked, like actors got down from a stage. The second occasion was the arrival of the drunk. He came feeling his way across the window, moving clumsily like a lobster in the aquarium of a seafood restaurant. That hand on the glass gave a relief to the drawing and another significance to the window, as I realized later on once back in Paris. I had left New York shortly afterwards without returning to East Village, and the drawing lay among others in the studio.

It returned to my mind because in the midst of my winter's work of finishing and painting the remaining copies of the market sculpture (thirty-two apples, eighty oranges, 108 leeks, 160 faces, etc) I felt I needed some 'light relief' and the midday scene in St Mark's Place seemed just the thing. However, I was aware that a deal of concentration would be involved, and for a time I was content to imagine the sculpture as it would be when finished. At the same time, I described it to one or two people, giving them the impression that it was already half-done. One night, sitting on the glass-enclosed terrace of a café, I was speaking of it again to friends just arrived in Paris. 'And the best of it,' I concluded, 'is the hand pressing against the window, just like here before our very noses.' My friend's wife is a sculptor,

and her approval of the idea put me to shame and the next day to work.

I've related this in a random succession of events to show with what 'irresponsibility' I finally sat down – to do what? Solely, I must admit, to reproduce as guilelessly as possibly, and within drastic limits of scope and scale, my brief vision of that vivid thoroughfare. The general concept of the sculpture was accordingly simple. It would consist of a windowed box in which I could stage the scene and place the various *dramatis personae* just as they had played before my eyes. The notable difference would necessarily be that, whereas I had sat within and watched them without, now they would be inside and I myself the outside spectator.

Given these conditions, what kind of sculptural interest could I hope for?

Essentially it would have to stem from the heteroclite nature of that crowd of figures. In the foreground, an uninspired Hindu, a mystical intellectual, the drunk, the smoker, the lovers, the hippy, a bum. Behind them, the two policemen, a cosy black woman, a Latin-type running, the man with the feathered helmet, a bruiser and his Portuguese pal. On the sidewalk opposite, though hardly to be seen, are nevertheless the man who sits on the steps (all day and every day according to Tony), a girl in hot pants, a dog, an

Arab, a black man stooping for a cigarette butt, a girl off to visit the shops, the cook serving a pizza to a truck driver, a loafer, a black mammie with her little girl, a bearded guy, an old man, a young black man and, at her window on the second floor, a dejected blonde. If I can group these people together I also have to consider that they must reorganize themselves in a dozen other ways so as to present a coherent picture to the viewer, who will change his angle before the window. The moving eye will give momentum to the separate elements so that they can come and go in a continual metamorphosis, sharply emphasized by the colour employed. This bristling between the figures should be measured and intensified by the rigid windowbars and by the geometry and lettering of the façades across the street. If the little space can come alive, its inmates might seem to breathe. Accordingly I must accept all incidents, all accessory facts, as vivifying, since they enrich the outlines; their crenellation claws and stirs the air around. (As I have said, I was at the outset fascinated by the turreted roof of the police car.) Similar attempts to tap the vitality of outdoor life have been evident in most of my street scenes and more particularly in my market sculpture, where I first used colour to detach and personalize a quantity of separate elements

I sat down to sculpt the East Village scene along precisely similar lines.

While I was engrossed in the making of my little peepshow, various thoughts came my way which I'll mention for what they're worth.

There was an Arab looking rather lost on the sidewalk opposite. In the sculpture he stands close to the Irish cop beside the police car – a couple of inches away. Now there's a greater gap than two inches between an Arab and an Irishman. So there comes a push of space between them, or so it seems to me. And accordingly between the other racial and social types which mingle in that exotic street.

A difference in sentiment or in expression also creates a gap. Travelling from the convulsed face of the drunk to the pacified grimace of the smoker represents a break in space and time, yes, a journey. I once noticed this on an alabaster Roman column featuring on alternative sides the masks of tragedy and comedy. There was no knowing the slenderness of that column. I had forgotten this.

In the same line of thought, it occurred to me, while I was painting the sheet-iron chimney beside the drab lace curtains, that the more I made it look like a chimney and the closer I could get to making a curtain – the more, in short, that they showed likeness to themselves – then the more they would differ from each other. They would thus tend to move apart to a minute degree. Minute but immeasurable, so therefore why not infinite?

I've already said on another occasion that I expect a work of art to speak of everything. What I saw through Tony Provenzano's window gave me an inkling that there may be a sculptural way of expressing it.

Exhibition catalogue, Pierre Matisse Gallery, New York, 1974.

A Tragedy in the North. Winter, Rain and Tears

SHORTLY AFTER CHRISTMAS 1974, ON A WARM SUNNY DAY in the South of France, I read in the local newspaper about the mining disaster at Liévin, a small town in the Pas-de-Calais. An accompanying news photo showed brick buildings of the mine and, on the cobblestones gleaming with rain, an anxious, milling crowd.

I was born and brought up in similar surroundings and at once felt nearer to this painful scene in the north than to the near-idyllic one of the festive Provençal interior in which I was sitting. That very day I began a small low relief based on the newspaper photo, and subsequently painted it in the colours I felt would be appropriate.

The following spring, I happened to be passing through the Pas-de-Calais and decided to visit Liévin's tragic mine. I made the colour drawing at that time, on the spot. Once again, I was seized by the poignant beauty of simple nineteenth-century industrial architecture, and I decided to undertake a large work based on the tragedy, which would also be an act of fidelity to my own past.

Immediately on beginning work, I felt obliged to eliminate the pit-shafts to concentrate on the human figures. Moreover, although I come from a district in England of bricks and paving stones, it is not a mining district and I felt some hesitancy about so specific a subject. I thus enlarged it into an industrial catastrophe and finally chose as a title *A Tragedy in the North. Winter, Rain and Tears.*

So, to indicate the mine, there remains only the slag-heap, that black, manmade mountain, that enigmatic symbolic pyramid whose sloping sides are echoed repeatedly in the composition, be it in the gables of the buildings, the climb-up of the curbstones or the arms of the young woman in front of the torn features of her face. The slag-heap finally appears by direct contrast in the white handkerchief of the woman on the left.

André Malraux spoke of low-relief or high-relief sculptures which allow the reunion and the representation of people who do not know each other, as compared, in his way of thinking, to sculpture in the round, where the protagonists either know each other or are in direct contact one with the other. (This remark considerably enlightened me, coming at a time when I was doing my first street scenes and passing crowds.)

In a scene of tragedy, the unwilling actors recognize each other in their suffering. The bonds of such feeling are translated by their looks, which criss-cross space, forming axes every bit as active as those of lines and volumes. The looks converging on the woman in the foreground make up

another triangle of forces, invisible, of course, but which I imagine, as in comic strips, tracing dotted lines linking up the various figures. I banked a lot on this triple chain to restrain the woman crying and running out of the sculpture. For an identical reason, the outstretched arm of the Pole (much of the mining community in northern France is Polish) imposed itself on me as I went from the small sculpture to the big one. It would be an advanced element to restrain the fleeing woman. Then it assumed an importance all of its own, because a head-on form is sculpturally the most dynamic and reacts sharply in reply to each movement of the spectator. Furthermore, the hand ensures the contact with the public. I should say here that I want people to look at a large sculpture of mine not as an object, but rather have the impression of being in the work and of participating in the action. And what matters just as much to me is not uniquely the subject of the work, but the public's comprehension of it. Even though this is a condition that is difficult to fulfil, and thus considered today as almost irrelevant, it is an essential aspect of a work of art. It's no use talking about the high endeavour of Piero della Francesca in Arezzo if you don't remember that he was also illustrating the involved History of the True Wood of the Sacred Cross for a rural congregation.

As for myself, I work diligently on a sculpture hoping that it will satisfy to varying degrees each person who looks at it; young or old, cultured or not.

In a large group of multiple figures, I generally seek to make use of different expressions and emotions to give variety and animation throughout its spread. Here, of course, in a scene of general grief, expressions can scarcely differ. All that I can allow myself is the smile of the old man who attempts to comfort the little girl.

Is this sentiment? If so, I must defend it. Our age is familiar with sensational art which appeals to the senses alone. Is there no place for an art of sentiment which could speak to the soul? Beyond violence and sexuality, I believe my fellow creatures seek sentiment. No serious art being at hand nowadays to provide it, people have to turn to the sort of pictures on sale in department stores or the romantic trash of much cinema and musical comedy. They're not necessarily duped by the level they have to stoop to, but at least they find the essential, which is the sentiment of a warmer life. At all events, a work of art deprived of an ethical content plainly loses all reason for being.

At the same time, I am convinced that if one could portray extreme emotion, one would attain to the essence of sculpture itself. And that if emotions are to be examined, they should be sharp and simple like a botanical section. Narration must be upheld by a rigorous web – no expression without underlying geometry.

Thus these cobblestones, like the lozenged pavements of early perspectives, count out space all the better to carry the figures and fix the drama of a little community thrown one morning into disorder and grief.

Exhibition catalogue, Pierre Matisse Gallery, New York. April 1980.

Jean Dubuffet

I KNEW JEAN DUBUFFET BRIEFLY AT THE END OF THE 1970s, though I had heard a great many things said about him over the years, particularly from Robert Haligon, my moulder, and François Delagenière, my photographer, both of whom had worked for the artist, though on a much bigger scale.

Robert Haligon is the grandson of Louis Haligon, Rodin's moulder and enlarger. Following on from his father, Victor, who died young in the exercise of his profession, he was the third in this Parisian family of highly skilled moulders which continues to this day with his two sons, Olivier and Gérard. It was Dubuffet who convinced Robert in the 1960s to make the proofs of his moulds in synthetic resins like epoxy and polyester, rather than in plaster. Dubuffet wanted to enlist the sculptor César in putting up financial support for Haligon, who was already working for him at the time, but César didn't go along with the idea. About this time, Robert was forced to give up his Paris workshop, which like all workshops involved in the arts was situated in the fourteenth arrondissement, his departure being required by the development of the Gare Montparnasse. Fortunately, his father had bought a plot of land at Périgny, a village perched above the delightful river Yerres, not far from Brie-Comte-Robert, some thirty kilometres east of Paris. The money he had made working for Dubuffet was used to build a workshop there, and not long after this, in order to be as close as possible to his moulder, who was starting some important work for him, Dubuffet bought the neighbouring piece of ground. This at once gives you an idea of how possessive and intrusive the man was. (Dubuffet later acquired at Périgny more ground overlooking the Yerres, where he built his gigantic landscape sculpture *Falbula*.

The town council was overjoyed, thinking it would have a local monument that would attract a vast international public. This would certainly have been the case had Dubuffet not barred access to it, the outcome of all this being that Périgny is now separated from its river by an almighty blanc-mange, the view that confronts most of its inhabitants when they look out of their windows.)

The Haligon workshop had long been famous for its enlargements, and an artist like Joan Miró would see his terracotta statuettes the size of a man's fist, which had been lying around in drawers since before the war, transformed into giant sculptures, their surfaces tightened and corrected, which did a great deal for his fame when they were cast in bronze and exhibited at the Galerie Maeght. Dubuffet, passing the doors of the workshop as he drove up and down the lane in his little red Austin, would be confronted with work being done for other artists, and one evening he stopped and went into Robert's to announce: 'Haligon, from now on you work only for me.' Robert must have turned pale, so Dubuffet told him he would be back the following day to have his answer. Clearly, this could only be no, and Robert explained to him that the Haligon family had always exercised their craft in total freedom, even in Rodin's day. 'In that case, I'll sink you,' said Dubuffet charitably, severing relations on the spot. It came as a great shock to Haligon, not only because of the financial loss but also because it came from an artist whose work he revered.

It so happened that at that very moment in 1970, I had just completed my large sculpture *The Departure of Fruits and Vegetables from the Heart of Paris*, an elegy for the demise of the central fruit and vegetable market of Les Halles. I had already met Robert, who was a neighbour of my friend and fellow countryman the sculptor William Chattaway in Paris. I only sculpt in plaster and had long been distressed to see the marvellous light of that medium vanish the moment it was cast in bronze; all the more so since my relief sculptures at that time depicted outdoor scenes – cities and landscapes. I wanted this large new sculpture to be polychrome, and I persuaded my New York dealer, Pierre Matisse, to put up the money to have it moulded in resin at the Haligon workshops, for I knew that its white surface was a perfect support for acrylic paint, having tested it beforehand.

This influx of money and work came at just the right time for Robert and his workshop. The six months required to mould and assemble the sculpture were full of complications, the seventeen pieces being difficult to fit together, and the workshop didn't enrich itself. Nevertheless, it was turning over and, in the end, the gap was filled, and other works by other artists – with Niki de Saint-Phalle entering in strength – found their way in. Dubuffet, meanwhile, was uniting his own personal team of moulders at his workshop in Périgny.

The story told me by François Delagenière painted a similar picture. He had been Dubuffet's official photographer for ten years, working in the studios at Vence where the artist had his assembly line, the finished painting being passed to the workshop next door where François had his cameras, the photographs then going on to the archives department, while the works went off to the framer and the packer. For a peccadillo, this marvellous photographer had been dismissed! I was the main beneficiary of this, since François took the definitive photos of my major works and, in the beginning, did so free of charge out of fondness for my work.

The context in which I made Dubuffet's acquaintance, therefore, was anything but auspicious. The meeting came about at his private view at the Galerie Claude Bernard in October 1978. As I have related elsewhere, Claude had put an end to his years of discovery to exhibit celebrities: Balthus, Francis Bacon and – Jean Dubuffet. The latter was famous but unapproachable for the public, and his presence in the gallery involved sitting alone on a bench while the visitors lined up along the walls stared at him in fascination. I had time to look him over. He was small, of course, stooped (I was unaware that he had suffered for years from severe spinal trouble, making it very painful for him even to stretch out his hand), bald and had a tic that was distinctly odd but enlightening. He had a big mouth, which was constantly being opened and closed by powerful jaws. Had his tongue darted out, he would have been the spitting image of a giant lizard, and I immediately thought he could have been a prehistoric beast making its way through virgin forest, masticating everything in its path and regurgitating it in its onward march. Which was exactly the behaviour that had been described to me.

Shortly after this, I saw the other Dubuffet. I had been introduced to him by Claude Bernard, and he sprang to his feet, his mouth now breaking into a smile of great charm. 'So you're the magnificent Mason? Tell me, when can I visit your studio?' I was rather taken aback by his approach, totally unexpected, and the thought flashed through my mind that Dubuffet had got me all wrong. Perhaps, from the point of view of Art Brut, he had thought my sculptures, seen in reproduction, were made from unusual materials, breadcrumbs or whatever. To my reply that he had only to choose his day and hour, Dubuffet the dynamo floored me with 'tomorrow morning, nine o'clock'. At ten past nine the following morning he was at the studio, bent double again, only this time to apologize for having been delayed by traffic.

I've received quite a lot of important people in my studio – great poets and writers, great dealers, great artists, among them Alberto Giacometti, Balthus and Francis Bacon – but never have I had facing me a man so feverishly intelligent, so quick to take in and appraise the work presented to his gaze. The studio was dominated by my great composition *A Tragedy in the North*, a polychrome work inspired by the mining disaster at Liévin. Each detail – each paving stone, I might almost say – was scrutinized with positive appreciation, and he concluded his inspection with the remark: 'You've managed to put into your work a popular, public dimension that I've never been able to do.' Later, I showed him my coloured sculptures of landscapes of the Midi, and Dubuffet waxed lyrical in his praise: 'There are only two younger artists I appreciate. There is you here in France, and there is Claes Oldenburg in America.' I was pleased to hear the name of this artist, since at the beginning of his career I, too, had found him the most interesting of the Pop artists, after seeing his retrospective at MOMA in New York in 1969, and, since I'd only just started working with colour, he had influenced me. (This was before the huge blow-ups of everyday objects, like the lipstick, the hammer and the scissors, which left me completely cold.) At the end of his visit, Dubuffet declared: 'So, you must have a big retrospective in New York. Where do you want to exhibit?' I didn't reply straightaway, and Dubuffet went on to say: 'The Guggenheim. That's it. It's there and nowhere else. I shall write at once to the director, Mr Messer.'

The following day, I received a letter from him: 'I was extremely impressed by my visit… Your works are very moving, I like them all enormously and they will remain very much present in my memory… Your own person inspired the greatest sympathy in me and, adding to the effect of your marvellous works, is a comfort and a stimulus to me.' More astonishing still, he took the trouble, with rare delicacy, of writing a similar letter singing my praises to my dealer Claude Bernard, which made a tremendous impact on the gallery. He also sent me his catalogue from the Fondation Jean Dubuffet, inscribed 'To the marvellous Mason with the friendly admiration of Jean Dubuffet', and invited me to his home in the rue de Vaugirard, where he pulled out drawer after drawer to show me a stupefying quantity of drawings.

This was the high point of our friendship. He later wrote me a letter congratulating me on my forthcoming exhibition at the Pierre Matisse Gallery in New York and hoping that my Provençal landscapes which had so impressed him would be shown. He no longer mentioned the *Tragedy*, which was a hundred times more powerful than these low reliefs. Further letters were exchanged, followed by the explosion. 'How dare you call me maître! I who have spent my entire life avoiding official sanction. I thought you more intelligent and you disappoint me.' That was the end, since I didn't reply to such bad faith on the part of an artist who exhibited only in official museums and galleries and befriended each minister of culture in turn. In any case, I had understood that my usefulness in Jean Dubuffet's life, the pleasure of boxing me in for a short moment, had come to an end.

Nevertheless, there was what might be described as an amusing sequel. At the time of my exhibition in New York, I was contacted by Mr Messer, the director of the Guggenheim Museum, who had indeed received a letter from Dubuffet asking him to organize a retrospective of my polychrome sculptures in his museum. He invited me to come to the Guggenheim to present him with the different aspects of my work. A date was fixed, and I decided I would give Mr and Mrs Messer a slide show accompanied by my own commentaries in the lecture hall of the museum, in the presence of my wife and of Mr and Mrs William Louis-Dreyfus. William is my patron and my principal collector, and since he lives only a few blocks up from the Guggenheim on Fifth Avenue, he offered us a small reception at his home afterwards. Mrs

Messer repeated several times that 'Dubuf' was her best friend, and I began to understand that his letter to the Messers was not merely a suggestion that they put on the big exhibition for me, but an order. After the slide show, which, I think, was of quality, the pictures of my works resplendent with bright colours on the large screen, Mrs Messer declared that she had immediately grasped the attraction my sculptures might have for 'Dubuf'.

The trouble was, I didn't like the Guggenheim Museum. Its winding spiral structure struck me as quite ill-suited to the architecture and frames of my large works (in 1980, the tower with its level floors had yet to be envisaged). In a gesture that I today admit was probably over-hasty on my part, I whispered into Mr Messer's ear, during our short walk to the Louis-Dreyfuses' home, that, of course, I was in no way soliciting an exhibition at his museum. The look he gave me, veiled in astonishment, steeped in gratitude, was pleasant to behold. The temple of abstraction was not to be profaned by narrative art.

Though my encounter with Dubuffet was short-lived, I was witness to several high points in his career as an artist. In 1947, I visited his epoch-making exhibition at René Drouin's astonishing gallery on the place Vendôme next to the Ritz, where we made the acquaintance of Art Brut. (The delightful Drouin later went from this, the biggest gallery in Paris, to the smallest, in the rue Visconti.) On my first trip to New York in 1968, I stayed at Pierre Matisse's home, and the walls of my bedroom were lined with portraits on paper by Dubuffet's hand, for it should not be forgotten that Matisse did a great deal for his career in the days when he was part of his gallery, not that this prevented their collaboration from ending very badly.*

In 1969, benefiting from the fact that Alberto Giacometti had been unable to carry out his project for the Plaza of the Chase Manhattan Bank in New York, Dubuffet conceived and had made in the workshops at Périgny the *Group of Four Trees*. I saw them the year they were installed and thought

* When Pierre Matisse came to Périgny to inspect the work being done at Haligon's on my sculpture of Les Halles, he pricked up an ear on learning that his former artist had bought the neighbouring piece of land. He immediately wanted to buy something himself at Périgny, just to annoy Dubuffet. He announced from New York that he was about to buy the Grande Ferme. Too late. It had been sold the day before.

it a briliiant idea to place huge trees made of resin on a site where there wasn't a tree growing anywhere. My only regret was that Dubuffet's characteristically thick lines were still black, where green would have been sublime.

I was present when Dubuffet's *Ghost Monument* for Houston, Texas, was put together in Olivier Haligon's new workshop at Brie-Comte-Robert, Dubuffet having gone back to work with the Haligons after finding the quality of his *Four Trees* poor. Before this multifaceted, twelve-metre-high work went off to the States, Olivier Haligon had it assembled behind his workshop to show it to the artist. The latter seemed very pleased and asked if he could make an urgent telephone call. When he returned, he explained to the Haligons that he had wanted to phone his mother to tell her about it. His mother! Dubuffet was eighty-one at the time.

Basically, however, these sculptures and monuments made at the end of his life were just enlargements of polystyrene cut-outs that are easy to manipulate with the aid of heated tools, the almost insane multiplication that his fortune enabled him to finance and a reflection of his desire, likewise growing with the years, to crusade ever more all around him. The long *Hourloupe* cycle wearies, despite the striping, intended to be dynamic. Those black lines running everywhere reveal the basic nature of Jean Dubuffet's art. It is graphic, entirely graphic. This omnipresent drawing, however, remains at all times two-dimensional and flat. Rendered in sculpture, his slabs of polystyrene stuck on top of each other never attain the three-dimensional spiral of true sculpture.

The edifice of the *Tour aux Têtes*, which overlooks the Seine from the Ile Saint-Germain in the west of Paris, is all too easily revealed to be a giant blow-up of an object of modest size and equally modest interest. The monotony of this last period is all the more surprising if we compare it to the veritable firework display of inventiveness that characterized the Dubuffet of the post-war years. No doubt, this immense repetition and multiplication corresponds to his will to overrun the world, to extend his work and his name everywhere. Previously, in the fruitful decades of the 1950s and 1960s, it was more like the world, with its myriad mysteries, that had penetrated into him.

Jean Dubuffet is clearly a major figure of late twentieth-century art.

The artists of his generation belonged to modern art – Giacometti, Balthus, Bacon. He, on the other hand, belongs to contemporary art. His mockery makes him part of that race of contemporary artists for whom art is not a quest, not a faith, being less important than their own persons. He surpasses them in his rich early periods, and he differs from them in having originally been a gifted painter and draughtsman with a perfect classical training – in the manner of Derain, Louis Deladicq has said, and the remark is just if one adds that, in Dubuffet's case, the line is wirier and the result more lively. The explosion of his personal style, neo-naive and caustic, came in a burst of colour in 1943, the darkest year of the war.

An astonishing figure!

The Picasso Bequest, the Grand Palais, Paris, 1979

I HAVE READ ATTENTIVELY THE PRESS OCCASIONED BY THE re-emergence of Picasso's work on a large scale at the Grand Palais. With scant variation, the critics have written the same articles as in the past. There is the same astonished, even stunned, admiration, which doesn't call for too many explanations; with, here and there, it's true, some barbed criticism, which even goes so far, in one case at least, as to speak of the overall 'failure' of Picasso's work.

I have myself, over the years, had time to form several somewhat contradictory views on the matter. There was a long, totally devoted period in my youth, during which I was able to meet the master and show him my early works. This was followed by a period when I stood back and, shortly afterwards, by one of harsh judgements. The latter coincided with my familiarity with Alberto Giacometti, who for many of us had become, if not an antidote to Picasso, at least a new standard who seemed to ring truer, to be more in tune with the human condition. Naturally, my doubts were not promoted by Giacometti himself. Despite everything, I always kept one eye open on the pole from which I had distanced myself. For there was something in it that strongly attracted me and which still tugs at me today. Except that I am now in a better position to know what it is.

The moment I embarked on my period of large compositions, my thoughts focused almost exclusively on Picasso. Why? Because Picasso is essentially a painter of compositions, of history paintings even, which in the past were considered the *summum* of artistic activity – as no doubt they are.

Picasso is a painter of compositions, a history painter and a painter of large formats. The three things go together. They also have certain obvious corollaries. To compose means to create, and still more to invent. The artist of compositions doesn't study, he doesn't analyse. Human behaviour is neither a still-life, nor a landscape, nor even a man if he's posing. To realize the great subject, the artist paints from his own mind, which has no precise form. To put it across and have us believe in it means inventing forms and styles. This is a good description of Picasso.

To compose is also a form of speculation more intellectual than sensual. On a large surface, ideas are numerous and must be organized so that each idea relates in a significant manner to all the others. The intrinsic value of an idea counts less than its relationship to the other elements of the composition, like the characters in a play.

There is this that is particular about Picasso's idea of composition: it is not at the outset an idea of plastic construction but, broadly speaking, as in all narrative art, an object, a form, later a symbol, representing an aspect of our ordinary, everyday life. The entities – a table, a window, a ladder, a sponge, a horse, a bull, a child, a woman – will take their place in a human drama which always seeks to transcend the ordinary and the everyday and attain to the universal, to joy or death.

We can already see that the singularity of Picasso lies not so much in the forms he invents as is in the very goal of his work, which sets him totally apart from his contemporaries.

That he is a history painter goes without saying, the epic *Guernica* being the only successful example of that genre in our century. It fulfils its role of reaching out to the general public (something which every artist in the past considered vital and most artists of the present despise). It attains to universality because it speaks the language of sentiment, which alone touches the hearts of men. (Needless to say, all his paintings have this effect of exercising a direct hold on the public, and the howls we hear even today

Picasso painting *Guernica*, 1937. Photograph: Dora Maar

themselves testify to their impact on the spectators.)

Let me go back to what I was saying about large formats. We obviously accept that Picasso is a painter in the grand manner. But, at the same time, we judge him in a far more modest perspective.

The Picasso–Giacometti duality wasn't viable precisely because the latter is a master of small forms. His works – his sculptures, paintings and drawings – have the seductiveness of 'fine objects'. Their specific density is greatly enhanced thereby. Furthermore, the particular genius of that artist focused on a given point, on a single problem, with an essentialist rigour. There you have it. Giacometti's art is an art of essence. This marvellous density seemed to reveal, by comparison, an alarming void in Picasso's forms. Even his most faithful admirers could feel it.

Today, I think we misconstrue the debate. Notice the striking quality of any Picasso reproduction. Why? Because reducing the size of the image increases its gravity, gives it the added density.

I was struck by a review of the exhibition in one of the big French dailies. Remarking that, even after his death, Picasso still disturbs, they cited the verdict of a nineteen-year-old student: 'I'm disappointed,' she said. 'I see paintings that are better reproduced in books. Here you have to stand six metres back to see anything.' I'm filled with admiration by such a perceptive reaction. Of course you have to stand six metres back! For the simple reason that almost everything we see here is a piece in a larger composition. The forms tend to spread. The lines of force reach straight out to the four corners of the painting, ready to spill over onto the next one. They burst out of their frames.

So many disjointed late works, with few genuinely major achievements – might this be Picasso's 'failure'? In terms of all that he was capable of, this is clearly the case. With the coming of old age, did the king reveal his alter ego, the clown? Perhaps that, too.

In terms of his time, however, and of the cooling of the artistic mind, the answer can only be no. It is an artist of sentiment we have lost. I'm not talking about his private life. He aimed his art at the public as a whole. His many 'periods', as they used to be called, can no longer disturb us. They seem to me the most natural progression towards his definitive personal style. Bizarrely, some people see Cubism as the high point in his career, a rigour never surpassed. Be wary of such people! They're aesthetes. Cubism was a school of purity and rigour. Like abstraction today, of which it was the direct forerunner, an artist can interest himself in it, can learn the secrets of his craft from it as he once did in the master's studio, then come out and fashion an art capable of speaking to the world of the living.

As Picasso did, whose different styles paved the way for the volcanic fusion, the blaze of warmth in defence of his country. A sentiment that was truly without precedent. Truly admirable. One eruption each century? Now everything sleeps.

Joseph B.

I N THE WINTER OF 1981, I WAS FEELING MORE ASTHMATIC than usual. I wanted to breathe warm dry air, and I knew that the fields around my house in Provence would be a touch too damp in the month of December. The ideal destination was Egypt, but that would have required a certain amount of planning and here I was leaving on impulse. Sicily! That was what I needed and, having hit on the place, I phoned my friend Sandro Manzo, an Italian from the south who had long made his home in Rome where he ran his art gallery, Il Gabbiano. 'Ah,' said Sandro, 'Sicily during the Christmas period. Not easy, but I'll try.' Later, he phoned back to say that, not without some difficulty, he'd found me a room at the Hotel San Domenico at Taormina. 'Thank you, you're a pal.'

When the plane landed at Catania, I laughed because the passengers had burst into applause the moment we successfully touched down. A demonstrative people, I thought to myself. Once inside the airport, however, I changed my mind when I saw people, not talking out loud but walking up and whispering a few words in the ear of their interlocutor. Mafia behaviour, I corrected myself, equally approximately.

The activity of the common people was put aside the moment I arrived at the Hotel San Domenico. I realized at once where I was – in one of the classiest hotels of the Mediterranean. A former monastery on the water's edge, it was enormous and the price of the room could not be otherwise. The director claimed he knew my work and was fond of artists.

At dinner there were seven of us in the dining room, and I now knew that the hotel had five hundred rooms (my thoughts went out to Sandro). After a short stroll through the streets of Taormina, I also knew that this wasn't the climate I was seeking. Warm, yes, but with a damp, stifling, maritime warmth. My mind was made up, I would leave at once. Nevertheless, I couldn't possibly forget that at the centre of Sicily is the little town of Piazza

Armerina, near to which is the ancient villa of Hadrian which contains some very fine, very large floor mosaics, a few reproductions of which in Georges Duthuit's book *Le Feu des signes* had made a strong impression on me. It would be criminal to leave without seeing them.

The following day, on leaving the hotel I asked the taxi driver at the head of the queue to drive me to Piazza Armerina. This seemed like an enormous journey to him and would only be possible if he could stop off on the way at Catania to inform his wife. I thus visited a very poor neighbourhood in that town and, during the few minutes while the driver was away, marvelled at the Christmas lighting, the most sophisticated neons, which covered each house. They were of a religious character, of course, the Italian Christmas consisting exclusively of the Nativity.

It was Christmas Eve, and on arriving at Hadrian's villa I found myself alone in the enormous solitude of antiquity. But soon the idea took root in me that the Emperor and his company had gone hunting and would be returning at the end of the day to repeople these rooms, which remained more or less intact. The mosaics stretched out over the floor for hundreds of metres depicted the entry of Noah's Ark, with larger than lifesize characters holding or leading gigantic animals and birds. Since I was alone, I was able, with complete freedom, to fetch some water and splash it over the mosaics to recover the colour in all its freshness of the admirable work of these ancient artists, no doubt Greek.

Once these few magnificent hours were over, I went back to the taxi and we started on the journey back. At some point, the driver, an ill-shaven young man in a singlet, glanced round and asked: 'Signore, do you know Joseph Beuys?' Utterly taken aback by such a question from such a person, all I could say in reply was: 'No, I don't know him personally, but I know who he is.' (And how! He was at the height of his fame at the time.) 'But why in heaven's name do you ask?' 'Because yesterday, Signor Beuys made the same journey as you.'

I made enquiries at the hotel. Joseph Beuys had spent one night there, had amazingly taken the same taxi to see the same Hadrian's Villa and had left Sicily.

153

Manet and Cézanne

I N SPRING 1981, ON A TRIP TO LONDON, I RETURNED TO THE
Courtauld Galleries to see Manet's *A Bar at the Folies-Bergère*, which I
hadn't seen for more than thirty years. I might even say that I was driven
by a great desire, without really knowing why.

It's true that, when people ask me from time to time about my early
days in the profession and my first loves, I never forget to mention this artist
and this painting. In the beginning, I studied painting, and Manet's work
seemed to me a fine example of painting that was beautiful and true, though
I only knew it from reproductions, which in those days could be rather
approximate. My admiration for his work had culminated in an attempt to
make a composition largely inspired by *A Bar at the Folies-Bergère*, my setting being the more down-to-earth one of the Cadena Café in Oxford High
Street (I was a student at the Ruskin School at the time). In the foreground
of my painting, I had put myself sitting at a table, and my girlfriend leaning
forward to serve me, with a chignon and a lace-collared velvet dress, was
perfectly in tone. Our bodies were reflected in the large mirror behind the
table, along with the interior of this luxurious café, its clients lit by chande-
liers. It was, in fact, my last painting, at a time when I still thought of myself
as a painter, for I was about to switch to sculpture under the aegis of the
school's secretary, who had studied before the war with Despiau.

If I consider that, broadly speaking, my sculpture, even today, can be
described as the vision of a painter rendered in three dimensions, it is easy
to think of this painting as the prototype for the work that followed. In the
foreground are lifesize figures, while the middle ground and background are
occupied by figures that have been considerably foreshortened – in my
painting by the depth created by the reflection in the mirror, in my sculpture
by perspective, so accelerated as to cover what is actually 200 metres in
1.5 metres.

I will end there my personal preamble and speak instead of that visit to
the Courtauld which accentuated and crystallized so many of my thoughts.

A Bar at the Folies-Bergère is Manet's last composition, painted when he was fifty. He died the following year. At the Courtauld Galleries it hangs in the centre of a wall in a room that, though not large, is outstanding in terms of content. The painting measures 96 x 130 centimetres, which is not too big either, but the composition is particularly rich and dense.

To either side of it are several Degas pastels belonging to his early period, thus neither big nor colourful.

The opposite wall is entirely taken up by a row of Cézannes, each of good quality.

I'm not going to describe Manet's painting in detail, since it's too well known. I mention only its seductive frontality, as the main figure, the blond-haired young woman, looms up before you, looking you straight in the eyes. In fact, this space jutting out between you and the painting is even more effective than the movements depicted in the painting (I'd almost say that paintings which don't have this dimension become 'regardless', and that the astonishing power of the *Mona Lisa* lies solely in the way it is projected forward by the woman's gaze, the actual handling of the work being rather poor). Then I will ask you if you've ever noticed the two legs dangling from the top-left corner? Those of a trapeze artist with green boots, like an inversion of the bottles of Bass strewn about the marble bar below. Moreover, the crowd reflected in the mirror is looking at her, including the woman with the opera glasses.

If you walk backwards from the painting and look at it from the opposite wall, it expands and moves towards you, flooding the room with vivacity and life and light.

Let us now look at the row of Cézannes. The opposite phenomenon occurs: they withdraw into the wall! This is partly due to their vertical construction, which respects the surface of the canvas, and partly to their lack of light, which Cézanne replaces by colour. But it is more certainly due to their uniformity. Cézanne pursued a problem that he considered he never solved. Since the problem never changed, all his paintings look much the same.

A Bar at the Folies-Bergère, on the other hand, is unique. Manet painted a dozen unique compositions in his life. He aimed at the masterpiece, putting absolutely everything into it. In between, he painted this and that, sometimes of no great consequence. Then he rallied himself for something major. Cézanne compiled an analytic body of work. In Manet we're dealing with synthesis – of light and shade, form and colour, and, above all, life and art. He renounces nothing. Each thing has its true significance and its autonomy as pure painting. The young woman of the *Bar* is 'painted' – and how! – but she also has a glint in her eyes and a gaze. The same can be said of *Olympia* and *Le Déjeuner sur l'herbe*. In the latter, the seated nude even has a look in her eye that perfectly explains, to my point of view, the reaction of the official procession at the Salon des Refusés in 1863, since it is one of the utmost impertinence. Manet, it's said, was a great womanizer. He cannot conceive of a woman who doesn't look at him – or at us.

The moment I got back from London, I went to the galleries of the Jeu de Paume to take a fresh look at the Cézannes and put the opinion I had formed at the Courtauld to the test. At the head of the stairs leading to the first floor was Cézanne's large *Femme à la cafetière*. Large? Monumental! Yet had I been told that the woman was in fact the coffee pot or the coffee pot the woman, I wouldn't have raised any objection. Both are objects. This is fine for the enamelled coffee pot; but what about the woman?

There's a fundamental difference, that is to say, between Manet and Cézanne, a difference far greater than that between Manet and his predecessors (Delacroix and the Spaniards) or between Cézanne and his successors (the Cubists). This frontier renders null and void the widely accepted idea that Manet is the first modern painter, in other words the first to destroy the subject. The argument makes no sense. He loved the subject more than himself (I'm thinking of Ruskin, who told his first students that they would never love art well if they didn't love what it mirrors better).

Yes, the break is situated between Manet and Cézanne. Somewhere between these two, and for the very first time, life loses ground to art. Content becomes less important than form. The beauty of Manet's art comes from its perfect equilibrium of one with the other, from its being a complete art – not, certainly, for the first time in history, but it's a rare moment nonetheless. This great painter, moreover, did not willingly place the accent on art as a world of its own (today totally crystallized, alas). He doggedly sought to remain in contact with the world about us, which in his case meant the well-to-do middle classes. This has always been seen as a weakness on his part. As I see it, it's the moving adherence of the man to the world in which he belongs, in which he believes. Do people still know that it's important for man to believe and, for the creative artist, paramount? To believe in something outside oneself. The work guided in this way is rich in a content that will ensure its entry, sooner or later, into society. This generous movement of loving others sweeps away all the narcissistic, introspective drivel.

On Light

THE SUN IS THE SIGN OF REALITY. THOUGH IN WORKS OF art you seldom see it, you feel its presence everywhere in the play of shadows. Shadows are fleeting. They mark time. I get the impression that Cézanne, who painted in sunlit regions, wasn't interested in them. Doubtless because he was aiming at eternity. Perhaps it is precisely this lack of shadows that detaches his landscapes from nature and purifies their construction, making them *cose mentale* – and, soon, abstractions (in other hands, it's true).

If the absence of shadows marks an unreal eternity, their presence underlines a palpable immediacy. In narrative compositions this helps capture the spectator's attention and gather him into the action. The cast shadow makes us believe in the existence of the thing painted. Metaphysical and Surrealist painters used it to make us believe in their wildest dreams. But in their case the orb that lights their way is terrible and no longer moves. Dalí's paintings are everlasting nightmares.

Responses by Raymond Mason to
Questions by Michael Peppiatt

You talk a gread deal about 'content' in art. What would you say is the 'content' of your work? What is it essentially about?

If, as you say, I talk a great deal about content it's simply to make up for the fact that the others hardly talk about it at all. Doesn't it strike you as odd that for so many decades art has been a question not of 'what' but uniquely of 'how'?

Right at the start when I wanted to be an artist it always seemed to me important to know what to say before knowing how to say it. At art school I was incapable of mastering a technique *a priori* and felt it keenly at the time. Later on, the movements of modern art left me bewildered and unbelieving. Based on the outer look more than the inner thought, art stemming from art, they still seem to me the exact expression of what art cannot be.

As far as I'm concerned, the only movement of an artist is towards life, towards the others. I seek to express and, if possible, to exalt the world immediately surrounding me and which I know. I know its looks and I know the reason for those looks. At the beginning of this century, European artists, in their pursuit of all that was new, started to lay their hands on arts which did not belong to them, confiscating forms without the slightest idea of what they contained, of their *raison d'être*. Negro art, primitive art, oriental art, calligraphy, and so on. All attracted by the outer look. That was the big error. To think that art is just a simple excitement of forms and colours, figurative or not. And so we arrive at the absurdity of mistaking decoration for real painting, just as others are led to consider as sculpture what are nothing more than mere objects. Paintings and sculptures are not objects but vehicles for human thought. And the contents decide the nature of the container. I mistrust talk of 'painting' and 'sculpture'. For me their importance resides not in their existence as such but in what they are employed to say. I've always detested people talking about them as though they were floating freely in the air. Advancing painting, progressive sculpture… Then there's

this idea that modern art is in constant movement and that artists must follow the movement or be outstripped. A bit like crossing a ford where one
passes over the stones as lightly as possible.

Lots of artists paint canvases in this fashion. It isn't the stone which
matters but the direction, the tendency they say, the movement. My point of
view is exactly the opposite. For me a work of art must crystallize movement. The thought must enter the material, gain weight and permanency,
resist centuries.

What in fact can a work of art contain? At this hour of simplification
the reply seems to be – the least possible. Here, once more, I'm 'against the
movement', because for me the reply is *everything*. And it seems just as evident for me that I should address it to *everybody*. I work diligently on each
sculpture, in the case of the big ones for several years, intending it to satisfy,
naturally to varying degrees, every person, young or old, cultured or not,
who looks at it.

What can I say about *my* content? Well, as a boy in Birmingham I lived
and played in the streets. Did this decide my predilection for out-of-doors?
At all events, the city scene, the buildings, the life outside provided me with
subjects until my middle forties, with an occasional interlude when being ill
in bed limited me to drawing my left hand, which I later sculpted, or an
operation on the back kept me involved with torsos for a year or two.

Since then, I have been occupied specifically with the human theme
and, now that I think it over, with the doings of humble folk. This is clear
and simple. What is decidedly less so, in an epoch of declining beliefs, is the
choice of a subject of a universal nature capable of interesting and speaking
out to the general public, to the entire world. For what matters to me is not
only the subject of the work, but the public comprehension of it. Even
though this is a difficult condition to fulfil and thus considered today as
almost irrelevant, it is a necessary dimension of a work of art, an essential
ingredient of the content which the artist must consciously consider right
from the start.

From all I've said it must seem obvious that I am a worshipper of the
visual world and a figurative artist. But after the outer world, there's the
inner thought, and real art cannot exist without the combination of the fig-

urative and the abstract. The stupidity is to have imagined dividing the two. For me, the elaboration of the inner structure is all-absorbing and is probably my best contribution to present-day art.

At the same time there's another element I want my work to be essentially about. I won't satisfy anybody if the sculpture is not *beautiful*. The subject of the work situates it in the world and in history. Beauty transcends that reality and brings happiness.

What artists have impressed you most? And in what enduring way?

Lots, of course. But more or less of the same type. And rather casually, not by direct study or copying. I'm not an assiduous frequenter of museums and probably haven't been more than twenty times to the Louvre in thirty-six years.

A permanent admiration has been for Manet, since I loved him as a youth and still do. In particular his last masterpiece, *A Bar at the Folies-Bergère*. (He aimed at masterpieces, which is an additional reason for my admiration.) The juxtaposition of the foreground figure of the barmaid with the tiny figures of the crowded theatre, an entire world, has been a direct influence on much of my sculpture, so it seems to me now. Indeed, the majority of artists who impress me are painters.

The mural painters of Italy – in fresco, I mean. From Giotto to Gian-Domenico Tiepolo, if you can imagine such a slice. And we'd better go back as far as the Villa of the Mysteries in Pompeii. When I was doing my last sculptures in bronze I was influenced by Michelangelo, but I was thinking of his *Last Judgement*. And the room of Brueghels in Vienna, a much greater painter and colourist than one imagines, and on a greater scale, too. (The only art which really interests me is that of composition. All those I have mentioned express themselves by numerous ideas and personages with interlocking significance, and do this in breadth and sharply defined colour.) Poussin and Seurat sometimes. Van Gogh always, because, with him, art becomes alive. Of modern artists I say at once Picasso because he was, at his best, a compositional genius. These works never begin as an aesthetic idea but, as in all narrative art, group together different entities like a table, a window, a ladder, a sponge, a horse, a bull, a child and a woman,

which then take their place in a human drama which seeks to attain to universality, to joy or to death. When one thinks back, his work of the 1930s can
be seen as totally different in scope and in objective to the other artists with
whom he is so commonly grouped, Matisse, Braque, Derain, etc, and the
world public accords him its acclaim precisely because of that.

More enduring influences have been those of Giacometti and Balthus,
because I have known them over the years and my tissue has been necessarily modified to a degree that I myself cannot judge.

Giacometti, whom I met first, was the saviour, the only rallying point
possible in the luxurious art world of Paris. He was the example for a young
man who felt that the image of the world had to be worshipped. He showed
that it was possible. His conversation and his judgements were those of a
modern Socrates.

Balthus in those days was difficult to meet. It was my English-Scottish
blood which triggered off our relationship. England he reveres, and he
speaks its language with a better accent than mine; Scotland, too, in the
shape of a pair of plaid trousers I was wearing, saying that he was a Gordon,
like his forebear Lord Byron.

Our meeting was the moment in 1956 when he had brought all his
works from his château in the Morvan for his first retrospective. He was
touching up each canvas by Paris light in the old studio of Francis Gruber in
the Villa d'Alésia. Typical Balthusian scrupulousness. When I saw the
whole of his work together, its breadth – giant canvases composed with calm
mastery – convinced me that he was the other pillar with Giacometti on
which could be built a new art of the figure and the figurative world.
Happily, a quarter of a century later Balthus is still very much alive and
active, and we could have met last week at the opening of his big exhibition
of drawings and watercolours in Spoleto in Italy, since he was, most untyp-
ically, present.

To be influenced by Francis Bacon would be, once again, robbing an
exterior without participating in the high ritual of its contents. At the same
time Bacon the painter of the flesh, Bacon the colourist, once seen, can never
be forgotten – so the influence is there, inescapably.

How would you characterize your development as an artist since your arrival in Paris?

When I arrived in Paris after the war, I had already made the change from painting to sculpture. Probably less than I thought, because when I exhibited in a group show at the Galerie Maeght in 1947 I was showing coloured sculptures – much to the dismay of Monsieur Maeght, who had seen them in white.

Thoughout the 1950s I made a series of drawings and low or high reliefs of the cityscape. In these years I had two exhibitions at the Beaux-Arts Gallery in London simply because Helen Lessore who ran it had the very rare gift of reading into a work of art and detecting its intrinsic value, heedless of the artist's youth or lack of fame. A handful of well-known names can now testify to this. But then she closed down in order to paint, and I never exhibited in London again.

In 1960, I opened a gallery adjacent to my studio in the Latin Quarter with my wife and named it after her, Janine Hao. I'm more interested in art than in my own person and find great pleasure whenever I come across it. For six years we worked humbly to present artists, all good, famous or not. The marvellous American painter Anne Harvey, Gaston Louis-Roux, who is now appreciated in London, Léopold-Lévy, the genial poster artist Cassandre, Balthus and many others.

We had begun with an exhibition of my own work which was visited towards the end by the Paris dealer Claude Bernard, and my opting for sculpture was finally officialized, so to speak, when I entered his gallery in 1963, because in those days it specialized only in sculpture. My first exhibition there in 1965 fixed me as a black and white draughtsman of the city scene with the extension into sculpture of such subjects. The centrepiece was a giant sculpture, *The Crowd*, which was at the same time an accumulation of all my past scenes and the final abandonment of all decor, giving emphasis to the human element alone.

Pierre Matisse of New York took me on in 1967 and financed a large showing in 1968 of all my work in bronze. Was it the hammering of the two-ton bronze versions of *The Crowd* during the hot summer in Rome which tired me of this material? Not exclusively. I had already decided that my open-air scenes lost much of this quality when translated from plaster into metal, ceasing to be scenes, becoming objects. About this time the English sculptor William Chattaway, the only compatriot artist I know in Paris, introduced me to Robert Haligon the plaster-moulder and enlarger (his grandfather had enlarged all the works of Rodin, who contented himself with his perfect clays at one-third size). Monsieur Haligon was already well advanced in the techniques of moulding synthetic resins, thanks to his work for Jean Dubuffet. Epoxy resin seemed exactly the material to render my plasters permanent, since it has the same warm white colour as plaster of Paris. However, a cast never has the specific intensity of an original, and one day I painted onto the epoxy cast to give it more accent and realized at once that I had hit on a satisfactory solution to my various problems. The light weight and the tensile quality of the resin would allow me to do my large compositions, and the act of painting its surface with matt acrylic paint had revived my long-buried love of paint and colour.

After finishing my two copies of *The Crowd* in bronze, I moved almost immediately onto a larger sculpture based on the disappearance of the market of Les Halles from the centre of Paris. This eventually emerged two years later as a three-dimensional fresco in vivid colour, *The Departure of Fruits and Vegetables from the Heart of Paris*. Helen Lessore commented at the time that I had moved from the Mediterranean tradition to the Nordic tradition.

This move to polychromy gives me intense pleasure, but, of course, complicates the elaboration of my sculpture a great deal. Colour is essential in order for the viewer to believe in the scene. At the same time, the size of the major compositions, without being artificially blown-up, is big enough for him to feel that he himself is participating in the action. The slightest movement of the spectator is echoed in the depth of the high relief by the figures and forms riding one across another. The use of colour heightens a hundredfold the spatial possibilities of recall and repetition between the pieces. This rustling, this continual metamorphosis, provokes a sense of liveliness and, I would like to think, of life itself, since this is the object of art, to capture the spark of life, no?

What would you say was your debt to England and English art?

If I reply in all seriousness that I think there is no more 'English' artist working today than myself, you will understand that, whether I am right or wrong, at least I consider my debt as total. This said, it needs a little qualifying.

First of all, there is the fact that I have been living outside my native country a long time – thirty-six years. At one stage, I had not spent more than forty-eight hours in England in twenty-one years. It's obvious that you don't consciously make an English art under those conditions. So, if what I do is essentially English, it is in spite of myself, or rather it springs from a natural inside source and is not willed. I probably wouldn't even have noticed the fact until recently, had not a few eminent voices told me with force that that is what I am.

Picasso had praised my *Barcelona Tram* in the presence of other artists and then added: 'You're an English artist.' I admit I felt dismayed. He noticed it, of course, and assured me that he had the greatest opinion of English art and reeled off a list of names from Hogarth onwards. Balthus was more persuasive in convincing me that I was a son of my fathers. He is, as I have said, a pronounced Anglophile. A younger contemporary of mine, Sam Szafran, a first-rate artist and erudite, later gave me a volume called *Peinture anglaise*, a most remarkable book, which reminded me that some of the paintings I appreciate the most are in Birmingham Art Gallery.

The specific English tradition to which I attach myself most voluntarily is that of narrative art. Is it the complement of our great tradition in literature? At all events, the national talent seems to flower at its most personal there. From Hogarth to William Blake, from Samuel Palmer to Ford Madox Brown, from Stanley Spencer to Francis Bacon, and countless more, the line is unbroken. (I thought in the past when people were shocked by a Francis Bacon that it was because his narrative power was too strong. He described too well a situation in which they did not want to be. Are they not 'conversation pieces' of a furious kind, so many of his triptychs?) This is to say that I do not consider the English landscape tradition as our essential art. In point of fact I don't think of landscape as a great art form. After all, you can put a tree here or there and nobody knows the difference. Turner is not for me the foremost English artist but indeed out first international star, a

precursor with a great future inasmuch as the content of his pictures is based on the Void and Nothingness. Let's forget all idea of narration as a minor art, as illustration. Its essential force comes from its indissoluble link with human behaviour. Hogarth is considered, or rather disconsidered, as literary. Rubbish! There is not a form, not a line, in his saga of eighteenth-century London which is not considered and chosen plastically, as the *Analysis of Beauty* proudly maintains. To mention one example among so many, taken from the last episode in Bedlam of *The Rake's Progress*. Behind the prostrate Tom Rakewell, a fellow inmate gesticulates. The upraised hand, fingers well spaced, is instantly repeated in the half-opened fan of a peering lady visitor and re-echoed with great finality by the vertical iron bars of the door. Isn't this simply an admirable artistic concept? And isn't it time to face the fact that these repeated patterns of lines are only exciting because attached to the living hand, the fan, the door? That the same network of lines without human implication does not thrill, just as decoration does not astonish. This is the lesson that English art can give to the world. I'm glad to see many artists in this country engaged in doing so, the nonsensicality and non-communication of abstract art having caused fewer ravages there. Although out of touch, I know that a lot of what I say here has already been publicly discussed by Hockney, Kitaj and their friends.

What would you say was your debt to France and French art? How does the description of 'Anglo-French' artist sit on you?

I was almost inclined to reply, as to the previous question, and say 'total'. And then 'Anglo-French' would sit on me perfectly.

The influence of the French school and the Ecole de Paris came early on, as with all young artists. If the move to Paris was an intelligent one, I can say so because it was a decision made for me by close friends and not by me at all. It enabled me to sit, if not at the knees or the feet, at least at the table of the great artists in question. So there was no distortion in my appreciations. But this wasn't terribly important. More so was the bracing vigour of Paris life. In those days it was real freedom. That is to say, you could live or you could die and the French wouldn't care less. If you made a mark you were promptly applauded and accepted as one of them. No chauvinism whatsoever. If you didn't, if you foundered, nobody mourned.

And that's how it is for me to this day. I've said already enough for you to size up the unrepayable debt I owe to France and my love for the French. I say this with force because so many of my compatriots like French countryside, French buildings, French cooking and French girls and don't like the French. Whereas they, dear souls, have a steady, unflickering admiration for the British. I'm not French, I've never considered taking a French passport. I have an English accent and yet I'm an accepted, even privileged, member of their community. The French state has made several important acquisitions of my work. I've even been decorated. And the younger French art curators, like Gérard Régnier (Jean Clair) of the Pompidou Centre, have transformed my career.

As for 'Anglo-French', I came across this description applied to me for the first time a month ago by an Italian critic of the Venice Biennale. The Italians have the pleasant gift of rounding off corners. Then I saw it repeated in the English press and I was most impressed. I wonder whether one can be Anglo-French? Or dog-cat?

Why do you colour your sculpture? Some people prefer it uncoloured. What do you think about this?

I have already said that for me the importance of sculpture is not in its existence as such but in what it is employed in saying. The conclusive proof that the sculptors of antiquity, the Middle Ages, the Early Renaissance and much of the Baroque did not think in terms of 'sculpture' but of what their sculpture was intended to represent, is provided by the fact that they painted over their subtly wrought forms in strident colour, applied with vigour. They neglected nothing to make it warmly human. A sculpture in colour is more human than one in marble or bronze.

And so with me. And so with many others – early Oldenburg, what a treat! Sculptures are inert. My aim is to make them alive and valid. I shape my big compositions as dynamically as possible and I colour them because I want them to please and to plead to living people. Yes, my friends often shudder when they see me preparing to paint over a work which has taken me a year or two to sculpt (Phidias's friends must have shuddered much more). However, they are generally in agreement with the final result. The people who never are and would always prefer bronze are aesthetes and, as such, live in a pipe-dream. There are other reactions which intrigue me more: the critics who have discussed sculptures of mine from all angles without mentioning the colour; and more frequently, those who apparently see only colour, or local colour, and talk of historical fresco, characterization and even caricature without perceiving that there's a sculpture behind it all. Yet for me it is all-important that narration should be sustained by a rigorous web – no expression without underlying geometry. As such I feel a strong link with the quattrocento.

What future works do you have in mind?

I live a sculpture entirely during the time it takes to conceive and make it. I have never been able to work on two different sculptures at the same time, which is perhaps a pity since, if the work gets stuck, I can do nothing but brood by its side. Once a sculpture is finished, painted, photographed under my supervision and exhibited (the text of the catalogue is written by me), once, in short, I have done everything to send it out into the world,

I stand as empty as the studio which surrounds me. The sculpture which has departed can be of no help to the one which will follow. Which will follow when and how I have no idea. None.

What feelings does a retrospective of thirty years' work in a public gallery awaken in you?

If the last sculpture is ready in time for the exhibition in November, if it's all I hoped it will be, then I will be happy to show my compatriots, my friends and my one or two enemies the work of thirty years. Years which have flashed by like so many months. I thank the sympathetic members of the Arts Council and you yourself, Michael, for making it possible.

It will be my first retrospective, which seems perfectly in keeping. I am now sixty. Ideally a retrospective should be as late as possible, so as to be as dense as possible, without – and this is just for his personal pleasure – the artist being actually dead.

Exhibition catalogue, Serpentine Gallery, London, 1982.

Raymond Mason, *Barcelona Tram*, 1953

Francis Bacon

MY FIRST CONTACT WITH THE WORK OF FRANCIS Bacon, as for many people in London (where I was living at the time), took place opposite a single painting of his hung in Rex Nan Kivell's Redfern Gallery in the spring of 1946 and painted the same year. It was simply called *Painting*, but it was quite certainly one of his first masterpieces. The image of a man huddled up under a black umbrella, and the presence of carcasses of meat, was poignant but powerful, the painting marvellously rich and textured and essentially enraged. Everything about it contrasted sharply with much of the British production of the period and its insularity brought about by the war.

I left almost immediately for France, where I settled permanently, as a result of which for several years I heard no more of Francis Bacon, since his name was still unknown here. I can no longer situate exactly a trip to London when I saw at the home of the art critic David Sylvester the impressive painting depicting two naked men prudently referred to as *Wrestlers* but manifestly in the act of making physical love. It was the first time I saw Bacon's enormous talent for rendering flesh tones, one of his most specific contributions to the art of painting.

My first one-man exhibition of sculptures and drawings took place in 1954 in London, at the Beaux-Arts Gallery in Bruton Place, just behind Old Bond Street. It was run by the remarkable Helen Lessore, who was herself a painter and had the gift of discerning the intrinsic value of a work without bothering about whether the artist was young or old, known or unknown. Nearly all the artists of her choice, in fact, had no reputation to speak of before being linked with her gallery, among them Lucian Freud, Frank Auerbach, Michael Andrews, Leon Kossoff and... Francis Bacon.

The exhibition included my first important work, the high relief entitled *Barcelona Tram*. From the outset it was well received by the public and by a number of important artists, and I had the pleasure of learning from Helen that Francis had liked the sculpture and wished to meet me. The three of us gathered for dinner at Helen's home, together with David Sylvester. The latter

I had known in my very first year in Paris, where David had lived for a short spell. I was never on close terms with this mandarin of the arts, but neither have I varied in my opinion of him as a remarkable analyst of the artists of his day, who, after a brief spell as secretary to Henry Moore, made himself the ardent appreciator of Alberto Giacometti and Francis Bacon, his transcriptions of their conversation being models of their kind. At the moment of my exhibition at Helen's, David was an art critic for the *Times*, in which he had devoted a few fine-sounding sentences to my work, heralding the arrival of a new sculptor.

The dinner was a complete fiasco. Instead of having a serious discussion with these two men of exceptional artistic interest, I set out to amuse them by recounting my madcap adventures during the war. Nothing could have interested them less, and I can still remember the look of dismay on the face of Helen, who had expected better of the evening. Nevertheless, there was no reaction on the part of Francis and David. I even remember the remarkable politeness with which the former listened to me. It must have been a very close shave. Over the years, I have often seen that same polite, gentle look on Francis's face, particularly at the beginning of an evening, suddenly replaced by a malevolent, aggressive mask.

No, I had begun a friendship with Francis, one made rather intermittent, it's true, by the fact that we lived in different cities and countries. Moreover, I was not a night bird and, being short of money, didn't frequent restaurants or bars and drank only in modest quantities. This kind of thing annoyed Francis slightly, and at one of our very first meetings he took me to the Colony Room in Soho on a superb summer's afternoon to sit at the bar, with all the curtains drawn, and drink one straight whisky after another, while Francis waited for the moment when I would fall off my stool. The experiment failed because of the choice of drink. Being half-Scottish, I have never had the slightest difficulty downing large doses of scotch. This is not the case with other spirits, and I could tell a story about gin and tonics with Francis that turned to my disadvantage.

My second exhibition at Helen's, in 1956, was less well received and, on David Sylvester's part, frankly ill-received, this time around in the *Listener*. From that moment on, no English critic mentioned my name for twenty-six years. While I was in London, I saw Francis of course, but one particular day comes to mind, when a gathering of artists had assembled at the Beaux-Arts Gallery to protest against a government measure taken against them. I was rather surprised to see Henry Moore walk in, arm in arm with Francis Bacon, and stand listening at the back of the room. Francis's patience for this kind of mildly politicized gathering had its limits, however, and after a quarter of an hour I heard him say to Henry: 'It's all shit. Let's go.' Henry didn't agree. He had made the effort to come, so he meant to stay. Whereupon Francis seized him by the arm and literally dragged him outside. It was amusing to see these two silhouettes, Henry wearing tweeds as always, Francis in blue jeans, leather jacket and tennis shoes, his style of dress for thirty years or more.

In the 1970s, I started to see Francis Bacon more often. My dealer Claude Bernard was going out of his way to attract him to his gallery, and Francis came regularly to Paris. Moreover, he envied me, he said, living permanently in the city. This surprised me, since to me Francis was the quintessential Londoner, as at home in the little patch of clubs and restaurants around Soho and Mayfair as William Hogarth, Henry Fielding and their friends had been in the eighteenth century. No, no, he insisted, he loved French cuisine, but above all he loved Paris. From the point of view of beauty, he added. I would never have imagined that this familiar of the underworld, with its vice and its criminals, liked to stroll about with his nose in the air, admiring the architectural beauty of Paris. The explanation for this is actually very simple. Bacon's lifestyle made living in Paris impossible for him. Going out at night, drinking more and more, being found in the streets blind drunk, was only possible in London where everyone knew him. It's a long time now, not since the 1920s, that famous Parisian artists no longer stagger through the street or clutch at lampposts for support.

That said, he owned a studio in Paris, in the rue Birague next to the place des Vosges, that Claude Bernard had found for him. To make the place habitable, the dealer had sent round the gallery's carpenter, Michel, to put up some bookshelves – next to nothing in reality. Michel, however, was a young working-class lad, healthy, vigorous and, it could be said, rather good-looking. Francis had clearly enjoyed having him around and, when the work was completed, to thank him gave him – a triptych! This caused great con-

sternation at the Galerie Claude Bernard, where they dreamed every day of selling such a work. Furthermore, Francis, knowing Michel would be tempted to sell his Bacon, had paid for the frame and also given him the name of a potential buyer. Needless to say, the moment came when Michel, needing to get the roof of his home in the suburbs redone, sold his triptych to pay for the work. When he saw Francis again a few months later, he confessed the thing to him with a mortified air. 'You did the right thing, Michel,' said Francis, patting him on the shoulder. 'I'll give you another one.'

The Bacon exhibition at Claude Bernard's was a huge success. There were so many visitors that the dealer had to change the carpeting in his gallery. It should be said that, after the retrospective at the Grand Palais in 1971, Parisian art-lovers were unanimous in considering Francis Bacon the most important painter in the world. This, despite the existence of two Frenchmen called Balthus and Dubuffet. But as I keep telling my fellow countrymen, Parisians are the least chauvinistic race on earth and not the other way round. A thousand times less chauvinistic than Americans at any rate. At that period, I went out for lunch or dinner with Francis on several occasions. He used to pay for everything and everyone with so much gusto that I was thunderstruck when some friends of mine reported back to me that Francis had said: 'That Raymond fellow is terribly Scottish, don't you think? He never invites me out for a meal.' It was true, of course, and I later tried countless times to make up for it, but without success. He was always the one who paid.

Shortly after his triumphant exhibition at Claude Bernard's, I was preparing what was to be my best – and last – exhibition at that gallery. The centrepiece was to be my large polychrome composition on the mining disaster at Liévin in the Pas-de-Calais, *A Tragedy in the North. Winter, Rain and Tears.* This sculpture had absorbed me for fully two years, the time needed to conceive it, sculpt it in plaster, translate the latter into resin along with all the relevant touchings-up, then paint it with every nuance of colour possible. One day the work was completed and, giddy with fatigue and pleasure, and even, I confess, with pride, I went out of my studio to draw a deep breath in the main doorway onto the street – something I never do, and did, therefore, for the first time that day. At that precise moment, it was quite extraordinary, who should came walking along my pavement but Francis Bacon, way off course, God knows what he was doing there. I pounced on the opportunity of this miraculous encounter and, grabbing him by the arm, said: 'Francis, I have something to show you.'

Once in the studio, the great artist and generous soul revealed themselves: 'But, Raymond, it's magnificent. A sculpture at last. Not a beam forming a right angle and painted orange.' He was referring, of course, to Anthony Caro, and we had a good laugh. Obviously, it was an enormous pleasure for me to be able to show my great work to this crucial artist, my fellow countryman, at that precise moment. All the more so since Francis revealed that he had been thinking for some time that I might help him make some sculptures, since he saw them in polychrome. After which Francis went further, assuring me that he would come back the following day with his friend Michel Leiris to show him the sculpture. This he did, and I was able to confirm what I had long suspected, namely that Leiris, without the guide-marks provided by a few famous men – Picasso, Giacometti, Bacon – was singularly ill-equipped to judge works of art. Mine, at any rate, left him deeply baffled, being a brutal slice of life that could hardly have been more remote from his own personal introspections. In the foreground of the work, a man stretches his arm out horizontally to hold back the weeping woman who is almost outside the composition. As I see it, this outstretched hand is also supposed to capture the spectator's gaze and draw him into the action. Michel at last opened his mouth and said: 'Yes, he's very touching that man holding his hand out to see if it's still raining.'

Francis was present at my private view at the Galerie Claude Bernard in November 1977, and at the dinner offered for a hundred people by Claude Bernard at his home on the place de l'Étoile, among whom were his friends the Leirises and our mutual friend Helen Lessore. More cordial still was the dinner held for the opening of my official retrospective, organized by the Arts Council of Great Britain at the Serpentine Gallery in London in 1982. The meeting with Francis at the private view had already been amusing. I can still see him walking up to me with a sheet of pink paper in his hand: 'Raymond, David [Sylvester] woke me up this morning with a telephone call to tell me, "Here's what Mason thinks of you," and he then read me a passage from your interview with Michael [Peppiatt] in which you say that I'm a narrative artist, and as I am not, I've written my response down here.' Bacon is indeed, in my eyes, the last representative of the great English narrative tradition, following on from artists like Hogarth, Blake, Ford Madox Brown and Stanley Spencer, to name only the more important ones. Narrative has nothing to do with anecdote or illustration but conjures up very strongly an interest in human behaviour. It is obvious that, on a more anguished and sensational plane, a typically English 'conversation piece' exists in Bacon's work, and to my mind the moment you say triptych you say narrative. At the time, Francis didn't read me what he had written, and I very much regret this because people then dragged him off for a drink and I lost sight of him. When I caught up with him again some time later, he had already visited the exhibition and announced to me that he liked it a lot and that, though he didn't agree with what I had said about him, he was in perfect agreement with what I myself was doing. Then he added confidentially, though under the influence of alcohol (in Francis's case, however, this changed nothing in his speech or wit): 'You know, Raymond, I'm not a narrative artist because I have nothing to say to people. My only wish is that they get as much pleasure looking at my paintings as I had making them.' It was nicely put by this remarkably intelligent man. It wasn't a quip, but a serious *mise au point*.

Throughout the private view Francis drank more and more, and at the end held his arm out for his glass to be filled – then, misjudging the trajectory, threw the contents over his shoulder. When we left the gallery, which is in Kensington Gardens, it was a pitch-black, late-November night. We were on our way to the famous restaurant Rules in Covent Garden, and we needed a taxi – several taxis, in fact, since there were seven of us. Despite being drunk, it was Francis who rushed into the flow of traffic on Kensington Gore and came back with a taxi. At the sight of all these people trying to pile into his vehicle, the cabby cried out no, that he had just been fined the day before. We climbed back out, and once again Francis disappeared with astonishing speed – he was seventy-three in 1982 – and came back with a second taxi, which, something unthinkable in France, agreed to take all of us. The banquet was a huge success, thanks to my patron William Louis-Dreyfus, who had chosen the Hogarth Room, a medium-sized private room, its wooden panels decorated with Hogarth prints, for us to dine in at Rules. My wife Janine had somehow managed to have all her jewellery, along with our thousand pounds in cash, stolen from the hotel the previous day, so I began my thank-you speech by stressing that so happy were we to be there that my wife had given away all our worldly belongings to the poor and needy of London. Zoran Music, who was present at the dinner, recently told me that Francis had taken out his sheet of pink paper during my speech and made notes on what I was saying. Francis was on fine form from start to finish. He told his neighbours at table what had happened to him in the Tube that day. (This *habitué* of taxis in the Tube!) The man sitting next to him, the clinging type, was going on and on about the evil done to our lives by propaganda, all those lies and false promises. 'Isn't that right, sir?' he said, tugging at Francis's arm. The latter, thoroughly exasperated by this time, replied: 'Dead right you are. Just think of Christianity.' The man stood up with a start and got off at the next stop. I should point out that Francis Bacon was an extremely witty man, just like the other two 'mavericks' of modern art, Giacometti and Balthus. (They were called the three mavericks by Alfred Barr of MOMA, a maverick being a bull that lives apart from the rest of the herd.) One evening, sitting together on a sofa during a party at Claude's, Francis noticed the entrance of a very distinguished-looking gentleman in a navy-blue blazer, with a deep, oily tan. I explained to him that he was a close friend of Claude B., was very rich and lived all year round on his yacht in the Mediterranean. 'Ah, a skipper,' said Francis in a drawl. Then, looking a second time at the tan: 'Looks more like a kipper.'

In the summer of 1985, the Tate Gallery presented a complete retrospective of Francis Bacon's work. Invited to the private view the evening before, I crossed the Channel to attend. We were able to begin our tour of the exhibition before dinner, and I found myself captivated by the quality of the paintings which followed on from the more monochrome period of the *Popes* and which, by contrast, were very richly coloured, the surfaces skilfully worked, often with a palette knife in a thick impasto. The subjects were extremely varied, the canvases of relatively modest proportions. This happy moment took me up to, and including, the Van Gogh series, *The Artist on the Road to Tarascon*, etc.

Thereupon a friend pointed out that the buffet dinner was already in full swing. I left the exhibition saying to myself that never had I imagined Francis was such a great painter, because what I had just seen seemed to me on a par with the greatest painters of the past. Once the dinner and its numerous encounters were over, and not knowing what time the Tate closed, I attacked the retrospective a second time, starting at the end. In the last room, which comprised numerous late triptychs, my initial enthusiasm was not renewed. A triptych in art is a high point, something exceptional. Repeated with a great uniformity of motif, making them virtually standardized products, these triptychs were no longer unique but a kind of readymade, a Francis Bacon, a saleable object. A uniform, orange-coloured background – a colour to be used sparingly – dominates these last canvases, though each of them, of course, contains a figure or a passage of painting worthy of this artist. I admire the sensational triptychs of the *Sweeney Agonistes* period, and some of those featuring George Dyer are masterpieces of poignant art. And who could possibly forget the subtle, modern colouring of the triptych in the Moueix collection?

I am not at all saying that Francis Bacon's work declined towards the end. Myself a member of the Marlborough Gallery – his presence as their star artist was one of my motivations in joining – I would witness his last works arriving from the studio and was thus in a position to observe that the handling was broad and sweeping and more than ever assured. But the repetition was there, and when you think about it, this is exactly what the condition of contemporary art and the market demand. A standardized product, instantly recognizable. Most artists do not seek truth, which being independent of their own person would gradually transform their art, but the perfecting of a style that will glorify their name.

These misgivings about Francis's later work had surfaced in an unfortunate manner a few years previously. It was shortly after his visit to my studio that I mentioned earlier. Just as he was crossing the courtyard on his way out, Francis remarked that he had never met my wife, and that, in order to make her acquaintance, perhaps we would be so kind as to dine with him and a few friends the following evening at La Grille, a bistrot in Les Halles that in the 1970s was highly reputed. This exquisite thoughtfulness, typical of his British courtesy, and his perfect generosity touched us, particularly Janine, who, after further demonstrations of the same order, has always remained an unconditional supporter of Francis. Naturally we accepted.

The long table for eight at La Grille was a congenial sight, with bottles of Chirouble standing uncorked in the middle of the white tablecloth. Francis was accompanied by his great friend and boon companion Sonia Orwell, and by Michel Leiris and his wife Zette, owner of the Galerie Louise Leiris, formerly the Galerie Kahnweiler and Picasso's gallery therefore. In addition, there was Geneviève Picon, an old friend of ours, and John Russell, the leading art critic for the *New York Times*, who, himself English, had known Francis for many years and had just written a book on him. I was placed at one end of the table, with Madame Leiris on my right and Sonia opposite, a vis-à-vis I found extremely agreeable. At the time of her marriage to George Orwell, a few months before his death, Sonia must have been a spectacular beauty. Thirty years later, she still possessed an attractive silhouette, blond hair, a rosy tint and lively blue eyes. She was sporting a pretty silk blouse, with vertical pink and grey stripes, buttoned at the neck with a Renoir-style ribbon. I had complimented her on her appearance, and she had replied, laughing, that she was just an old drunk. 'A drunk, Sonia! No-one would suspect you of drinking a single glass in the year.' 'Oh Francis,' she cried to the other end of the table, 'this man is adorable...' Backing up my gentlemanly remarks with a wave of my heavy hand, I knocked over the bottle of wine standing open before me. Its neck came to rest between Sonia Orwell's breasts, spilling all the way down her beautiful silk blouse. With a howl of displeasure, Sonia sprang to her feet and, her eyes bloodshot with rage, showered me with the crudest insults she had picked up from the years of drinking in bars. It was a relief when John Russell addressed me to enquire after Pierre Matisse and his new wife, Tana. To hear what he was saying, I was obliged, being deaf in one ear, to lean forward a little to my right, since he was sitting opposite my neighbour Zette Leiris, and I had failed to notice that I was leaning on the latter's plate, which now stood at forty-five degrees to the table. After a few caustic remarks on her part, the dinner carried on and would perhaps have taken a more normal turn had I not seen fit to call across to Francis over everyone's head: 'Francis, when you think about it, you're a mannerist artist, are you not?' It was a conclusion I had come to on seeing his latest paintings at the Galerie Maeght; namely, that they were no longer an ever closer search for truth, but the pursuit of a style of painting. Granted, but why in the devil's name come out with so unflattering a thought apropos of a man so amicably disposed towards me in the middle of so promising a dinner? Janine looked at me, horrified, tapping her temples in my direction, while Francis, under the blow, leaned over to Michel Leiris to ask him what 'mannerist' meant in French. Michel, who hadn't heard my remark, replied without hesitating that the term had originally been pejorative, which Francis, of course, knew perfectly well. I was horrified by my stupidity and, to try and make up for it by persisting in my folly, threw in for good measure: 'But, of course, the most mannerist of them all is Picasso.' (This was rather cunning on my part. I knew that Picasso was the only point of reference, the only artist with whom Francis wished to be compared.) But it was too much for my neighbour Zette Leiris. She stood up, saying 'The man is mad,' and left the table. Everyone was standing in fact. The dinner, which had hardly begun, was over. Janine told me later that Zette had said to her: 'How I feel for you, chère petite madame. I know your problem only too well.' We took her remark to be a reference to the fact that her husband, Michel Leiris, had for years undergone treatment as an alcoholic, and that his wife had assumed that I, too, was an uncontrollable drunk – which was more flattering, I might say, than being the idiot I felt myself to be. Sonia Orwell, on the other hand, had grabbed Janine by the arm, saying: 'Come on, let's go and finish the evening without this stupid moron.' I went home alone. During the night, I decided to give Francis the best drawing of mine I had to hand. The following day, I dropped it off at the Hôtel des Saints-Pères where he was staying. A week later, I received a letter from Francis in London thanking me for the drawing and expressing astonishment at the gift since he couldn't remember a thing, he claimed, about the evening at La Grille, 'since we were all drunk'. As I have explained, we had had but a glass or two and were therefore not drunk, but it was a charming way of excusing me. Still, every time I see a photo of Francis's studio with its incredible disorder, I shudder at the thought of my good drawing lost for ever under all those layers of paint.

In 1986, an important Rodin exhibition was held at the Hayward Gallery in London, the official exhibition halls of the Arts Council of Great Britain. The curator was Catherine Lampert, and a month or two before the show she had asked me to come to London and give a talk on Rodin – in other words, to present the point of view of a modern sculptor on this turn-of-the-century giant. I must confess that had I been able to choose my subject I would never have opted for Rodin, who has never influenced me, since I am not a modeller but a constructor, concerning myself very little with my surfaces, which I leave rough; whereas for a modeller of genius like Rodin the surface was crucial, which deprived his work, in my view, of architecture and replaced genuine structure with a melody of muscles. But since the request was backed up by the person who had organized my retrospective in 1982, and since Rodin in his day had been the very incarnation of 'sculpture' and I naturally had things to say about sculpture, I agreed. Moreover, the more I delved into the subject, the more I found things to say in his favour, and in all it became one of my best meditations on art.

I informed Francis that I would be giving the talk, and he promptly told me he would come to it and asked me to dine with him afterwards. This was impossible, unfortunately, because I knew the Arts Council would be keeping me on for dinner, and doubly unfortunate since I knew that their kind of restaurant could not possibly compete with Francis's.

The Rodin exhibition, which was dense and concerned more with the intimate than the monumental Rodin, contained the series of erotic drawings made at the end of his life and seldom seen in public. The talk was held in the Purcell Room, the concert hall adjacent to the Hayward. There was a good turn-out, perhaps some hundred people in all, including persons of quality, among them a high-up member of the Tate Gallery, the directors of the Arts Council, my friend the poet Roy Fuller – who later wrote a poem about myself and Rodin(!) – and a great many friends in the arts, including Sarah Wilson from the Courtauld Institute. But up to the moment the talk was about to begin, no Francis Bacon. But yes, here he came with Helen Lessore, and to my surprise they positioned themselves at the back of the hall, a long way back from the others. I spoke, as is my custom, without notes. It's a perilous exercise when it's a question, as here, of talking for an hour and a quarter, but the contact with the audience is better. Anyway, I managed to stay the course, since at the end I was asked to speed up to leave room for the concert that was to follow. In short, I put a lot into it, and it was with great pleasure that I met my friends afterwards for the cocktail offered by the Arts Council. Equally, it was with great displeasure that I heard Francis say he hadn't heard a word of what I'd said. I turned to Richard Morphet from the Tate to have his verdict, and he assured me that he had heard every word, finding the whole thing very novel. At this point, I got cross. I had gone to the trouble of crossing the Channel and making all this effort and, out of sheer coquettishness, so as not to be with everyone else, Francis, half-deaf like all people of his age, had knowingly positioned himself in a spot where he couldn't hear a thing. 'Yes,' I said to him, pointing at Richard, 'some people are more intelligent than others.'

Nevertheless, we all, including Francis, had dinner together in a restaurant, supposedly French but in fact Thai, though the dishes, wines and champagne in reality were not so bad. After dinner, someone convinced us to finish the evening in a black nightclub in the East End, and at two o'clock in the morning I found myself down a basement, with skull-splitting music, surrounded by huge black men, everyone standing shoulder to shoulder. It was exactly the kind of ambiance I loathe, especially as the following day at noon I had to give a second talk, this time at the Tate Gallery, on 'The School of Paris'. Without saying goodnight to anyone, I left and found myself in a deserted, run-down street in the middle of the night. I didn't know where to go or how to, when, like a mirage, I saw a parked taxi, with its driver slumped asleep over the wheel. I don't know if he had been planning to carry on driving, but faced with my insistence he turned his lights back on and drove me to the West End. I later heard that, some time around four in the morning, Francis, well-oiled of course, pulled from his pocket hundreds of pounds that he waved above his head, wanting to settle the bill. Fortunately, his dealer's daughter, Barbara Lloyd, was standing next to him, and she always keeps a firm grip on any situation.

It is important to know that Francis Bacon had suffered from very bad asthma ever since he was a child, having contracted the illness from the proximity of horses in his father's stables in Ireland (his father was a horse-breeder, and an allergy to horses is prominent among most asthmatics). He lived for the greater part of his life in a studio in Reece Mews, above what had formerly been a stable. A London mews is a lateral passageway running between two streets of large Victorian houses. It was there that carriages, horses and their coach-drivers were quartered. I am certain that, decades later, the smell of horses persists, and Francis agreed. He also agreed that he should find a studio somewhere else, but needless to say this was never done. I was asthmatic myself, and whenever Francis heard about a new inhaler he would give me a ring to find out if I knew about it.

My first visit to his home in Reece Mews made a powerful impression on me. Next to the double-doors of the stable (converted into a garage, though never, of course, to shelter a car belonging to Francis) was his own door, which opened onto a narrow, almost vertical staircase. Passing a kitchen where the washing-up in the sink reached halfway up the wall, you entered the bed-sitting room. The floor was bare and had visibly not been washed, let alone polished, for months, perhaps years. At the end of this long room was the unmade bed with the bedspread pulled across. Nearer the doorway were a few chairs and a low table where Francis plonked down beautiful cut-glass tumblers. I recognized his Savile Row suit hanging from a nail in its protective plastic bag. The studio next door is familiar to everyone from photos. His work space was reduced to a strict minimum and, in view of its size, it is a miracle that he was able to produce such large and richly coloured canvases, painted with so much force and style.

All in all, his home life was scarcely more scintilating than that of Giacometti. Out-of-doors, gourmet meals in the finest restaurants in London replaced the hard-boiled egg that Alberto made do with for lunch. The latter's overindulgences were coffee and cognac.

Francis Bacon, quite apart from his painting, was an exceptional creature in all respects. In addition to his terrible asthma, he sometimes led the most dangerous life imaginable in his homosexual frequenting of the fringes of society. If one then adds to this the provocative manner in which he liked to display large sums of money about his person, the fact that he lived a long life without being attacked, the physical robustness that enabled him to fall over dead drunk then wake up a few hours later and paint at dawn with the elegance and brio that we know – all this, the sickness and dangers he overcame, seems to constitute an enchanted life. In my eyes, it is also a sign of tremendous courage.

He died, aged eighty-three, of heart failure, following a final attack of asthma, but with no sign of senile decay, for – and here is still something else – he retained his youthfulness to the very end.

Late Picasso, 1953–73

THE OCCASION IS THE EXHIBITION AT THE POMPIDOU Centre, Paris, featuring the works of the old age and extreme old age of Pablo Picasso (born in 1881). Before entering I am told by several curator friends that these works are overwhelming.

I came out without being overwhelmed. Like most of the other people in the rooms, I had gone rapidly from one painting to another without any one of them stopping me in my tracks or satisfying me fully.

That evening at home I meditated on this. Hadn't I been unjust? Here was the epic case of a genius face to face with death but struggling with all his force not only to continue a great life but to relive its quintessence in the sexual act, and this with a rage and a frenzy without limit. Hence the *terribil-ità* which only the great genius can manifest and, in our century, certainly only Picasso. Nobody could strike a canvas with greater vigour. The science and attack of great form is intact. This hand painted *Guernica*.

At the same time, these terrible strokes seem to me like so many desperate blows of a walled-in prisoner. Which, in point of fact, is what he was. His historically famous friends were dead. He was alone with Jacqueline Roque, a woman of no particular distinction, who shut him up in her own little dimensions. Thus the permanent evening guests were the painter Edouard Pignon and his wife Hélène Parmelin, completely second-rate people.

I remember my dismay in the 1950s when I saw Picasso's recent work appearing. He no longer elaborated a painting but fragmented the subject over a series of canvases, the last one the starkest and generally the least interesting. We had moved into the age of Picasso the magician where, at the drop of a hat, the work appeared, hailed by a court of flatterers. The Clouzot film, *Le Mystère Picasso*, probably turned the artist's head for good because, from then on, one canvas followed another – we know with what speed; more applause – without any thought, any improvement. Picasso the great composer was no longer active.

When the tragical scene of the last years was set, solitude within four walls, the system, alas, didn't change. The blows that rained were, like those of the prisoner, always the same. Canvases of identical dimensions and similar subject were covered in a single session.

Can a great painting, a work of art, be produced at top speed? Or, more pointedly, at top speed all the time? A painting or more a day. I don't believe so. Picasso at the end spent more time on an engraving 15 x 20 centimetres than on a painting 130 x 195. It's absurd. I might as well add that these engravings, which seem to delight everybody, don't capture my interest either. What do they show? That Picasso at ninety years of age retained the same virtuosity as when he was forty or fifty. (Virtuosity alone because the nobility of the *Vollard Suite* does not reappear.)

But, good God, the great affair of the ageing man is wisdom, not pretending that he is not old, which is stupidity. The great artist approaching the end opens up to this new dimension of wisdom. His work gets both blurred and radiant, and he himself loses footing. His 'I' disappears before 'Him'. Picasso had neither this humility nor this wisdom before the eternal. His 'I' remained monolithic. Of course, all Picasso's work was autobiographical, but this fundamentally positive factor transforms itself into megalomania beneath the excessive flattery I have described. The first signs of this immense vanity were the rehandlings that Picasso decided to bring to the greatest works of artists universally admired – Velázquez, Delacroix, Manet. The catalogue of the present exhibition speaks of 'exploratory cycles exhausting every possibility of recomposing the masterpieces of the past'. Flattery not yet dead, because in point of fact Picasso's commentaries are most superficial in a waggish vein and effect no penetration into these works, deeply worked and dense. And what is the appropriation of other artists' works but the detestable projection of 'me, me, me'?

Michel Leiris compares, with his usual haphazardness, Picasso to Mozart, and I'm sure everyone will agree that there is no possible connection between the two. But between Picasso and Don Giovanni, yes, certainly. *Mille e tre* describes perfectly this exhibition. And the Don finishes badly.

Picasso faced the lonely later years ill-armed. Wisdom is replaced by impetuosity, and our hearts bleed because this dénouement could have been admirable. Perhaps the most famous man on the entire planet, poorly clad in singlet and shorts, turns his back on the world, shuts his door and paints for ten years to the day of his death.

And this is how the exhibition can be seen as overwhelming. Simply by the duration, the accumulation of the hundred and fifty paintings all together. *Mille e tre*. The catalogue. (And maybe this is also why the art professionals find it all so rich.) But individually there is hardly a veritable work of art in the lot. This impression is accentuated by too much space in the hanging and the Old Master frames, as though it were a question of masterpieces.

Video Text

IT ALL BEGINS WITH DRAWING. A BLACK DRAWING ON white paper. If I draw in India ink, it is to ensure that the line is well and truly black. The drawing is the first contact. It's also the thought and later the project.

The moment I arrived in Paris, I found myself living in the Latin Quarter. Most of the houses were rendered with plaster and painted a light colour. The dark openings of doors and windows formed a sort of black drawing, and the whole had a graphic impact I found profoundly and permanently appealing. For several years, then, I made drawings of the streets and, of course, of the people in my neighbourhood.

When I later rendered these views in sculpture it was in low relief, as though, almost imperceptibly, the white paper of the drawing had filled out to form a relief on which the pen strokes were replaced by hollows and incisions. Gradually, these sculptures became bigger and deeper, tending towards the high relief. (While I'm about it, I'm going to give a very simple definition of these terms 'low relief', 'high relief', etc. If I take, say, a tomato in my hand, it's an object in the round. If I place this object against a wall, it becomes a high relief; it retains the plenitude of its form but it's now attached to a background. If I throw the tomato against a wall it splatters, becoming a low relief, that is to say part of the surface of the wall.)

With my street scenes in high relief, I was immediately dealing with depth and perspective, and the simple, austere character of the façades in my neighbourhood took on added significance. I had always been struck by the fact that, when seen head-on, a façade is punctuated by the black rectangles of well-spaced doors and windows, but when seen at an oblique angle, on that same façade, those openings closed ranks dramatically and the lines became as thin as stigmata. This alternation of 'well-spaced' and 'close-together' struck me as a perfect description of space. I place a few well-spaced lines on a surface, that surface faces me; I place them close together, the surface turns and flees. You'll notice that I talk about drawing on my surfaces. A plain surface strikes me as inactive and inexpressive; a surface punctuated with lines, on the other hand, is articulated by the movement of the spectator. This transition from the full form to the fine line was used in radical fashion by Alberto Giacometti in his busts of his brother Diego in the 1950s. The head was flat: full in profile, but fine as a razor blade head-on. The shoulders formed the counter-movement: broad head-on, but next to nothing in profile. The formal metamorphosis is almost total. This is an important factor in sculpture. A spherical form, on the other hand, changes very little or not at all when turned, or when we turn round it.

In my first low relief, the scheme was equally simple: a head seen head-on, the eyes hollowed out with shadow, outside a house, the door and windows hollowed out with shadow. The side of the house flees in a diminuendo of windows and doors that have become mere lines.

Before long, however, the figures in my views of houses and street scenes started multiplying. Their undulation was captured by the rigour and geometry of the façades, recorded there as on the temperature chart of a hospital bed. Yes, at the outset, I was above all fascinated by the movement of the street. Before I'd even started on my drawings and reliefs of street scenes, I had built a sculpture in wood which I called *The House of the Soul*, and on the plinth I had placed on thin sticks the horizontal form of a spiral. For me it represented the people walking along the pavement outside the house.

Later, as my interest in the crowd grew, I often drew on the boulevard Saint-Michel, and since I'm quite tall, I could see over the heads of the people, and their eddying movement would ripple towards me like so many spirals. The spiral is likewise a sculptural factor of great importance, because continually transformed in space. It will continue to play a crucial role in all my sculptures, and the outstretched arms in some of my more recent work are all so many spirals advancing towards the spectator. In my landscape sculptures, the clouds very often unroll according to the same form. The spiral was also a major presence in my stage set for *Phèdre*, in the succession of vaults in the central palace. As late as the sculpture of the *Grape-Pickers*, rows of vines sway back and forth in the form of a helix.

My street scenes culminated in *The Crowd*, in which nearly a hundred figures surge towards the spectator. My passers-by had come to represent humanity. For the first time, there was no scenery and, for the first time, I felt

I had a message to convey. The work overflowed in a general context of music and literature – Beethoven, Mussorgsky, Hugo, Manzoni and, of course, Michelangelo. In the sea of people of *The Crowd*, the influence of the ocean can be seen. Moreover, is it a coincidence? Perhaps not: I was born under Pisces, as were Mussorgsky, Hugo, Manzoni and Michelangelo, and many other artists who have treated the crowd, among them Daumier. At any rate, once *The Crowd* was finished in plaster, I worked for a long time on the crest of the sculpture, where I sought to define a group of people breaking like a wave. On several occasions, in fact, I found myself sculpting the form of a wave. A few years before *The Crowd*, there was *Falling Man* and, later, the first frieze of my sculpture about the departure of the central fruit and vegetable market from Les Halles in Paris reproduced this same cascading fall. The sea, of course, was already present in my stage set for *Phèdre* in 1959. At the time of its conception, I was at Ménerbes in the Vaucluse, and I was studying my wave effects on the fields of vines set in motion by the wind. In my recent sculpture of grape-picking in those same fields, the clusters of windswept leaves re-enact the image of a raging sea.

The hand also seems to play an important role in my work. In 1960, I was laid up in bed with sciatica and could only draw with my left hand. I later made a sculpture of it, and as soon as it was done, the art historian Patrick Waldberg saw an analogy with my first sculpture of the Luberon mountains, the ridges of the latter separated by deep ravines suggesting to him the parted fingers of a hand. Afterwards, hands in my sculptures became as expressive as faces. Hands holding crates in Les Halles, the hand of the drunk in the sculpture of St Mark's Place, an outstretched hand, a hand with a finger pointing – its presence everywhere astonishes me almost. The hand I studied in my bed had been preceded by the giant hand of Venus in the stage set for *Phèdre*. Only recently, while I was working on the large composition of grape-pickers in my studio, there was my maquette for that stage set lying in a corner. Looking at it one day, that maquette with its hand, I was rather taken aback to see that in the large sculpture behind it, the five rows of vines also formed an even bigger hand, coming down the field towards us. And I was precisely engaged in fashioning the hand of the woman picking grapes that she holds up to shield her eyes from the sun – to take a better look at us.

And I wanted the fingers of that hand to form a counter-movement, as it rose towards the crest, with the rows coming down from it – what I didn't know was that they had the form of a hand.

These are the kinds of considerations the artist encounters when looking at his own work. I'm speaking here of certain aspects which may be concealed from the public. I've already described in detail the different analogies in some of the large sculptures, particularly in *The Departure of Fruits and Vegetables from the Heart of Paris*, where a large grid seems to lock together the market gardeners, their produce and the rich and prolix architecture of the church of Saint-Eustache towering over them. I've remarked before on the fact that the main stem of the cabbage leaf at the centre reproduces the serpentine 'Line of Beauty' dear to my fellow countryman Hogarth, but, heavens above, here too, while rummaging through photos of old works for my retrospective at the Pompidou Centre, I discovered that line, still more pronounced, in the middle of a high relief that I called *The Idyll*, inspired by the Luxembourg Gardens; and this I had forgotten, for the work in question was destroyed many years ago.

And the role of colour in all that, you may well ask. I always say that the need to paint my sculptures can be explained by the fact that I began my life as an artist as a painter. More simply, colour reflects my desire to come as close as I can to reality. As for its being applied to sculpture in particular, I think this: my first polychrome work was the sculpture of Les Halles in 1969. Shortly before this, I had finished *The Crowd* in bronze. I had reached the end of the path which leads from drawing to low relief, to high relief and ultimately, with *The Departure*, to sculpture in the round. I couldn't paint my forms before, for ancient and medieval sculpture teaches us this: that to be able to hold the paint, the form must be finely worked, full and taut. The paint must be applied in a lively manner so as not to obscure the form.

I never forget drawing. I seek form in all its plenitude, colour in all its richness.

I want to make a total art.

August 1985.

Rodin – An Opportunity to Discuss Sculpture

WHAT ARE MY CREDENTIALS TO SPEAK ON RODIN? Well, I'm a sculptor, and a figurative sculptor at that, and I happen to live and work in France. And I recently learned that Rodin had to abandon his military service because he was short-sighted. I left the Royal Navy for the same reason, so there is a link.

Then I was told that I was being asked to do so by my dear friend Andrew Dempsey* and I owe him a lot. Moreover, when a sculptor is asked to say something on Rodin it's impossible to refuse. The man *was* sculpture in the late nineteenth and very early twentieth centuries.

If he was a late beginner we know why. The stupid Ecole des Beaux-Arts professors turned him down. He never got into the school which could alone assure commissions and work for its successful students. It was a glaring injustice, because Rodin had shown right from his earliest drawings at the Petite Ecole that he had the gift of God, the hallmark of the great artist. He was a born draughtsman. These early drawings are laboured in their search for total articulation but their labour was rewarded as, I might add, labour, at least in art, always is.

At all events, Rodin was out in the cold – and even out of his country – for eight years in Belgium, doing decorative work for other sculptors. This doubtless steeled his character for other struggles ahead. When he re-emerged on the Paris artistic scene, his other artistic gift was there to stun the officials. The young man who was not allowed into the Beaux-Arts humiliated all the academic nonentities who were, by his sovereign modelling of the human figure. Where did this impeccable training and understanding of form and surface come from? His years of hack work explain nothing; on the contrary. So what tenacity of purpose, what will power, has been displayed to achieve all this by solitary work! I make a point of this because I

---

* Andrew Dempsey was assistant director of the Arts Council of Great Britain for London exhibitions and responsible for the 1982 Raymond Mason retrospective at the Serpentine Gallery.

have a great admiration for this early, deadly serious, Rodin.

At the time of my being asked to give this lecture, two important and illuminating exhibitions of sculpture were being held almost simultaneously in Paris. 'French Sculpture of the Nineteenth Century' at the Grand Palais and 'What Is Modern Sculpture?' at the Pompidou Centre.

The first was an eye-opener. It is a fact that nineteenth-century sculpture was French, only I'd associated it with academic commissions. I was wrong. True, by the nineteenth century there was no more style, the great subjects of the church and the court had collapsed. There was no more style, but there was still a technique. So the Frenchmen of the last century were free to work unhampered in any direction, sometimes to a ludicrous degree, yet always with the means to express it. The great range of work they produced made the nineteenth an open century.

The Pompidou Centre showed the essential sculptures of modernity, that is to say, our century, and, from Brancusi onwards, they stripped themselves down to a single object, finishing with the aridity of Arte Povera, Conceptualism and Minimalism. A century, in fact, progressively closing in. And from which all anthropomorphic influences are excluded, as the curator of the exhibition, the American Margit Rowell, so coyly put it. Translation, no human figures.

Inasmuch as Rodin was, in the first half of his life, a sculptor of heroic groups and, in the second half, the sculptor of the single figure and even the single figure progressively shorn of arms and legs, he clearly has his place in both centuries. The current tendency is to dice interest heavily on the late Rodin, because the more arms and legs he saws off the more he resembles Brancusi. My interest in Rodin is precisely that which is not modern, because therein we can rediscover what we have lost. In a similar way Cézanne is assimilated to modernism – the first Cubist! Yet Picasso and Braque threw straight out of the window the essential nature of Cézanne, the *recueillement*, the meditative prayer. He had painted nature all his life almost on his knees, as an act of worship. I once saw the collection of Gertrude Stein, who had bought many Picassos and Braques when they were first influenced by Cézanne. It is sad to state but, compared with paintings by Cézanne, they were mere posters. And what I say about Cézanne can be said about Rodin. In the first place because he said it himself. 'The whole of art lies in nature and the need to express life.'

The opening paragraph of Catherine Lampert's* catalogue study was so good that I felt there was no point in my crossing the Channel to say any more. She puts the multiple aspects of Rodin in a nutshell and explains perfectly why, a hundred years later, people are still flocking to look at his work. It is as simple as this. Rodin was interested in the human form as an expression of human sentiment. This is precisely the main thing the wide world is interested in. Present-day creators can eschew the great river of sentiment and ignore the principal subject which surrounds them – the motion and the emotion of their fellow beings. But let them be warned! They will, as far as the world in general is concerned, be ignored. Another reason why Rodin's sculpture, serious and often sad, appeals nonetheless to the public of today is that it supplies them with food and drink, spiritual nourishment. The major works provide a full meal.

These major works, *The Burghers of Calais* and *The Gates of Hell*, are not in the present exhibition. Of course, as Catherine points out, *The Burghers* can be seen below the Houses of Parliament, and the *St John the Baptist* at the Victoria & Albert Museum, but like *The Gates of Hell*, they are not in the show. I am personally convinced that, without *The Burghers of Calais* and *The Gates of Hell* in their complete form, the world's imagination would never have been struck as it was and we would probably not be talking about Rodin at all at this present moment, and certainly not to the extent we do.

This exhibition is thus Rodin the inner man. The plaster he handled, the smaller bronzes, the drawings are sensitively and very correctly shown in an intimate light. Not the outer man and the big works he fought for years to complete. When one reads the life of Rodin there are lots of things which can displease but, if I turn to the sculptor, I am at once all admiration before his absolutely uncompromising attitude in defence of his art.

Because Rodin aimed at, strived for and attained the masterpiece. The

* The selector and organizer of 'Rodin, Sculpture and Drawings'; Hayward Gallery, London, 1 November 1986–25 January 1987, and the author of the catalogue.

heroic fibre we associate with his work is not his subject matter, it is his total battle to produce something unique. He had to fight for time, often years, against different committees. 'A work of art, as anyone who struggles with one knows, needs unrestricted reflection and calm,' he wrote. We know he reimbursed the Société des Gens de Lettres the money they had advanced for the Balzac monument rather than hasten his pace, saying superbly: 'It isn't the Société des Gens de Lettres which refuses a Balzac it hasn't seen. It's me. My principle is not to want to know whether my work pleases other people if it doesn't first of all please me. I have made three studies of Balzac. Very complete, almost finished. They didn't satisfy me, and it's true I broke them up. Having been the artisan of my work I have appointed myself its judge.'*

He had to fight his times, the French society of the period, until they accepted his uniqueness. This is certainly something that we artists can learn from Rodin because it's one of the things that has been lost. The capacity to produce a work of art capable of standing alone, rich in intentions, totally realized and recognizable to all. Today critics are only interested in trends, i.e. when there are thirty or three hundred artists doing the same thing.

A major work is a totality. A great theme fires the artist's first thoughts. More often than not, literary and historical because in this way he has precise knowledge with which he can deal – and by history I mean the moment lived by man, this very day, as well. Throughout all the vicissitudes and difficulties of creating the work over months and perhaps – but nowadays rarely – years, this theme will be held up and maintained like a standard in battle, until it can be delivered in material form to public appreciation. The essential pieces of Rodin's sculpture, *St John the Baptist, The Gates of Hell, The Burghers of Calais*, the monuments to Victor Hugo and to Balzac, have great literary and historical sources. These works have a *meaning* which has been captured in sculpture. However, and the point is important, at no time does sculpture take precedence. If the *Burghers* are the suffering burghers from start to finish, so is *Balzac* the genial Balzac. It is not just a sculpture, however audacious. It is Rodin's Balzac.

---

* Letter of Rodin to the newspaper *L'Echo de Paris*, 23 October 1893.

I have mentioned already several times *The Burghers of Calais*. It is the outstanding monument of Rodin. I can't agree with Catherine when she talks about *The Gates of Hell* being the greatest public sculpture of the nineteenth century. It never appeared before the public of the last century and only now appears before visitors to different museums throughout the world, who are not the indifferent mass we call the public and for whom a public sculpture must make a declaration, capture the attention and win the heart. In any case, Rude's *Departure of the Volunteers*, otherwise known as the *Marseillaise*, which is on the Arc de Triomphe, is infinitely more public and popular.

But *The Burghers* did make this conquest, and this great statement now seems totally obvious. Yet, my God, what a tortuous path it took! And right from the beginning.

I have always carried with me and enthusiastically imparted to others what I now realize is false information about the original conception of this work. As you all know, the six burghers were important members of the city of Calais, volunteers to carry its keys to the city gates and the besieging English troops under Edward III when, in exchange for their lives, the city would have been spared. Fortunately for them, and for us, the Queen had a softer heart and obtained pardon for the six heroes.

Rodin put me wrong in the beginning because authorized sources like Paul Gsell and Rilke tell us that he intended his burghers to be separate and placed at ground level in Indian file on the public square of Calais. This was in his initial communication to the mayor and his committee. And when you examine the group today, you see that they each have a separate base. But I had extended this beautiful idea into seeing the burghers stretching all the way from the City Hall to the gates where we English were waiting for them. The first, the mayor, would have arrived at the gates all erect with the keys in his hands and, several hundred yards behind, Eustache de St Pierre slightly bent in sorrow, then the third in greater movement and anguish, and so on down the line. Only the other day I came across the source of my idea. Why, it was Henry Moore! Talking to Alan Bowness, he said: 'The final grouping of *The Burgers of Calais* is an arbitrary affair. So far as I can follow the story of the commission, Rodin's idea was to make separate figures and place them one

by one on the route the Burghers took.'* But in his same initial communication with the committee, Rodin *also* said that his burghers would also look
very effective in a group placed on a very high base! Given this remarkably
opposed choice, the committee chose this latter. We have photographs of a
temporary plinth Rodin had made in Meudon where the burghers are
silhouetted against the sky. And he even proposed putting them on a pylon
out in the sea! Given the detailed study Rodin had devoted to his personages,
to the point of sculpting each one nude before attacking the final figure, how
could he have envisaged putting them somewhere where his miraculous
modelling would be invisible? But he did. And the version here in London,
which was far too high, was put in place by Rodin himself, who thanked the
English for allowing a sculptor to put his work at a height he himself deemed
fit. Thank goodness we had photographic albums to get us up close!

In any case, high or low, preferably low, *The Burghers of Calais* is unforgettable. I ask for a great statement. Here it is. And now that the figures *are*
united there is something unique about this absolutely freestanding sculpture facing in all directions.

As a sculptor, I'm more interested in movement than mass. It occupies
space better, is more alive, more surprising. This is to be found in *The
Burghers* where the figures ride, one across the other, in continual metamorphosis. The poet, and erstwhile secretary of Rodin, Rainer Maria Rilke was
marvellously attuned to a work of art. He writes of *The Burghers of Calais*
thus: 'If you move around the group, you are surprised to see, rising from the
undulating contours, great and pure gestures which stay aloft, then subside
into the mass like brought-down flags.'†

This metamorphosis in space is the essence of sculpture, bringing
liveliness, indeed life itself, to inert material. Rodin excelled in this vivid
occupation of space, and I can see now that it is my debt to him. I had always

---

* Interview with Henry Moore and Alan Bowness from *Rodin. Sculpture and Drawings*,
Arts Council of Great Britain, London 1970. Rereading Rodin's remarks to Paul Gsell, I now
see that he speaks specifically of 'the degrees of heroism of the Burghers', which seems to me so
significant and so *spatial*.

† *Auguste Rodin*. by Rainer Maria Rilke. Translation by Raymond Mason.

thought that it was my link with Giacometti, whose articulation in space, perhaps his sole contribution to sculpture, was formidably effective. Think of the busts of his brother Diego, with the head of razor thinness placed in counter-movement to the width of the shoulders. When you look from the profile there is a total transformation. Or, in a different way, think of the *Nose* of Giacometti which turns and wavers before your moving gaze, as does the hand of his *Man Pointing*. But here we are back with Rodin and precisely the *Monument to Victor Hugo* with the dramatic, outstretched arm addressing the sea – and also you, the spectator, at once implicated in the sculpture. All Rodin is in this turreting, this out-shooting of arms and legs. We know he loved walking through forests and had a passion for trees – and also for great cathedrals, those forests of stone. I find I have done a succession of advancing hands and arms myself over the years, culminating in the foremost pointing figure of the Montreal monument, who emerges on street level with his arm like an advancing spiral to meet your gaze and which from its profile makes a horizontal counter-movement with the sheer vertical rise of the edge of the building.

I talked about photographing details of Rodin's sculpture earlier on. Last week, at the inauguration in Paris of the new nineteenth-century museum, the Musée d'Orsay, I was looking at the original plaster of *The Gates of Hell* which the Rodin Museum in Meudon has now had to concede to Orsay. I had seen it on my visits to Meudon, but there it was lit by rather indifferent daylight and now you see it sharply lit. The white plaster with black shadows reveals a hundred details quite invisible in the bronze. I liked this work for the first time last Wednesday. And I wasn't alone. Soon we were quite a group of sculptors enthusiastically commenting on something we thought we knew all about long ago.

Such a single-minded, obsessional pursuit of detail stifles criticism. Layer after layer of bodies, and then maybe a very last one, an inch or two high, turning her back to you and disappearing into a tiny hole, a grotto. And I say to myself, My God, isn't this man saying something in relief which has never been said before? Instead of figures emerging from a dark background into light, here they do the contrary, deepening the relief *ad infinitum*.

Maybe all this could be made visible to the general public by careful work with a movie camera. In fact, I seem to remember that it has been done. But I've never yet seen a film on sculpture which showed any sign of knowing how to pass from, not one form to another – that they do all the time – but from one coherent image to another. I don't go to the cinema but I'm sure that nobody films the visual excitement of movement when travelling, say, around the city. Out of the window of a Paris bus I see the flat spread of doors and windows, and then we cross a side-street and, like magic, all these forms thin up, group together and disappear into the distance, then return to normal when the bus continues along the street. Or looking backwards as you travel down a long street. A factory chimney or a pylon begins to appear and climbs higher and higher as you retreat. Because there can be a meaning in movement, too, and a part of sculpture is its strict ordinance.

Oh yes, I've mentioned twice the nineteenth century, but please don't think that my heart resides therein. I was greatly shocked to see that the academic painters take pride of place in the Musée d'Orsay, while our hero-friends the Impressionists and Post-Impressionists are squeezed together up in the attic, another Salon des Refusés. My hatred of the *pompiers*' insipid, superficial paintings, each one done with a trembling desire to please, grows in proportion to the present-day infatuation for this rubbish. The sculpture of the period comes off better. One forgets how many good sculptors there were at that time. Rude, Carpeaux, David d'Angers, Dalou, Roger Bloche, Préault. But the *pompiers* were there, too.

Another important aspect of movement in Rodin's sculpture is the actual drawing and indentation of his surfaces, the delineation of muscles, etc. An inscribed surface turns more drastically, its lines closing sharply together, just like in the side-street I have just described. When a work is punctuated in this way it loses its contemplative, static nature and becomes a cry. I will have a final word to say about this graphic nature of Rodin's sculpture later on, but, for the moment, I will continue to talk about the purely sculptural aspect of his work since that is probably why I was invited to come.

I said earlier that the sculptors of the nineteenth century still had a technique. They had more. They had every trick of the trade and a host of clever and dedicated craftsmen installed in Paris to help it flourish. Plaster-moulders, modellers, enlargers and reducers, marble-cutters, etc. As soon as Rodin began to earn money, he put it to good account by setting up his own studio of plaster-casters and, later on, marble-carvers who were simply the finest up-and-coming talents of the day, just as would have done a Florentine master who had the young Leonardo da Vinci to wash his brushes and the young Michelangelo to make the tea. But here it was a question of Bourdelle, Despiau, Pompon, of Maillol I'm not sure, but we know Rodin's eagle eye had spotted the youthful Brancusi, who had refused, saying with a Romanian peasant's sagacity: 'Beneath the shade of great trees nothing grows.' And then he had recourse to outside specialists like Lebossé and Haligon for his enlargements and reductions. (He was selling reduced versions in all sizes of his well-known pieces.) When I arrived in Paris forty years ago, there was still plenty of plaster and marble dust coming from the workshops in the Montparnasse district south of the city, where all such craftsmen had their addresses.

I'll deal first of all with the question of enlarging, because it was an inherent part of Rodin's actual technique. Rodin's initial clays were modelled with infinite subtlety at one-third size – don't forget he was short-sighted – with a view to being enlarged. At this very moment, one of the machines which was made by Louis Haligon for Rodin's work in 1895 is enlarging my pieces for two big outdoor sculptures for Washington, D.C. The machine is simple. Suspended by pulleys and free to move, it consists of a pivoted steel bar with a point near the pivot which caresses the surface of the model and a second point inscribing a bigger arc at the further end of the bar which, in the hands of the workman, scratches into a block of dead plaster or clay the larger version. In truth, it is not a machine but a tool where the craftsman's skill is paramount. It is said that, once enlarged, the forms are broadened and generalized. Nothing of this order really happens. If, as was the case with Rodin, a sculpture is blown up three times, it suffices to step back three times to see the work exactly as it was originally. Closer to, it looks grosser and, to permit a normal, close examination, the surface should be entirely reworked by the artist. But grosser can also mean stronger and Rodin did *not* rework his surfaces in order to benefit from the increased power. This process is successful for him, and disastrous for most others, because of his consummate science as a modeller. The power of *The Burghers of Calais* and the *Balzac* compared to the non-enlarged *Gates* is obvious – *and* as compared to all the other sculptures by other sculptors of the period, which, I must emphasize, were arrived at in exactly the same way. All that remains are the phenomena of the feet and the hands, which look large simply because in the small scale one tends to emphasize such extremities – even Rodin.

Incidentally, Henri Lebossé, Rodin's principal enlarger and reducer, had his studio in the rue Moulin Vert, a little street in the fourteenth arrondissement of Paris behind Montparnasse. Rodin was naturally a constant visitor to that studio. Diego Giacometti, right up to his death last year, lived in the rue Moulin Vert, and his brother Alberto's studio was fifty yards away in he rue Hippolyte Maindron where it crosses the rue Moulin Vert. Etienne-Hippolyte Maindron was a famous academic sculptor of the nineteenth century who, at the demand of Rodin's family, had been the first to discern the talent of the young boy. As for Rodin himself, he has an avenue and a square in his name but, as they are tucked away in the residential sixteenth arrondissement, in forty years I've never put a foot in either.

Rodin's plasters in tremendous quantities are the product of his team of plaster-moulders who cast every step of his clay modelling so that each individual sculpture fragmented into many others. Deftly cast, the clay was intact and could be continued. Its original stage had been preserved. The wealth of the famous artist thus did away with one of the major difficulties of modelling, which is that, as in painting, in order to advance, to improve, the artist must cover up and often ruin the happy effect of the previous day, whereas the writer and the musician have the possibility to preserve their original versions. Unless as rich as Rodin, the sculptor no, and the poor painter never. (This might seem a detail, but in fact it's the key to the whole extravagant behaviour always attributed to painters. After their solitary day of anguish and, at times, exaltation, come evenings of pleasure to celebrate a triumph or forget a failure.)

But this multiplication of plasters could move away from the guiding thought of the works. When Rodin used them as a treasure-trove in which to dip and dabble over his assemblages, the result seems to me arbitrary and the absolute contrary of composition, which is the inner structure of a work and the intellectual *ne plus ultra* of art. I am out of sympathy often with the amputations of the plasters which present-day critics see as a first step to modern sculpture, i.e. the destruction of the image. I know that Henry Moore thought that *St John the Baptist*, once he had lost his head and his arms, and become just the *Walking Man*, was more convincing because the idea of walking or advancing is given more essentially. Perhaps, certainly even, but the meaning of the prophet has gone.

The title *Walking Man* makes me think of Giacometti's sculpture of the same subject, and then I am forced to think of another famous walker, Johnnie Walker himself and his familiar silhouette, a sculptural pun on the name of the whisky distiller. Why? Because time and time again, I have sat in bars with Alberto Giacometti and found him looking fixedly at a Johnnie Walker figurine on a shelf above the bottles. 'That,' he would declare with emphasis, 'is what one should do in sculpture.' And, when you think of the movement of his own walker, well, he damn well did! He liked the vitality of the thing and the fact of it being in colour, because, as you know, Giacometti made several exursions into colour with his sculpture. After all, he had begun as a painter. I too like the Johnnie Walker because of that, and really it's a superb little job and I'd like to know who conceived it. And also because of the association with Alberto. And knowing this, my friend the Beaubourg curator, Jean Clair, turned up the other day with an excellent early example of the figurine, and it now stands on my window sill. *St John the Baptist*, Johnnie Walker. Mind you, if I have the latter, Henry Moore had the former, and probably the original-size Rodin, in bronze. And if Rodin took off the head of this sculpture, he certainly made up for it with the *Balzac*, which is the triumph of the head, to the point that, if the first is a body without a head, here we have almost a head without a body.

The most interesting, the most difficult thing in art is the human head. It is the extremity to which the great artist always moves when fleeing abstract forms of art. And the most extreme point of all is the expressive head. Part of the greatness of Rodin is that he exalted the head. More so than Michelangelo. I think we can say more so than Donatello. By his busts and by his burghers but, most of all, by the sublime head of Balzac, which rivets our attention on this work in a way that only a head, *the* head, can.

To complete my examination of Rodin's sculptural technique with the marbles, I don't have a qualm in saying that I don't like them, because Rodin didn't sculpt them. Did he ever sculpt? Yes, certainly, enough during the years of hack work to know that it wasn't his thing. As a young and necessitous artist he sent the bust in marble of the *Man with Broken Nose* to the Salon, but he paid a marble-carver to do the job. And yet people, even authorities, believe he did. I remember walking through the Tate Gallery in, maybe, 1954, with the famous Parisian gallery owner Pierre Loeb, the dealer of Miró, Giacometti and Picasso – and a great collection he had, too. In any case, it was at the time the Tate was appealing for £15,000 in order to buy Rodin's *The Kiss* in marble for the nation. Passing in front of it, I muttered something about 'all that money for a sculpture Rodin never touched', and Pierre Loeb stopped dead and said: 'What are you talking about?'

I see no reason to go along with the recent re-evaluation of the marbles. That this reappraisal gives a fresh field for art historians and curators and dealers is one thing. It can't give strength and vivacity to works mechanically executed by marble practitioners from subtle clay forms which need the shimmer and the dark tone of bronze to come to life. With the whiteness of the Carrara marble, not only are they dead but already in the graveyard. No, I have often said that only Michelangelo, by the intensity of his thought and his drawing and his direct carving, can transform moon-white marble into something almost black. Think of the *Moses* in Rome. My point of view is thus the contrary of that of the art historians. I am really glad that Rodin did not sculpt these works. It would be too damaging for his reputation. I must laugh in agreement with Alexander Calder, who said that they look like shaving cream piled on the floor.* Henry Moore called them smarmy. As *marmo* means marble in Italian, let's apply the Italian negative to get 'smarmo' – not marble. I wonder whether Henry meant that?

So let's get back to what Rodin really did, with his own miraculous hands – or rather, hand, because I must discuss the astonishing final episode of the late drawings. And, to get a perspective on the matter, just think of the

---

* These comments are to be found in the introduction by Albert E. Elsen to the catalogue *Rodin Rediscovered*, National Gallery of Art, Washington, 1981–82. Daniel Rosenfield in his chapter on 'Rodin's Carved Sculpture' in the same catalogue writes positively of Rodin as a marble-carver.

extraordinary mutation of this man's career. I said at the start that he belongs to the nineteenth *and* the twentieth centuries. Why, it's almost as though, at the turn of the century, he became a new, a different, man. Consider this list:

Early Drawings	*Late Drawings*
Essentially male	Totally female
Historical subjects with tragic overtones	Uneventful and repetitious, pleasure-loving and playful
Public statuary addressing itself to the world	Private; personal satisfaction
Lengthy effort	Cursory and rapid

Obviously these late, cursive drawings and the astonishingly small sculptures of female dancers – though let's not forget the *Nijinsky* – are a definite step into the twentieth century, but, without Rodin realizing his new role as a modern artist, I wonder in fact whether he was really worshipping at the shrine of femininity in these thousands of sheets, as his friends tell us with such awe and envy? For me, these gracile, stereotyped drawings are not sensuous images of women. They are Rodins. The essential element of worship is that the worshipper forgets himself. His heart goes so completely towards the adored subject that he himself is emptied. I think we witness with these drawings a vast joy the aged Rodin was giving himself, producing drawings under the most pleasurable circumstances. They give us pleasure, too, but I personally don't look at any individual drawing any longer than it took Rodin to make it. But they are Rodins. And we know he preserved them carefully and gave them just as carefully. Now I think of it, I wonder why the Rodin Museum keeps all this vast quantity of drawings. They'll never be shown. There's no point, they're so alike. Why not sell a lot of them since they are perfect, standardized products? Rodin was a great believer in the dissemination of his message, and his studio churned out copies of his statues in all sizes and all materials; and it's certain that it was this, rather than money, which kindled him. The drawings would be better on view in drawing rooms or other museums than in trunks in the rue de Varenne – where, in any case, they could always keep, say, three thousand.

But I don't want to be carping. The world would be a poorer place without them. Indeed the most alarming thing I know about Rodin as a draughtsman is the fact that, while he possessed several admirable Van Gogh paintings which he liked 'because they evoked nature', he considered that 'poor Van Gogh couldn't draw'. Rodin produced his thousands of drawings convinced that he could. Van Gogh, one of the greatest draughtsmen of all world art, truly humble, a true worshipper, certainly never felt that. However, Rodin the great master wasn't destined to leave us like that. The very last of the late drawings again turn a page. Here, the present exhibition scores heavily, because these rubbed and crayoned drawings are never seen and they are the best. They have the simple, crumbling grandeur of late Michelangelo drawings. And once again they become works which have a meaning. Truly erotic, they relate the final obsession with the female sex. They are burning declarations of desire into which no aestheticism enters.

Now that we have reached the final point of this phenomenal outpouring we can realize that these late drawings, these bodies spinning in space, were the tactic of a lifetime. Despite the palpable aspect of his sculpture, Rodin was essentially a draughtsman. His system of modelling was the multiplication, to an extreme, of linear contours. (He said the contrary, but don't believe him.) A linear drawing of the head or of the body in space, followed by a second linear contour one degree rotated and so on, and on. And from all angles. We know how, as a young artist, he would climb ladders to get a bird's-eye view, of the sixty drawings of Victor Hugo's skull, of the Pope who refused to have someone, even the aged Rodin, above him in this way.

This means, and it is important, that Rodin was a visual sculptor. You don't touch a Rodin, you look at it. He was nourished by the painters he loved. (I belong completely to that family. For me, too, when I think of Michelangelo, I'm thinking of the Sistine Chapel.) *The Gates of Hell*, you don't caress the gates, do you? So now we arrive at why we don't touch a Rodin. Because he was making sculptures, he was not making objects. A sculpture is not an object. A sculpture speaks of our human destiny. And, above all, it is a vehicle for human thought. It speaks of our human destiny. Out of the material emerges something immaterial which you cannot touch.

A last quotation from Rodin. 'All masterpieces would be quite naturally accessible to the public if it hadn't lost its spirit of simplicity. Even so, the artist must live with a sentiment for the people, must possess "a soul of the crowd" in order to conceive and create the masterpiece. He must perceive through the crowd, even if it is only ideally present.'*

All I have just said is why Rodin is loved by the public, whose interest in girders, cubes, a hundred steel squares placed side by side, is as minimal as the so-called art of the same name.

Lecture at the Hayward Gallery, London, Wednesday, 10 December 1986.

Hogarth

WILLIAM HOGARTH HAD STRONG FEELINGS ABOUT his fellow men. This basic interest in others made him the model citizen, the first real artist to paint the big city. Centuries later, his paintings and engravings of the people of London are as vivid and as fresh as life itself, and the buildings that surround these scenes are not poor fictions conjured from a painter's mind but genuine constructions with powerful orifices that give relief to the figures. English art began with a man of the utmost originality.

Leaving to others the pleasure of evaluating Hogarth the moralist, I prefer to pay homage to the artistic talent which enabled him to put his messages across so well. It is because of those messages that Hogarth is today credited – or discredited, rather – with being literary. What stupidity! There isn't a form, a line even, in his saga of eighteenth-century London life that is not chosen for plastic reasons, as the painter proudly affirms in his treatise *Analysis of Beauty*. It's true that his art is narrative, but let us forget the idea that narration is a minor art, mere illustration. The essential force of narrative art is that it is a mirror of human behaviour. The true tradition in English painting, far more than landscape or the individual portrait, is

* August Rodin, *Les Cathédrales de France*.

precisely that of narrative art, where the national talent flourishes at its best –
from Hogarth to William Blake, from minor painters like Rowlandson and
Cruikshank to the Pre-Raphaelites and the major artist of that movement,
Ford Madox Brown, from Stanley Spencer to, yes, Francis Bacon. Hogarth's
dominant contribution is not the character study (don't mention the word
'caricature'), but his science of composition. In dealing with city life, he often
had to treat thronged pavements and crowds. His articulation of grouped figures is magnificent, as is his handling of smaller gatherings, as in the progress
of the rake and the prostitute. If Hogarth was enamoured of the outside
world, he was no less concerned with pure aesthetics, revealing himself to be
a true artist, reconciling outward reality and inward thought. Figuration and
abstraction necessarily go hand in hand in any true work of art. Only in our
modern age have they stupidly been separated and opposed. To capture the
spark of life, a painting must express movement – Hogarth was hostile to
landscapes because they don't move. He thought the most active form of
movement was that of the flame (whereas I, as a sculptor, opt for the spiral),
and thereby arrived at his famous serpentine 'Line of Beauty'. He illustrated
his theory in large, powerful engravings in which he shows himself to be a
master of perspective, that arduous intellectual construction which allows
one to describe multiple figures in space. His compositions, however, transcend theories of this kind and come across as treasure-troves of infinite
invention. In the final episode of *The Rake's Progress*, in Bedlam, we see
behind the naked, prostrate body of Tom Rakewell another inmate, gesticulating. His raised hand, the fingers well spaced, is immediately repeated in the
half-open fan of a lady visitor observing the scene, then, in a final echo, in the
vertical bars of the peephole in the door. This gives us the same shudder of
delight we experience when contemplating one of Picasso's inventions. In the
last painting in the series *An Election*, the dazzling mound of supporters
holding up the happy candidate crosses a bridge the arch of which is followed
by that of the parted legs of the figure in the foreground. Here, as so often in
Hogarth's work (in *The March to Finchley*, for example), the red-brick
façades warm your heart, their windows overflowing with people. In a marvellous echo of this in our own day, there is the *Christ Carrying the Cross* of
Stanley Spencer, another one-hundred-percent Englishman, situated in his

native village of Cookham. Balthus is a self-professed admirer of Hogarth; *At the Tailor's* could easily be a Balthus from the early period when his figures make gestures every bit as dramatic as those on Hogarth's stage. One should never underestimate the histrionic element in art. The theatre speaks to the people, as does the great art of the past. The Greek pediments exalt Homer, the Romans speak of Rome, and centuries of Christian art have preached to the eager faithful.

I have a natural affinity with William Hogarth, though I've never made a particular study of him. While every bit as English as he, I have spent two-thirds of my life in France, where there is no painting by Hogarth and where – still more astonishing – there has never been an exhibition of his work. I declared thirty years ago that I wanted my sculpture to be understood by all, young or old, educated or not, not knowing that Hogarth had expressed the same sentiment, with the same aim, two hundred and fifty years previously. He never loses sight of that essential truth that life consists of comedy, tragedy and plain normality, and that it is through the contrasts they present that art takes on its full density.

Given the scale of his talent, it's a pity that Hogarth painted small. He belonged to the Northern and Flemish school, which is modest in size compared to the breadth of Italian frescoes and canvases. There is another reason for this, however: William Hogarth was a pioneer, the founder, despite every difficulty, of English art.

The Surprises of Public Sculpture

A T THE END OF 1976, THE CLERGY OF THE CHURCH OF Saint-Eustache in Paris contacted me to find out if I'd be willing to make a crib for the coming Christmas. This was quite impossible, I was in the midst of my labours on my sculpture of the mining disaster at Liévin. Not long after this, they returned to the charge, asking if I would be willing to lend them, to fulfil the same function, my large sculpture *The Departure of Fruits and Vegetables from the Heart of Paris, 28 February 1969*, a colourful and, I must say, good-natured work celebrating the famous market of Les Halles that had surrounded their church for eight centuries, justifying its presence in the background of the sculpture. This time, though I didn't refuse, I nevertheless expressed certain misgivings, pointing out that there was nothing religious about my work; but the people at the church assured me that the sculpture was perfect just as it was, and off it went to Saint-Eustache.

After it had been installed in the middle of the portico under the grand organs and lit to perfection by the reverend Père Denis Perrot, we noticed a frieze of fruit and vegetables running all the way round the portico and identical in volume to mine, made by the sculptors of old. At the midnight mass, the congregation, which filled the nave to overflowing, must have had something of a shock when, in the darkness that suddenly descended on the church, giant screens were hoisted on which the Pompidou Centre's audio-visual department projected images of the sculpture – now called *The Crib* – situated behind them, accompanied by an improvisation by the master organist Jean Guillou, the incumbent of the grand organs.

Intrigued by the use of my modern sculpture for liturgical purposes, my friend the art historian Michael Brenson, later to become the influential art critic of the *New York Times*, positioned himself for two days next to *The Departure of Fruits and Vegetables* to note the reactions of the faithful. I recount the one that tickled us most and which justifies this little story.

An elderly couple were examining *The Crib*: 'Yes, yes, it's very nice,' said the old lady at last, 'but where is the little Jesus?' After a moment her husband, pointing to the figure on the right walking away with his cart, replied without joking in the least: 'He must be the one pulling *le diable*.' (*Diable* means both 'little cart' and, of course, 'the devil'.)

The Crowd in bronze was installed on the steps leading to the Jeu de Paume in the Tuileries gardens in January 1986. When the summer season comes round, I often step outside to sketch the bustle of the city, and this time I had decided I would capture the attitude of people looking at this sculpture, which was arousing a certain interest.

One Sunday morning in the month of May, I turned up in front of the sculpture with my camping stool and all my equipment. Before placing the people, I began by drawing *The Crowd* itself and, after a while, felt the presence of a man observing my work. 'Are you a professional artist?' he asked. I gave a nod of the head. 'You can tell. What a line! Freehand. Amazing.' Then he added: 'But why draw a piece of shit like that?' Silence from the sculptor. 'It's yet another of those Lang things in our gardens.' It was true, Jack Lang, the Socialist minister of culture at the time, had been personally responsible for installing *The Crowd*. 'But today, thank God, he'll be given the boot.' This also turned out to be true, that Sunday being the election day when the Right were returned to power.

His rantings had given me time to get my wits back. 'I've been told that the work was purchased under Malraux.' 'Malraux?!' said the man, thunderstruck. 'Malraux!' He immediately beat a retreat, and behind my back I heard him hurrying away, his voice repeating ever more faintly in the distance, 'Malraux... Malraux...'

Giotto

THE ART OF GIOTTO IS FUNDAMENTAL FOR US ALL. Homage is due to the first great artist of Western art. In my own case, the homage should be all the more insistent since, without having made a particular study of his work, I feel myself to be greatly influenced by him. Those familiar with my work as a sculptor will know my interest for mankind in the plural. I'm a city-dweller, and to live in a city means to come into daily contact with great numbers. To capture artistically the activity of the outside world is a question of composition, and that is my main concern. Where could I find a better master than Giotto of Bondone?

Against background scenery, his figures embody a powerfully felt biblical narrative in the simplest and most effective manner possible. They stand out sharply in space, the chiaroscuro (a novelty at the time) modelling their volumes and turning them into sculptures transformed by colour. This sculptural conception, it has been suggested, shows the influence of the sculptors Nicola and Giovanni Pisano, the latter being present in Padua, but I remember the shock I received from the early Giottos at Assisi. *St Francis*

Preaching to the Birds, which seemed so pretty when I saw it in reproduction, was big and strong, and the birds were huge.

Nevertheless, however sculptural they might be, there is nothing stiff about their simple gestures, for the second element which we find so moving in Giotto's work, his psychological research, is rich and lively. The Florentines, as we know, were narrators, and Giotto has a way of dramatizing his altogether human figures that brings out their feelings and passions, so that in the great moments they attain to the tragic. I was proud, in my sculpture *A Tragedy in the North*, of the gazes passing back and forth through space, uniting the people in their collective sorrow, and I was dismayed to find that Leon Battista Alberti, in his fifteenth-century treatise *Della Pittura*, had already made this a recipe for composition. These interacting gazes, however, I had certainly taken from Giotto, as had Alberti himself no doubt. Profiles repeating themselves, one on top of another, then profiles face to face. Unforgettable once seen.

I willingly describe my large polychrome compositions as so many three-dimensional frescoes, and it is only natural that Giotto, as the founder of the *buon fresco*, should delight me with the extraordinary freshness of his tones, allowing the complementary colours – or, among clear tones, the unexpected appearance of a massive black – to sing out. Nevertheless, insisting on the active force of Giotto's art – so far in the past, so modern to our eyes – I cannot do better than cite a passage from John Ruskin's *Giotto and his Works at Padua*:

> On one principle lay Giotto's great strength and the entire secret of the revolution he effected. It was not by greater learning, nor by the discoveries of new theories of art, nor by greater taste, nor by 'ideal' principles of selection that he became the head of the progressive school of Italy.
>
> It was simply by being interested in what was going on around him, by substituting the gestures of living men for conventional attitudes and portraits of living men for conventional faces, and incidents from everyday life for conventional circumstances that he became great and the master of the great.

The vivifying moments of European art are due to a Giotto, a Caravaggio, a Manet, who felt the urgent need to draw closer to their fellow men and to represent what they saw.

Joseph Wright of Derby

I AM SPEAKING OF THIS ENGLISH PAINTER FROM THE second half of the eighteenth century on the occasion of an exhibition of his works at the Grand Palais in Paris, in May 1990.

Like everyone, I'm discovering his work rather late in the day. While interested in certain reproductions of his paintings I had seen on and off over the years, I received a shock, a great surge of emotion, when, after a lunch at the Tate Gallery in London with the Keeper of the Modern Collection, Richard Morphet, the latter insisted I see the current Wright exhibition, thrusting the catalogue into my hand.

The quarter of an hour of that day in London was like a revelation. Back in France, I read the catalogue from cover to cover, then took a long look at Joseph Wright's work two months later at the Grand Palais.

This painter from the Midlands, and a stranger therefore to the artistic centres of London, Paris and Venice, found himself at the exact spot from which the Industrial Revolution would spring up, changing the face of the world. Needless to say, the fact that this poet of the dawn of industry came from the Midlands makes him particularly dear to the heart of a native of Birmingham like myself, enamoured and proud of that past.

But it is the artist and his work that I am concerned with here. Unlike his English contemporaries Gainsborough and Reynolds or, slightly later, Constable and Turner, he was that rare thing, a 'picture-maker'. Being a picture-maker involves a science of composition, a work of the mind, which alone gives structure to a work, an architecture capable of withstanding time and ensuring continuity.

Let us put aside the numerous portraits by Wright which burden – or add a frivolous note to – the exhibition. They were his bread-winners, but only among the well-to-do, middle-class society of the Midlands. The great social centres of London and Bath were monopolized by the virtuosos of the genre, the Reynolds and Gainsboroughs whom I mentioned earlier. No, to work from a motif – from a human head or a landscape, that is to say – like Constable or Turner, was not Wright's path. He had excellent vision, he was capable of capturing a moment as few were in his century (see the famous gouache of 1774 of the eruption of Vesuvius), but he also had things to say. And the human figure and the landscape had to work together to this end. This is perfectly illustrated by the difference between the portrait of his friend Burdett – competent but nothing more – and the same Burdett who appears in *The Planetary* (1766), an unforgettable scribbler of notes. Each fold of his face and clothing is worked into the web of the composition, singing loudly in this static music.

Joseph Wright, in this early composition and in *Experiment with an Air Pump* two years later, was already a master at illuminating his paintings from a single source of light. Oddly enough, they are not remotely reminiscent of Caravaggio and his followers, nor of Georges de La Tour. Their light is that of the Enlightenment, the illumination of the mind, and it radiates from the faces reaching out to comprehend the future (Wright was close to the Lunar Society which united men of science in the industrial melting-pot of Birmingham and its north). A second point I have in common with Wright is the point of illumination. I have often sculpted groups of figures gazing in wonder on a fixed point of light or an ideal.

There's nothing very mysterious about the interrogation of light in Wright's work. Though oblique light sculpts the surfaces, creating areas of shadow, they are shallow and sketch a delicate network of accentuated lines which pin down the elements of the composition on the canvas, heightening the spectator's interest and convincing him of the artist's rich and complex discourse. As a result, each element, accentuated by its shadow, is situated imperially in space, the descending curve of a nose brought out by the horizontality of a buttonhole on the jacket next to it and the precise positioning of the button. The impartiality of this 'realism' makes Wright the absolute precursor of the mid-nineteenth-century painters. (The critic in *Le Monde* who compared Wright to Boucher and Fragonard understood nothing.) As with any true artist, the aim of these dogged labours was to capture the beauty of the world. Wright does this in a singular fashion, using personal subjects – handsome figures, powerful or womanly, seen in a working context, often in front of a fiery forge.

An unusual but particularly captivating element in his work is the moon, which intrudes on all his works that take incandescence as their theme, engaging a dialogue in all its whiteness with the glowing red. The moonlight in question is almost invariably reflected in the water, and Wright's inspired hand can be seen in the inventive calligraphy with which he places his reflections.

The catalogue, which I read attentively, didn't really satisfy me. As in most catalogues today, its author knew everything about Joseph Wright's paintings and nothing about his painting. The duality of moon and fire was scarcely mentioned. Yet in the paintings representing the eruption of Vesuvius, it takes on great symbolic force. What's more, it raises an interesting enigma. At the beginning of the nineteenth century, a school of Neapolitan 'Vesuvianism' centred around Posillipo produced gouaches of Vesuvius erupting, destined for the first English tourists. Though manufactured on an industrial scale, their artistic quality is undeniable. One interesting fact is that they always show the volcano spewing fire into the air, and the moon sowing its whiteness on the sea. The first painting by Wright of an eruption of Vesuvius dates from 1774, a quarter of a century earlier. True, the French painter Pierre-Jacques Volaire was already painting the same subject, but the duality of moon and flames had been invented by Wright in England long before his travels in Italy.

Wright's moon would shine once more on the sparks flying from the *Girandoles* of Rome, the fireworks display at the Castel Sant'Angelo, then, on his return to England, on a few recollections of Italy, a few burning cities and factories. One last time it would preside majestically over the cotton mills around Derby, their windows warmly lit, in the first painting to depict the coming of industry to the English countryside. Never has the moon been more superbly painted than by Joseph Wright of Derby. The sky itself, in all its glory and all its lowerings, has found in his work one of its finest interpreters.

Nevertheless, one must not overlook Wright's figure compositions. He was a complete artist and should be added to our Western pantheon.

Alberto Giacometti

LBERTO GIACOMETTI HAD SO MUCH PERSONALITY THAT one forgets to situate him in his time. Well, let me begin by saying that he was part of that large family of artists formerly known as the School of Paris. He was a foreign artist who had come from a remote valley in his native Switzerland to learn, to add his name to the list, to become a master in this city, the world centre of art. When he moved to Paris in 1922, it was exactly like Picasso twenty years earlier (there was this same difference in age): they didn't arrive by accident, but by choice, in preference to Munich and London for Picasso, Vienna for Giacometti, who initially spoke better German than French.

I myself had the honour of knowing that family, that school, when, as a young man, I arrived in Paris in 1946. It really was a school, in which the elders would welcome into their midst gifted or promising youngsters and give them encouragement – and criticism. I was struck by their spartan cult of art, for nobody in those days talked about money or a career, let alone their national flag.

This fine institution, envied worldwide, was neglected, sidelined from the 1960s on, when the Americans had the happy idea of creating American art. The only possible response to this was to become English art, French art… No-one talks about the School of Paris any more, though numerous foreign artists of quality are still working in the city. Look at the difference. In 1962, Giacometti, a Swiss subject, represented France at the Venice Biennale (where he was awarded the Grand Prix). In 1986, my sculpture *The Crowd* was installed in the Tuileries gardens, and the only critic who commented on it didn't forget to add 'the work of the English sculptor Mason' – this, after forty years in Paris.

When Alberto Giacometti arrived in Paris, he headed straight for the fourteenth arrondissement, the hinterlands of Montparnasse, where he would live right to the end of his life. At the time I met him, immediately after the war, the fourteenth arrondissement was a neighbourhood full of artists' studios, moulders' and marblemasons' workshops, etc. As you made your

Alberto Giacometti, *Yanaihara I*, 1960. Private collection

way along the street, the tap-tapping of the stonemason could be heard, clouds of plaster dust emerged from the doors and the pavement was covered with a trail of white footprints (a great Alberto speciality, this). I liked to enter the passageway of the Giacometti studio at 46 rue Hippolyte-Maindron to breathe the air of wet plaster and hear the sound of the Godin stove being stoked – the palpable signs of a simple, authentic working life. Sculpture? The whole area reeked of it. The street is named after a nineteenth-century academic sculptor, Etienne-Hippolyte Maindron, remembered for only one thing – it was to him Rodin's parents turned to find out if their son had sufficient talent to embark on an artistic career. Good old Etienne, he assured them that he did. Moreover, twenty metres from Giacometti's studio, the street intersects with the rue Moulin Vert, where his brother Diego lived just round the corner. In the same street could also be found at the turn of the century the studio of Henri Lebossé, the enlarger and reducer of Rodin's works, meaning that Rodin himself often went there.

Alberto Giacometti would tirelessly transcribe in his maturity the divine architecture of the human face, seized upon from earliest childhood in his father's art books – Egypt, archaic Greece, etc. His very first busts demonstrate this. To master this geometry of the absolute was the heart of his work, and where others see a struggle with the personality of the model, with his soul even, for me it is a dogged battle to render that geometry more logical, better made, more fluent and expressive. And more personal, too, of course. When he speaks obsessively of the root of the nose, he should be taken at his word – it is simply a problem of construction! Otherwise the root of the nose makes no sense. I open my newspaper this morning and I read this: 'Balthus says: "What interested Giacometti: placing a nose at the centre of a face."' And not only did Balthus know Giacometti extremely well, but he himself has painted some of the finest portraits of modern times and knows what he's talking about.

The face. Head-on, the oval, the median line. To either side, the circles of the orbits. The long triangle of the nose prolonged so as to enclose two further circles, the mouth and the chin. Then a forty-five-degree turn, and the symmetry's disturbed, drawing in space the most attractive outline in the world, the human profile, which in Giacometti's work cuts into air like the sharp crests of the mountains of his native valley. Some of his busts are barely wide enough to hold the perfect vertical of the median line; then comes the profile and the total transformation when that line shakes into relief.

Face, profile. At the same moment, the shoulders make a contrary movement. Or the transformation of an arm, the pointing finger of a hand, a nose. This spatial articulation is crucial in sculpture and gives vivacity and life, particularly compared with sculpture of rotundity, for when we turn around a sphere nothing happens. Furthermore, it is expressive, this articulation, it can carry a message. We find it all through French sculpture. In Rude, of course, in Pigalle, a favourite of Giacometti's, all the way back to Gothic, then back again nearer our own time with Rodin's sculptures, whose limbs push out into space like the branches of trees in the forest he so loved. Rilke writes of *The Burghers of Calais*: 'great and pure gestures which rise aloft, then subside into the mass like brought-down flags.' Then there is the monument for Victor Hugo, with the hand of the poet speaking to the sea. Talking about movement brings us to that remarkable moment in Giacometti's work, the figures on a square that he so quickly abandoned. Then, of course, to his figures of walking men that Yves Bonnefoy rightly relates to Rodin's *Walking Man*. But there's another famous walker, Johnnie Walker himself, with his familiar silhouette, a sculptural pun on the name of the whisky distiller. On more than one occasion when drinking with Giacometti, I would see him fixing a heavy eye on the figurine of Johnnie Walker on the shelf behind the bar. 'That's how sculpture should be made,' he always said. And isn't that exactly what he did?

I was not a friend of Giacometti's but a young disciple, the difference in our ages being too great. In other words, he was the only artist who counted for me at the time. For a young man recently arrived in post-war Paris, which in those days was dominated by a vaguely figurative painting made of forms taken from Picasso, colour from Matisse and impasto from Braque, Giacometti's approach seemed the only serious attempt at capturing the visible world. Over the years, I found that the concentration I had so admired in Alberto's work – and that I still admire, like you all – was preventing me from opening myself to the movements and emotions of the outside world. Little by little, I became keenly aware of this mass of humanity which swirls around me and knows so little about art. I realized I could no longer work alone on one side, with the vast world on the other. I felt less and less like an artist. Far from seeking to draw others to myself, I wanted to reach out to my fellow men. I needed greater scope and ambition, hence a certain impatience with the small scale of Giacometti's work.

It should not be forgotten that, with Alberto Giacometti, we are dealing with a pure product of the great aesthetic school, steeped since childhood in an artistic tradition. Giacometti was an aesthete, an analyst who was strongly drawn to metaphysics, that which is beyond the physical; all his work attests to this, linear and penetrating. As a Surrealist he was attracted to the object, and as a realist often to the fragment – *The Nose, The Hand, The Leg* are all so many titles of his sculptures. He would cut the body in half to make busts, like the most docile follower of classicism. All his life, he would copy reproductions from museums (fragments again). He worked in a closed circuit. But the great classical tradition was also, thank God, a humanist tradition, and it was this banner, lying around forgotten in the modernism of the 1930s, that was seized upon by Giacometti. The survival of the essence of that tradition, MAN, would make Giacometti in the years immediately following the war, with the burden of the concentration camps and the threat of the atomic bomb, the only artist who was really at grips with the time. Hence his fame.

Today, nearly half a century later, the situation of the arts has changed for the worse. In an art world in which pitiful objects and their fortuitous installations prevail, the human dimension, the vital force of Alberto Giacometti, seems more than ever the only valid guide.

Talk given at the Centre Culturel Suisse, Paris, 26 November 1991.

Jacques-Louis David

THE TWO-PART EXHIBITION IN PARIS AND VERSAILLES devoted to the French painter Jacques-Louis David (1748–1825) has just closed, and it is doubtful that the comprehension of those who visited the exhibition was equal to the event. If proper comprehension can only come from considering his comprehensive body of work in full, splitting it between two places so far apart proved fatal, few of those who had visited the exhibition at the Louvre having travelled on to the château of Versailles.

So the work of this painter who gave so magnificent a picture of the Whole has been broken up. The giant must now take his place among all those other artists who painted this and that but always in a personal fashion, and people today prefer the Ingres, the Géricaults and the Delacroixs to the Davids, which are deemed impersonal and cold. This is precisely what is unusual about this artist and what touches me: he didn't focus his attentions on his own person but on the outside world, the people, the multitude, the crowd.

From an early age, he seems to have prepared himself for this task. Turning his back on the intimacies and fondlings of *rocaille*, he straightened his figures and, by ceaseless labour and close study of the works of ancient Rome and Greece, learned to group them. Both were civilizations, let us note, therefore impersonal in their grandeur.

After the period of antiquity studied by David, the representation of human beings in groups survived in decadent Roman painting, before flowering once more in the Middle Ages, when Christianity touched the heart of the multitude, culminating with Giotto. In the quattrocento, starting with Masaccio and Piero della Francesca, it became the noble art perpetuated in frescoes and paintings through the two centuries of the High Renaissance. While the subjects were certainly religious, they were rendered as a tide of humanity, yes, a humanist art.

The decline of religious beliefs and the decay of the monarchy in the eighteenth century had discredited traditional subjects, but the young David made a bold decision, treating neither one nor the other. His lofty character nevertheless required a grand subject, and he found himself drawn to Roman and Greek mythology. This shift in taste, the moral hardening of the message, prefigured to an astonishing degree the rejection of the *ancien régime* by the coming Revolution. Let us not pass over these history paintings, which leave the frivolous modern spectator so cold, without noting this: David had opted for human representation and, better still, the human drama. Thus – and this is important, since he would never forsake it – his scenes are represented like a stage where, on the open side, we, the spectators, have our place. This would later be held against him in his *Tennis Court Oath*, where all the protagonists are grouped before an empty proscenium. Napoleon, that oh so intelligent monster, immediately understood the matter when he first saw *The Coronation*. 'It's not a painting,' he cried; 'you can walk in it.' Precisely. David didn't want us to look at his painting but to enter it, to take part in its action, his lifesize figures, like those found in the foreground of the great fifteenth-century tapestries, aiming at this effect. I have sought modestly, for almost thirty years now, to pull off the same effect, and finding it so sharply defined, so lucid in David's work, I express my delight. This great painter liked people (as seen in his painting of large crowds, and in some fine portraits) and walked side by side with them. David is one of the great masters of composition, as is perfectly obvious to anyone who knows how to read his paintings in depth – among whom, as we know, was Baudelaire. This concern for uniting things also involves uniting art and the public. The central facts of David's career are an astonishing illustration of this almost Utopian desire.

Between 1784 and 1785, David painted *The Oath of the Horatii* in Rome. The dramatic character of this large history painting made a powerful impression on his entourage. Before the end of that decade, history itself had become a drama. On 20 June 1789, the Third Estate, rejected by Louis XVI, took refuge in the hall of the Jeu de Paume at Versailles and swore a solemn oath as a constituent Assembly. The Revolution was under way. The elated Federations of 1790 won all hearts, and David rejoiced: 'O my country, my beloved country, thus we will no longer be obliged to go seek in the history of ancient peoples the wherewithal to exercise our brushes. Artists lacked subjects, were obliged to repeat themselves, and now subjects will lack artists.' He began making studies for a huge painting, ten metres by six, *The Tennis Court Oath*. The gesture of solidarity which runs through all his work flowered at a moment unique in the annals of mankind.

The painting (which can be found in the château of Versailles and needs visiting) would never be finished for political reasons, but we know from the finished drawing and from the various studies he made that David's genius would have been equal to the task. The scale on which the composition has been conceived is staggering and can only properly be described as *la pensée en dessin*. Hundreds of people find room within the strict framework of the hall. A preparatory drawing shows the fine network of tiles punctuating space and riveting the figures to the floor, while its vanishing lines – a beautiful idea, this – continue on in the raised arms, their vanishing points centred around the face of the astronomer Bailly, reading the oath. All the people in the final drawing are precisely depicted as regards clothing and gestures. The first few rows consist of recognizable portraits. Each member of this vast assembly is situated in space, and in solemn Revolutionary fervour, with astonishing virtuosity. Better still, there are large, open windows running along the top of the room to either side, from which intrude not only a large

wafting curtain – what a symbol! the insweep of history – but also the populace, whipped up by the event within and the storm brewing without. The
different attitudes struck by these men, women and children, their umbrellas
turned inside out by the wind, are laid down, as in the preparatory sketches,
with rich, vigorous lines that class Jacques-Louis David among the great
draughtsmen. This intrusion of the natural into the sublime we have
encountered elsewhere in the late eighteenth century. Where though? In the
work of Gian-Domenico Tiepolo in the Foresteria of the Villa Valmarana in
Vicenza, of course. Let us also remember that, at the same period, Mozart
composed *The Marriage of Figaro*, where the people likewise raise their voice.
This natural beauty is more moving than that of the grand style, for it comes
from life.

I have related the high point of David's career. During the Empire,
his magnificent talent gave us *The Sacre: Napoleon Crowning Josephine* and
The Distribution of the Eagles. I shall say nothing about these paintings, other
than to express my admiration.

This is the man on whom our wretched contemporaries, more apt to
love things than beings, pour scorn. To life, they prefer the aesthetic. To
wholeness, the fragment, petty like themselves.

History painting used to be considered the *summum* of artistic activity, where the artist, you can be sure, undertook his *grande tartine* with the exhilarating twin aim of both conveying meaning to the people and, if possible, making a masterpiece. Associating it with much-hated Salon art (and with the idea of all that effort), our contemporaries have distanced themselves in mockery from history painting.

Picasso, on the other hand, was born and raised in the academic tradition and, stinting neither on work nor ambition, painted the great history painting (and masterpiece) of twentieth-century art, *Guernica*. Unlike the Matisses, Braques and Derains, who painted for themselves, Picasso in that work painted for us. Nor should we forget the great Mexican fresco painters, Rivera, Orozco and Siqueiros.

11 February 1990.

The Creative Act

'The greatest picture is that which conveys to the mind of the spectator the greatest number of the greatest ideas' – John Ruskin

IF THIS THOUGHT ASTONISHES YOU, IT ALSO ASTONISHED me when I came across it two months ago, since it reflects more or less what I have thought for many years, though previously unaware of these words of Ruskin.

'The Creative Act.' Were the title of this conference 'The Act of Creating', it would be very similar to 'how to create', something I have long viewed with suspicion, finding the 'why create?' of more importance. No doubt this is the suspicion of a plastic artist, for if I say that I do not want to isolate the act of creating from the initial determinism and the final goal, this is because in the visual arts, unlike in your own professions, this is precisely what, to my mind, is too often done. In art it can mean 'the manner' and even that other factor which comes into the act – namely, chance. The magical effect of something not being there at one moment and present the next.

The creative act for me is the act of thinking about the life I see around me. The artist not only lives his life, he looks at it. He looks at it more attentively than others and, so to speak, in much larger quantities. Among the profusion of things stored up in this way, the vast repertoire of the history of art is particularly important to him, since it consists of forms and styles which have meaning. The true artist seeks a meaning in the world around him. He seeks truth there. The world taken in by the mind via the eye.

When an important subject comes to him, he will stick to the initial idea all through the elaboration of his work, but imperceptibly other ideas will attach themselves to it – turning it into something else perhaps, in relation to his original idea, but faithful to its spirit. It is imperative that the artist follow this path, for his real force resides in this liberation of all his faculties, what Ruskin – he again – called 'that marvellous foresight', his lyrical description of which can hardly be bettered: 'The most just, the most truthful [faculty] possessed by the human mind, since it is through its workings that the vanity and individualism of man are crushed. The latter becomes an instrument or mirror used by a higher power to reflect back to others a truth that no effort on his part could have divined.'

This means that creation is the coming together of reality, the intellect and that occult force, inspiration. One thing is sure: the creating is done *during*. It can neither be foreseen nor programmed, still less – I am thinking of my own profession – entrusted to a third party.

There is another respect in which the painter and the sculptor differ from you, the lucky poets, writers and musicians, in the creating of a work. To create they are obliged to destroy as much as they construct. To advance their painting or sculpture, they must cover over – if they paint or model – or remove – if they sculpt – the often happy effects of the previous day. You others, who likewise have second or third thoughts about your projects, can always keep your early drafts and return, if need be, to that original freshness. Now, if you cross out as much as Beethoven did, or compose on a keyboard, perhaps you will join us in misery.

My creativity consists, I think, in a certain multiplication, a desire to put everything in, to refract the theme indefinitely, appearing in fact more like its contrary: repetition. Or, let us say, returns.

Preamble to lecture, Institut Collégial Européen, Loches, 11 June 1982.

Balthus

I AM WRITING THIS IN 1996. BALTHAZAR KLOSSOWSKI IS eighty-eight therefore (although being born on 29 February enables him to divide his age by four and remain in a fairytale adolescence). He lives in Switzerland's biggest and most beautiful chalet in Rossinière, a small village not far from Gstaad in the Vaud. One of his closest friends and neighbours is Yehudi Menuhin, today aged eighty. The entire music world speaks of the latter's 'genius', and having watched and heard Menuhin perform when he was still very young, with the absolute beauty of his face and a depth of emotion in his handling of the violin unrivalled in this century, I agree, if by that word we mean utterly outstanding. For twenty years, however, this violinist has been unable to play his instrument correctly. Here the two men, Balthus and Menuhin (Balthus less good-looking than Menuhin when young, but more impressive today), speaking the same upper-class English, meet, since Balthus has not done a really good painting since 1977, when he made one of the most beautiful nudes ever painted. Nevertheless, he too was a young prodigy whose remarkable gifts as a draughtsman and painter were rightly remarked by the distinguished friends of his artistic parents, Pierre Bonnard, André Gide and Rainer Maria Rilke (for whom Balthus, in his early adolescence, illustrated a book they had done together). As for the rest of his career, I will not hesitate to use the word genius of it, for here, too, the work is utterly outstanding. At the same time, it is singular, different from everything around it, whereas Menuhin was simply better than everyone else. And again, because it concerns a creative work, I give my preference to the painter.

Do we need to seek far afield the reasons for an artistic decline? Both men filled fifty years with their enormous talent. Very few artists end their careers on a precipice, their late work being the loftiest, and personally I find very little of value in the last twenty years of Pablo Picasso's work.

During the first period of my life in Paris, from 1946 to 1954, I knew nothing about Balthus, barely even his name. Yet I knew Giacometti, who saw a great deal of Balthus in those days, and I could easily have run into him in the sculptor's studio. Furthermore, I saw a lot of Dora Maar, another of

Balthus's friends. I must have come across his painting only shortly before
meeting the painter himself, since both events took place in Carmen Baron's
apartment in 1955, when she moved back to Paris. I am not going to describe
Carmen, nor her very close ties with Balthus, nor her salon on the rue de
Varenne and the superb company of creators of every description who
frequented it, since I have already done so elsewhere. I shall limit myself here
to speaking of my meetings with Balthus, without analysing his work, for
that, too, I have already done.

Balthus at forty-seven was tall, slim, sharp-faced, with the kind of nose
that cleaves space and that you often find in actors, and had a piercing gaze.
The overall effect was a bit like Sherlock Holmes. He wore sports attire that
was casual but in perfect English taste. The evening we met, among a crowd
of celebrities – I was the only unknown present – I was wearing a pair of
Black Watch regimental tartan trousers, recently commercialized since that
valiant corps had been put in khaki. 'Are you Scottish?' Balthus asked me, and
here I recognized the high clear voice, thrown forward, again as would an
actor. 'Yes,' I replied, though in reality I'm only half-Scottish, on my father's
side. My lie was overwhelmed by his. 'So am I. I'm a Gordon, like my ancestor
Lord Byron.' My more recent ancestor, a golf champion at Saint Andrews,
didn't cut much ice under the circumstances, and in any case we soon moved
on from Scotland – which he, like myself, hardly knew – to converse gaily
till the moment came to take leave of our hostess. At which point the Anglo-
Saxon streak in Balthus's personality – which runs deep, he speaks the language perfectly – came to the fore. I walked him home, after which he walked
me home (very English, that). Then, since I am English, I walked him home a
second time, whereupon, in lordly fashion – oh yes, Balthus is on all occasions lordly – he walked me home yet again, and this time came into the studio. Thus, at three o'clock in the morning, he fixed his piercing gaze on the
only two sculptures of note to be seen, *Barcelona Tram* and *The Idyll*. Having
said that he liked them a lot, he went home to bed. Nevertheless, and I found
out later how unusual this was for him, he came back the following day to see
them in the light of day. Thus he knew more or less everything about me, my
work having scarcely begun, and I next to nothing about him, apart from two
or three paintings at Carmen's. I knew the man, then, but not his work, which

was amusing, for almost everyone who was familiar with the paintings knew nothing of the artist, who lived in the Morvan and seldom came to Paris and, in those days, only to Carmen's, where he had a room, and to the mansion of the viscountess Marie-Laure de Noailles, by definition select.

Only a few months later, a major event suddenly put me in the presence of all Balthus's work. Henriette and André Gomès, his dealers in France (in New York, he had been with Pierre Matisse since 1938), organized a retrospective at the former Wildenstein galleries on the rue du Faubourg Saint-Honoré. In preparation for this, Balthus had moved into a studio formerly occupied by Francis Gruber, whose widow, Georges, he was still close to. Here, in the Villa d'Alésia, he was busy touching up all his paintings in the light of Paris – a characteristic piece of meticulousness that came to nothing, as we shall see later. When he opened the door to me, I had the great shock of seeing huge canvases, dense with subject matter and sumptuously painted. Here was the contemporary but complete art I had been seeking for so long.

On another occasion, about to return to the Villa d'Alésia, I was just leaving my studio when I received a visit from the director of the Museum of Melbourne in Australia. With utter naivety, I suggested he accompany me to Balthus's – instead of keeping him prudently in my studio, as it was my own work he had come to see. It was doubly naive on my part, since when Balthus saw me arriving with a stranger he gave more or less open vent to his anger. Needless to say, the man from the southern hemisphere had seen enough to be overwhelmed before we found ourselves out on the street once more. All I know is that, a few years later, an important painting by Balthus was acquired by that very museum, so the master may have pardoned his foolish young friend at some point. It should be noted, however, that in those days Balthus cultivated a genuine disdain for the world of galleries, museums, curators and art dealers, with the sole exception of Pierre Matisse, for whom he felt esteem and friendship. At no moment would he have made the slightest gesture towards Melbourne.

The magnificent exhibition of paintings assembled at Wildenstein's was a complete flop! The fault lay with the Gomès couple who, on the very eve of the private view, had excelled themselves when André drove his car onto the pavement and crashed into a lamppost, injuring his wife. Thus, what ought to have been her hour of glory, the private view of her darling painter, found Henriette wrapped in bandages, with one bruised eye peering out. Worse still was André's stupid idea of lining the walls of the gallery, which were perfectly beautiful in their muted red, with lengths of hessian recently purchased at the Bazar de l'Hôtel de Ville and thus still covered with geometric crease-marks from being stored, the confusion of their surfaces killing dead the paintings hung thereupon. I saw Balthus walk into the room, glance round at the disaster, mumble: 'And to think I spoke so ill of Bernard Buffet…,' turn on his heels and leave.

The following evening, passing in front of the Café de Flore around seven, I noticed Alberto and Annette Giacometti sitting with Balthus at the table by the door, all three of them staring gloomily down at their coffees. I had something to say to Balthus, and I went in to say it. 'Balthus, you've got to get those pieces of hessian stretched.' In his most lugubrious voice, Balthus replied: 'It's ruined, there's nothing to be done.' I was protesting that all was not lost, that I would deal with it with friends, when Giacometti, looking up at Balthus, said: 'If it's a wash-out, Balthus, you know who to blame. When I see a Cézanne in a poor light I say, "How beautiful it is. It's a pity you can't see it better." A clenching of the jaws indicated that Balthus had felt the criticism, and my admiration for him immediately prompted me to say: 'No, those paintings must be saved, because when I saw them the other day at Gruber's I realized that you're the greatest painter of the day.' With a howl of rage, Giacometti stood up and yelled: 'And me? I am what exactly? I'm not a painter, then?' 'But Alberto, you're the sculptor. You know what I think of…' 'Vous êtes un con, un double con, un triple con!' The Flore, packed with people at that hour, started to empty, so put out were the clients by Giacometti's vociferations and remarks, while Balthus protested in Italian: 'No, no, Alberto, you know Raymond's not an idiot.' There was nothing to be done. 'He's a *con*, a double *con*, a triple *con*,' and so on until Annette broke in to say: 'Alberto, you're going to have an attack!' bringing her husband up short, whose face now took on a sheepish expression while he searched frantically in his pockets for a pill which he swallowed straight down. During this little interlude, I felt anger welling up in me. To have been insulted by this man who knew me to be his fervent disciple made me speak equally harsh words in his direction. But Giacometti's anger had subsided. He changed places to come and sit next to me, and put his arm around my shoulders. 'There, there, we're both *cons*. We're going to spend the evening together.' Which we did, dining in Montparnasse, then going on for drinks at the Rosebud in the rue Delambre till two in the morning, but the atmosphere never really warmed up and I was happy to get back, but unhappy, oh so unhappy with my evening.

It was around this time, moreover, that the friendship between Giacometti and Balthus, which had been very close and reciprocal, started to cool when the latter announced to his friends that his real name was Count Balthazar Klossowski de Rola and that he belonged to the Polish nobility. Nothing could have indisposed the sculptor more, who by nature was devoted to simplicity and truth. I remember a dinner at Carmen Baron's with Giacometti, when Balthus arrived late explaining that he had been held up at the Mobilier National. 'Doing what?' asked Giacometti. 'Looking for furniture for the Villa [André Malraux had just appointed him director of the Villa Medici at Rome], since it's completely empty.' 'It's better that way,' said Alberto firmly. Soon their relations were reduced to nothing.

Though often invited by Balthus to his château at Chassy, near Château-Chinon in the Morvan, I hesitated to accept, thinking that the man who said this at a party in Paris would be rather less welcoming when transformed into a fierce painter, obliged to open the gates of his château to me. Finally, I set off on the train with the invaluable Carmen, knowing that Balthus would be delighted by her arrival. His handsome abode had but a few items of furniture – it was Balthus's most impoverished period – being furnished, in point of fact, by his presence alone, but it was also the period when this great artist and great man was most purely himself. I shall never forget the austerity of the place, the smell of slightly damp walls and, with the windows open, the view and fragrance of the fields sloping down towards the valley. Balthus's landscapes were all painted from these very windows, and today I have only to see one of those marvellous works for memories of the painter and his home at the time to come flooding back, bringing tears of emotion to my eyes. I can safely say that nothing in painting moves me more than the canvases Balthus painted in this château lost in the depths of France, for, even more than their breathtaking beauty, it is the tenderness with which they are suffused that makes them unique in this century. It was at Chassy, too, that the last great works of his Paris period were completed, and I would enter the first-floor studio with the respect and exhilaration at other times reserved for a famous battlefield; it was here that Balthus triumphed over the giant canvases *The Room* and *The Passage du Commerce-Saint-André*. The vestiges of those memorable days and months were everywhere in evidence on the walls in recognizable traces of painting.

Do people give full weight to his decision to leave Paris, to the fact that he turned his back on his pre-eminent place in the rich art circles of the day? And all to be able to paint! Balthus's integrity and dedication are revealed by this decision; in those days time moved slowly in that isolated countryside and the artist's face-to-face engagement with his art could only be total.

However, château bought and decor planted, as if by enchantment appeared a beautiful young girl – Balthus's niece by the marriage of his brother, Pierre. After the completion of the satanic *Room* and the austere *Passage du Commerce*, the presence of Frédérique would lead to a new and equally important phase in the painting of Balthus. Within the Virgilian setting of reawakening nature arrives all the grace of youth; in the picture of the young girl at a window, ecstatically enthralled by the sunlit landscape, I see the ultimate unfolding of the message of the artist's much-beloved Piero della Francesca. The springtime of the quattrocento enters into Balthus.

I was at Chassy once when the Gomèses arrived. Balthus referred unkindly to them as 'my people', and there were countless anecdotes in which he poked fun at them in one form or another. For all that, he relied a great deal on them, not only for the sale of his paintings in Paris – which at the time wasn't flourishing, especially as Henriette could hardly ever find a buyer worthy of possessing a canvas by her precious Balthus – but also for the myriad services required between his château and the outside world. The sight of Henriette and André getting down from their car gave Balthus the idea that we could all go and visit Picasso at La Californie, his house in Cannes. Balthus and Henriette could intrude on Picasso's privacy without difficulty – Balthus on account of the friendship between the two painters, who thought highly of each other, Henriette because she had been the attractive young lady who did odd jobs at the Galerie Pierre Loeb before the war, when Picasso, Miró and Balthus were the artists of the house. The outing to La Californie came to an abrupt end, however, when Balthus, telephoning from a restaurant in the Midi on the way, was informed that Pablo was in bed with flu. We forked off in the direction of Colmar and the museum of Unterdenlinden to see the Grünewalds, which neither Balthus nor myself knew. Colmar also has some very fine restaurants, and we dined and lunched extremely well. The following day, Balthus and I were sitting on the stones which line the main square waiting for the Gomèses, who had gone to do a bit of window-shopping. When he saw, at a great distance, their tiny figures starting out on the square, Balthus yelled out: 'Look at them. Thomson and Thompson!' We all know that he was a great Tintin fan in the 1950s, and Frédérique, his companion, assured me that he was always the first downstairs in the château on Wednesday mornings to meet the postman bearing the precious weekly.

The return of De Gaulle to power in 1958 and the appointing of a cabinet in which André Malraux would be taking in hand cultural affairs changed Balthus's life. He and Malraux had known each other for years, and if at cabinet meetings it is said that no-one dared contradict André Malraux, I know that in private Balthus could permit himself to say: 'But no, André, you're talking through your hat.' This friendship resulted in Balthus's being named director of the Académie de France at the Villa Medici in Rome, which greatly annoyed the members of the Institut de France and the Académie des Beaux-Arts who were alone entitled to appoint the director of the Villa. They had, in fact, been on the point of naming the well-known *pompier* painter Yves Brayer (who lived in a beautiful studio just down the street from me in rue Monsieur-le-Prince) to the post. Beside himself with rage, the latter went round cursing 'this petit monsieur [Balthus] who won't even know how to entertain.' All those who have had the pleasure of being Balthus's guest will appreciate the joke.

Balthus's leaving for the Villa brought to a close a great period of my life, when I had enjoyed a privileged relationship with an older figure I admired and a man I loved. There would be no more of those delightful moments, like the occasion when my Citroën broke down on the boulevard

Montparnasse and we passed before the crowded terrace of La Coupole, myself at the steering-wheel and Balthus and my wife pushing the car. For one thing, the man himself would change. The contact with the Roman aristocracy, one of the most artificial in Europe, would exacerbate the blue-blooded streak in Balthus. Nevertheless, I myself have never been a victim of this and, over the years, have had many a demonstration of his wish to maintain our friendship intact. However, his entourage changed and, little by little – and this is the great tragedy – his art as well.

Balthus also changed his life after a while in Rome, forsaking the woman who had been his muse for ten years, Frédérique Tison, to wed Setsuko, a young Japanese woman. His love for Frédérique had been real – his paintings testify to this – and he gave her all that he possessed in France: the beautiful château of Chassy and the noble apartment at 3 cour de Rohan in the sixth arrondissement in Paris, his former studio.

In 1965, Balthus and I met up once more in Rome, where I was having two of my sculptures cast in bronze at the Fonderia Bruni (the oldest foundry in Italy, magnificently installed a short walk from the Via Appia Antica in the south of Rome). At the time, I witnessed the enormous labours undertaken by Balthus to beautify the Villa. Shortly after this, he came to Paris for his retrospective at the Musée des Arts Décoratifs, organized by François Mathé. The latter was given a hard time by Balthus who, arriving once the hanging had been completed, promptly rejected the lot and insisted the entire exhibition be moved to the rooms overlooking the rue de Rivoli so as to benefit from natural light. In all this to-do, for what reason I don't know, there was no longer room for the drawings and watercolours. This collection of works on paper belonged to Frédérique, for the simple reason that it was she who for years had gathered up the sheets of paper cast onto the floor by Balthus, who was wholly concentrated on the main business, the painting in hand.

The small gallery run by Janine and myself had existed for several years and had proved its worth in the eyes of the artistic public of Paris, so Frédérique, a friend we had known for many years, thought it would be a good idea to hold an exhibition of her Balthus drawings and watercolours there to coincide with the one at the Musée des Arts Décoratifs. Balthus

Rome seen from the Villa Medici, 1976

immediately agreed and, a sure sign that he looked kindly on the event, announced that he would be present at the private view, something he had refused to the museum.

So it was that our courtyard at 60 rue Monsieur-le-Prince was overrun one beautiful summer's afternoon by the cream of the Parisian art world. The works were very fine, and our well-lit walls showed them to their worth. As for their real worth, it was Balthus who decided that the drawings would be sold in groups of seven – 'Three good, four bad,' as he sardonically put it – priced at a million old francs (needless to say, all the drawings are good and have been in private collections or museums for years). Some weren't signed, so Balthus duly obliged, sitting next to me in my pretty red Austin with its mahogany bodywork and white-wall tyres, conveniently parked outside the door of the gallery. This was because he was angry with his main collector, the banker Claude Hersaint, the lucky owner of *Le Passage du Commerce*, who was in our gallery.

An event like the first ever exhibition of Balthus's watercolours and drawings did not go unnoticed, of course, and art dealers like Erica Brausen from the Hanover Gallery, at the time the leading gallery in London, and Jan Krugier from Geneva came and bought the best works. The most important visitor, however, was Pierre Matisse, who rushed over from New York to see this pirate gallery exhibiting works on paper that he, Balthus's official dealer since 1938, had never been able to obtain.

We had in our stockroom two or three small paintings by Balthus, still-lifes not completely finished but of excellent quality nevertheless, not that this prevented their author from describing them as 'daubings'. (It should be said that, in those days, artists like Giacometti and Balthus were very hard on themselves, and for years we heard the former repeating 'I can't do it' and the second 'I'm a failure'. Naturally, neither considered himself a failure, and if Giacometti was modest it was when comparing his works to those of Egypt and Balthus to those of Piero della Francesca, not to the productions of their contemporaries. This litany of self-reproaches reveals the marvellous nature of these two artists who considered that art was more important than themselves, that they had not attained, that day, all they had hoped.) When he went into the room to look at the paintings, Pierre Matisse noticed a large landscape sculpture of mine hanging on the wall, and his visit bore fruit the following year when I joined the Pierre Matisse Gallery in New York and all my sculptures were dispatched to Rome to be cast in bronze.

This foundry work occasioned a much longer stay on my part in Rome, so that I could work on the different stages of casting; it also gave me, of course, countless opportunities to see Balthus, since he asked me to come to the Villa Medici every evening and would gladly have lodged me there, except that I had to take the first morning tram from its terminus near the Opera to get to the Fonderia Bruni on the outskirts of town. I was so engrossed in my work, moreover, that I hardly profited from his kindly invitations. For the same reason, I never paid a visit to Gaston Palewski, the French ambassador to Italy at the time, whom I had often met at Carmen's in Paris and who had even written an article about my work for *La Revue des Deux Mondes*. This was stupid of me, since the Farnese Palace is one of the most impressive residences of the Eternal City, having been partly designed by Michelangelo and decorated with magnificent frescoes by Annibale Carracci. Balthus, on the other hand, went there often, since Gaston and he were very close friends.

I did get up to the Villa Medici from time to time, of course. It was invariably a great pleasure, and almost invariably Balthus would ask me to fix a rendezvous to do my portrait. For the same reasons of work, I would reply that it was quite impossible, and here my stupidity was just plain crass, since Balthus was an extraordinary male portraitist, and in those days I had a head which was worth the trouble.

Later on during my stay, a painful but amusing accident befell me. I had so much work on my hands that Arturo Bruni – and I raise my cap here to this *gran signore* of founders – entrusted me with the keys to the foundry so that I could continue at night. One of the workers, Romano – whose name was well chosen as he was a delightful Roman – would get up at three o'clock in the morning to drive me back to my hotel in his old Alfa Romeo! Before starting on my nocturnal labours, I would go out in the early evening to have a cup of tea in a bar on the other side of a large trunk road.

One evening, running back to the foundry, I jumped over the little wall as always, only this time I landed on a round stone. The result was a broken ankle, the comical part being that, at that precise moment, the great Italian boxing champion Benevenuti was facing the world-title holder in New York and the whole of Italy was watching or listening to the match. For two hours the streets were totally deserted and I lay there, incapable, without help, of standing up. The following day, once my ankle was in plaster, my worker friends made me some crutches from large pieces of wood. When Balthus saw me like this, with my long hair, which was very dark in those days, and my red shirt, dragging myself along on makeshift crutches like a medieval vagabond, he got more than ever excited to do my portrait. At this point, I really should have accepted, since it would be difficult to work at the foundry; but no, back I went, even climbing up ladders in my handicapped state.

Not only did I not have the portrait, but shortly afterwards my stepdaughter, Danièle, married Michel Boffredo from Ménerbes and they came to spend their honeymoon in Rome. Balthus kindly invited them to lunch at the Villa and, at one point, we were all standing together on the large terrace overlooking Rome. Michel was a gifted professional photographer and, while chatting with Balthus, I noticed Michel pointing his camera at us. I pounced on him to prevent him from taking a photograph of us, saying: 'Balthus doesn't allow photos'. That evening, in the course of a conversation with the newlyweds, Michel told me how silly I had been, since he had sensed that Balthus was perfectly content to be photographed with me in front of the magnificent panorama. He was right, I had felt it myself. So no portrait and no photo. My future catalogues have been deprived of some fine images.

I mustn't forget an astonishing moment. I often talked to Balthus about the founder Signor Bruni, who was now eighty years of age but could remember going to the Villa Medici as a young man with his father to mould for the sculptors staying at the Académie de France and marvelling at the beauty of its famous gardens. Towards the end of my stay in Rome, Balthus held a big exhibition, in the galleries he had recently created, of the work of his distant predecessor at the Villa, Jean-Auguste-Dominique Ingres. It was going to be quite an event, and the entire Italian government, along with the president of the republic in person, were only too happy to attend. 'You must bring Signor Bruni along,' suggested Balthus. This decided me to go myself, though I was utterly worn out with work. (That said, during the party the champagne flowed freely, and by my third glass my fatigue had vanished!) A huge crowd was massed on the steps behind the Villa, and I was stationed there with the tiny Signor Bruni at my side. Balthus arrived, leading his important guests, and with the Italian president on his arm. When he drew level with me, he ran his free hand through my hair, a sign of affection reserved for his friends, and said: 'Ah, ma non è il signor Bruni?' and, holding his hand out to him, 'Molte piacere, Signore.' The amazement of Bruni at the tribute paid to him in this way by the director of the Villa, accompanied by his own president, was a delight to behold, and is a perfect illustration of the gestures of which this great gentleman Balthus is capable.

Why have I waited all this time to evoke the crucial aspect of my visits to Balthus's studio? I am talking about the huge room at the end of the gardens once painted by Velázquez. The room was situated beneath the terrace of the Bosco, and its windows, though not very clean, overlooked a road beyond which lay the gardens of the Villa Borghese. If Balthus changed over the

years, his studios remained strictly the same. Chassy, Rome, La Rossinière –
it was always the same gloomy space devoid of objects other than paint-
brushes, gutted tubes of colour, cigarette ends and, turned to the wall,
gigantic stretchers. A single canvas stood on a very big easel. On it I saw the
beginning of the second version of a card game and, as always in the early
stages of my friend's paintings, I was struck by the majesty of the composition and the feeling that everything was already there. At the same time, I
knew that Balthus would spend one or more years working on it before he
was happy with it – or incapable of going any further. In recent years, this
tenaciousness has not been good for his work, this Jacob's struggle with the
angel being beyond the powers of an old man. The large painting *The Card-
Players* was to usher in the less successful late work. True, there would be the
magnificent exception of the nude of Michelina, the *Resting Nude* of 1977 that
I mentioned earlier; but, though large, it is not a composition, not the work
of a 'picture-maker' that makes Balthus so unusual in our slapdash age and
wherein lies for me his supremacy.

I am certain of this, for *The Card-Players* was the painting on which
Balthus was working all through the period in the 1960s when I was regularly
in Rome at the Fonderia Bruni. The foundry would be producing the bronzes
for my exhibition at the Pierre Matisse Gallery in New York in 1968, and at
the beginning of this great adventure Pierre Matisse had come to Rome. As
everyone knows, Balthus and Pierre were great friends, the painter having
been with the dealer since 1938, and I was present at their reunion dinner at
the Villa, when we were fussed over as usual by the charming domestic staff,
Luigi and Benedetto. After dinner, we settled down in the big drawing room,
and Balthus assumed, as I did too, that with our glasses of brandy we would
spend a long evening conversing together. We were astonished, therefore,
when after a quarter of an hour Pierre Matisse stood up to announce that he
was tired and had to go home to bed, 'and Raymond as well'. Once we were
outside, with all Rome at our feet, Pierre said: 'Come to Rome to listen to the
Count, no! Where shall we go?'

I mention Pierre in relation to *The Card-Players* because when the first
lot of my sculptures to be cast in bronze had been dispatched to New York
he had been very pleased with the work of the Roman shipper, whose head

office was on the Piazza di Spagna. He now wanted me to inform him that he had to go up to the Villa nearby to look at the nature and size of Balthus's painting, for it was now finished (this was in 1968) and he, Pierre, had purchased it.

At dinner that evening, I told Balthus about this, of course, and gradually his face and soon his entire person were shaking with laughter – so much so, that it was a while before he was able to get out these words: '*The Card-Players*! Do you know what I did this morning when I arrived in my studio? I painted the whole thing over with white'. This was said with obvious glee. And yet – and here I am not altogether certain, but everything at the time suggested as much to me – he had already received the money from Pierre and may even have needed the sum, I think, to buy the Italian château of Monte Calvello, a hundred kilometres north of Rome. I am not at all suggesting that the painter was pulling a fast one on his dealer, for Matisse received his painting a few years later and at once sold it to the Boymans-van Beuningen Museum in Rotterdam. I mention the incident to show that Balthus was not only capable of brinkmanship in his work, but positively revelled in it at times. It was his pride in being an artist, the nobleness of painting regardless of the work as a commercial object. This lofty attitude finally led him into dead-ends. Previously, it had borne him to the summits.

Balthus was very close to Federico Fellini, who lived right below the Villa in the via Margutta. Fellini is one of the few filmmakers to have drawn me into cinemas. In forty years perhaps, I have stepped into their darkened halls only six or seven times, and on almost every occasion it was to see a film by Fellini, so colourful, so good with colour. I would have loved to have met the man, and I was convinced, moreover, that Fellini would have liked my polychrome sculptures. Balthus was consistently evasive, and even on the evening when I was to give a slide-show on my work for the residents at the Villa he didn't lift a finger.

Finally came the moment for my sculptures, now cast in bronze, to leave for New York, and I for Paris, where Janine was waiting for me with a keen sense of having been betrayed by this prolonged absence. When I announced this to Balthus, he cried out in protest: 'What, you're not staying for our birthdays?' It's true, our birthdays are close together, his on 29 February, mine on 2 March, and now his wife Setsuko's on 7 March. Pisces all three. Several evenings running, he told me I had to stay for the 29th that leap year, and each time I explained to him that I had to go home. Once he was convinced of this at last, he turned to Setsuko and asked her: 'Well then, apart from Federico, who will be coming?' The bastard, he hadn't told me that Fellini would be at the dinner. I had my pride, of course, and I returned to Paris.

I have never been to Monte Calvello, and only once to La Rossinière. That one occasion was so unique that it explains in itself my reluctance to return. Janine and I had known Setsuko from the moment she first turned up in Rome at Balthus's side as a young European girl wearing Simpson's of London-style pullovers. It was Balthus, no doubt, who had wanted his wife to wear traditional Japanese dress. This is understandable, since Setsuko wears it with considerable grace, but when Balthus himself adopted oriental dress and, little by little, a ritual, a ceremonial was established at the big chalet, with oriental food and domestic staff, the whole thing took on a character so foreign to my nature as a Birmingham man that I felt no desire to go to La Rossinière, not wanting above all to risk effacing the memories of my early Balthus, the quintessential European, Mozart for music, Anglophile for literature.

Balthus, however, repeated his invitation so often, countering my excuse that I didn't like the snow with 'Come next summer, then', that a date was fixed for the middle of August 1989. Not long before this, Pierre Matisse had died in the South of France, which naturally left Balthus heartbroken, particularly as Pierre had been on the point of visiting the chalet for his annual inspection of his friend's work. My visit was pushed back a week or two, and when I warned Balthus that the last possible moment for me that summer was the following Wednesday, there was the added difficulty that Balthus and Setsuko had been invited to a big reception the following day, organized by the town of Vevey for the centenary of their honorary citizen Charlie Chaplin. I assured them I would stay behind at the chalet and read a book, and my arrival was thus settled.

To reach Balthus's home in the remote valley of the Vaud, the French and Swiss railways had combined to carry you in a TGV as far as Montreux where, without changing platform, you could take a small train belonging to the MOB which drops you off at the tiny station of La Rossinière, at the bottom of the garden of the chalet – a VIP treatment that seems only natural in the case of the Count Balthazar Klossowski de Rola. The chalet has been described many times over, and never better than by Giorgio Soavi in his book *Giorni Felici con Balthus*. Its huge timbered façades are fashioned like those of a Tibetan temple. The master of the house has had the inside walls sanded down to bring out the colour of what Giorgio calls a piling-up of biscuits, which also explains the crunching sound that underlines your every movement and footstep. The views from the windows are all so many Balthus paintings, since he had already spent a long time working in the region during the war.

I was greeted by Balthus announcing that everything had been arranged for me to accompany them to Vevey for the festivities. Heavens! I had nothing to wear apart from a sports jacket and trousers to match. Finding a bow tie at the bottom of my suitcase went some way towards retrieving the situation, and finally I was altogether in the tone of the crazy evening that lay in store.

The organizer of the evening came in person to collect the Count and Countess and their guest. Impressed by the chalet, he accepted the drink Balthus offered, unaware that in the latter's slow-motion ceremonial it would be followed by others. A good hour and a half passed before the man from Vevey dared suggest we leave, with further delays when Balthus was unable to find his sunglasses – without which, he said, he couldn't 'tolerate the photographers' flashes'. The organizer offered him his own pair and off we went. By the time we got there, however, it was too late for the cocktail beside the lake, and the screening of *The Great Dictator* on the pretty square of Vevey, where a large audience composed of numerous film stars and actresses had gathered to pay tribute to Charlot, was about to start. The evening was also designed as a tribute to the French Declaration of the Rights of Man, the bicentenary of which likewise fell on that day, and once the film was over actors were supposed to deliver – in various languages, including Chinese – the famous speech in which Chaplin pleads on behalf of friendship between peoples, speaking for the first time on screen.

We were shown to our seats, which were bang in the middle, with the aid of floodlights, for night had already fallen; and so the spectators saw filing past a Japanese woman in a sumptuous kimono, followed by the tall silhouette of Balthus (made even taller by the fact that he had clogs on underneath his long cloak) with his silver hair and dark glasses, holding in his hand a long silver-knobbed cane. Bringing up the rear, as best I could, was myself, inescapably English. To my great surprise, I also heard my name being announced on the loudspeaker as 'the famous British sculptor' – I was even more surprised to hear a volley of prolonged applause – 'who is accompanying the Count and Countess Klossowski de Rola'. Frenzied applause. The nobility plebiscited for the bicentenary of 1789!

The moment the film began, Balthus and I were doubled up with laughter at the comic genius of Charlot. (Balthus, who has always been a great lover not only of theatre but of cinema as well, often received film stars in Rome, and I remember a weekend spent at the Villa with the Hollywood actor Tony Curtis, with whom I struck up a brief friendship.) The interval came round and, wiping the tears from his eyes, Balthus asked me if I remembered the rest of the film and, when I replied that I did, stated firmly: 'Me too. Let's go.' Thus, to the stupefaction of the spectators, the initial scenario was repeated, with our trio slipping out under the floodlights from this important evening. This was all very well, but we would miss out on the large dinner after the screening; meanwhile, the driver who had collected us and would be taking us back to the chalet, not expecting to have to return so soon, was nowhere to be seen. It was late, I was very hungry, and I insisted on going into a trattoria right in front of us in the street. The idea was a good one, since we immediately noticed our driver sitting at a table having his dinner. I ordered a full Italian meal, and Balthus, as is his habit these last few years, a small plate of white pasta. When he inspected the dish being served up to me, however, he declared: 'Mmm, that looks delicious,' and, to the astonishment of Setsuko, was soon eating the same thing as me, and drinking quite as much red wine. We dined like two students, with lots of laughter and good cheer. This was followed by a quick drink with the driver, then hup! the latter put us in the car. During the journey, he interrupted our merry conversation to say: 'Messieurs, listening to you talking, I wonder if you knew a client of mine, the sculptor Alberto Giacometti?' That took the biscuit! The moment we got back, Balthus said: 'Just think! Not only have we spent a marvellous evening, but we had a driver who knew Alberto!' In fact, the marvellous evening was not yet over. I had brought with me in my suitcase a bottle of Drambuie, the whisky liqueur that Balthus had always been so fond of in the past; but merely as a symbol, a souvenir of the past, thinking that my eighty-year-old friend no longer touched spirits. The bottle was standing in front of us on the table. 'Ah, the Drambuie!' cried Balthus and immediately went to fetch the glasses. Anyone who has ever tasted this nectar knows how marvellous it is. Setsuko's lips, needless to say, had never touched the stuff, but she was won over at once. We drank the entire bottle, which was only, it's true, a half-bottle; but three glasses each was enough to render our frail Japanese lady incapable of making her way upstairs to bed. We carried her up.

Since then, I have not been back to the chalet, but for several years we would speak on the telephone, and I would often write to him, commenting on this or that photo which had appeared in the press. When they started to appear in quantities in all the magazines, I became disheartened, dismayed to see my friend the great Balthus brought down to the humdrum in this way. More recently, a doubt has crept over me: what if he was partly to blame...? I wrote one last time, having seen a very beautiful picture of him, with his wife and daughter, having tea with a tea service that is also mine, since it is made by an English firm called Mason. I complimented them on their beautiful appearance, adding, as a joke, that I hoped they thought of me whenever they had tea. Silence. To reply in writing is not part of the ceremony.

Contemporary Art – for Whom?... and for When?

CONTEMPORARY FRENCH ART IS NOT THAT OF ALL artists who are 'alive at the same time as me', but an art practised by a younger generation that is grouped and distinct because institutionalized.

While I am a fervent admirer of my age and of the art of my age, its current output doesn't satisfy me, being too simple and insufficient. I don't feel nourished by anything I see. The number of self-proclaimed artists is multiplying dizzyingly. Those who now write on the subject are also legion, not art critics but journalists, the majority of them female, who fill with their ecstatic sighs arts magazines of a superficial cultural standard. We are losing the specialist, the connoisseur. I am constantly surprised by the ease with which all this comes about, by the approbation of museum curators whose intellectual background ought to make them more demanding. The ambition of many young artists seems to me limited. At the basis of artistic ambition, there is the understanding of the immense path to be accomplished in order to raise oneself to the summits of art. One must be conscious of one's insignificance, for the serious artist is above all modest. This lack of modesty on the part of so many young creators limits the scope of their art, an artist's work being unimportant when its author is self-important. To say 'To hell with it!' to art is much easier than to say 'I'm game!' to the great elders of the past. I do not believe in the *tabula rasa*; on the contrary, true novelty can only be grasped if the fundamental problems of art remain unchanged. Marcel Duchamp's schoolboy gag of calling any old object a work of art is not a fruitful starting-point for the future. This subtle and engaging man was not, as one hears it said, the Leonardo da Vinci of our age. Leonardo is famous for his art, his theories and inventions having come to little.

Even if the famous blow struck by *The Fountain* – the urinal, in other words – was merely for a point in time – and I think Marcel himself thought of it in this way – it has opened an almighty breach in the seriousness of artists' work. Eighty years on, no-one would dream of undertaking a masterpiece of history painting like Picasso's *Guernica*, no-one would be capable of the tenacious struggle of an Alberto Giacometti, yet thousands and tens of thousands of young people present an object they have bought or found lying around and proclaim it a work of art and themselves artists. The method, it's true, lends itself to accumulation, an entire room can be filled with objects in this way. Philosophical, sociological and political arguments can be advanced to justify the way in which they are laid out, but the rich blood of great art never flows there and the objects remain objects.

The general drift of contemporary art, therefore, is away from humanist art. In state art schools, directives are issued to this effect. No more studies from life, no more diplomas awarded for figurative works. This refusal on the part of the young artist to create, starting from a sheet of paper, a bare canvas, a lump of clay, something on a par with, then better or more personal than, the art of the past cuts him off from the very stuff of human existence. The works he produces will lack the essential quality – human passion in all its complexity. They will have no profound hold on people. They will no longer belong to the noble genre of painting but will be decorative. They will not be sculptures, but mere objects. To make a humanist art, you have to be able to draw a human being. The great artists applauded by the public in our day – Giacometti, Balthus, Bacon – are still masters of the human figure.

Since I'm a sculptor, the reign of the object grieves me. An object is not a sculpture. An object is simple, whereas a sculpture is symphonic. Sculpture is a vehicle for human thought. It speaks of human destiny. The inanity of an object thinking it is sculpture is plain for all to see when placed outdoors as a public work. This public display is odd when you consider that most con-temporary artists are driven by the conviction that art is a strictly personal affair. No concessions, no question of repudiating 'one's own problematics'. To establish a dialogue would be to compromise. The work is placed aristo-cratically on the public square, and it is the public, the plebs, who must do all the work of following the artist's intentions all the way back to his mind. To quote an artist who is paid handsomely for his public works: 'One must make a work which comes from the artist. One must not make works for public commission, because you fall into a sort of academicism.'

We must pull ourselves together. We cannot continue sliding down this slippery slope of intellectual stupidity. Nearly all the works we admire in the history of art were commissioned by and for either the Church or the State. None was made by the artist for his own glory. To say nothing of Egypt and ancient Greece, do people really believe that Giotto made Giottos, that Piero della Francesca painted frescoes for twentieth-century art historians, or that Michelangelo himself did not extol the Bible? Each artist scrupulously respected the need to address his public and, thanks to his talent or his genius, succeeded in making a work of art. Each artist took up the challenge that our contemporary artists decline. Pierro della Francesca, the subtle, the rigorous, the 'abstract' as he has been recently called, had first to satisfy a rural congregation. Isn't this projection towards others, moreover, the reason for our continued interest, for the still lively pleasure we take in these works of the past? The outcome is clear and the problem intact. To make a large object – or to have made, as is more often the case – and then place it before the public is not making a public sculpture unless the artist and his work are steeped from the very outset in the human dimension, in the people they have to address. The work must be half-sculpture, half-public.

This doesn't at all mean that the artistic contribution has to be minimalized or watered down. I have never sought, in my sculptures destined for the general public, to make a 'popular' art. In his desire to express things simply, Fernand Léger, though a great artist as we know, reduced his late canvases to mere flags that say very little to people. The difficulty consists precisely in pleasing everybody, young or old, educated or not, and this can only be done by complexity and multiplication and not by reduction. My fellow countryman William Hogarth spoke of 'intricacy', meaning by this a body of narrative and formal thought so richly textured that it can never quite be unravelled. As a result, the work will always be rewarding. Are we even aware any more of how much can be put into a work of art? In an age of simplification, the reply would seem to be: next to nothing. For me, the reply has always been more burdensome: everything. In an age of minimalism, I plead for a maximal art.

Another feature of contemporary art is, of course, the American stranglehold on our continent and museums. The legend would have it that, at some point in the 1950s, art crossed the Atlantic *en bloc*, making New York the absolute capital of art. The enormity of this idea dumbfounds me, as does the acceptance it has gained among the artistic establishment here in France. When the New York School was in full swing, all the great artists in France, with the exception of Matisse, were still alive and active. Artists like Giacometti, Balthus and Dubuffet were doing their best work. In England, there were Henry Moore and Francis Bacon. The art of New York had become a reality, but none of its leading figures could rival those I have cited.

Contemporary American art, shaped by the spirit of the country, by its energy and its cult of success, is an extrovert art. The artist who does not ask questions but 'lets himself go' can do so on a big scale. Which, of course, is what the Americans do. It just so happens that I saw both the big exhibition of the New York School at the Metropolitan Museum in 1969, and, when I got off the plane in Paris, the posthumous retrospective of Alberto Giacometti at the Orangerie. The difference in scale between the work of the artists who doubted nothing and the artist who doubted everything was illuminating.

The sheer size of modern American art gives it force and brutality and explains, as with a triumphant army, why it has conquered. Art, however, is a rather more complex organism in which extroversion and introversion exist side by side. The quarrel of figuration versus abstraction was sheer nonsense. True art has always been both at once, a conjunction of the real and the formal. The reality of the outside world and the artist's inner thoughts should complement one another as surely as do man and woman. Herein lies the difficulty of art, and when it is shirked by the majority of young people, in their impatience for success, the result is work that is one-dimensional and lifeless.

At the same time, a great simplicity went hand in hand with those large dimensions. To my eyes, however, the single line on a vast field of a Barnett Newman was perfectly inadequate as a work of art. And we still had minimalism ahead of us...

But there you are, the works are with us, scattered about the country and filling our museum rooms – devoid of content, very soon devoid of interest. Since they are very big and, because of the mind-boggling reputations of their authors, very expensive, we have the grievous but amusing situation whereby the moment a contemporary art museum manages, not without difficulty, to find some new exhibition space, it is immediately filled by a giant work which takes up not only all the space but the entire budget as well. The budget being public money, one marvels at these expenditures which don't give a second's pleasure to the public in question.

It is the financial and commercial side of American art, in fact, that is arguably the most disturbing of all. An essential American art, advertising, nourished Pop art and found its archangel in Andy Warhol. Warhol was initially a commercial artist, a profession that in my day was considered inferior to, and quite distinct from, fine art. This is still my point of view, of course. This talented manipulator of photographic images had taste. But taste contributes very little to a work of art. Warhol did not lift himself up to real art but has brought down the latter to the level of publicity.*

This mixture of harsh criticism and disenchantment coming from an elder like myself is justified by a fact that can't be denied: *no-one looks at this art* which here in France dignitaries promote and justify. Though it is installed in prominent places, nobody's head ever turns in its direction. We know, moreover, the sound that accompanies people visiting an exhibition of contemporary art. They may recognize with excitement the artists' names, but the sound of their steps never stops. No work arrests them in their tracks to make them look.†

The essential thing is not that the work be new. This suggests the ephemeral – a new shirt, a new girlfriend, a new car. 'Astonish me,' demanded Diaghilev of his artist friends. A disastrous request. By definition, one is only astonished once. Art must give lasting satisfaction, permanent spiritual nourishment to the spectator. The work must be riveting and permit this long, long examination. How many contemporary works respond to this imperative? Almost none. Why? Because it is not a question of contemporary art, but of the contemporary without art.

'Dossier: L'art contemporain, pour qui?', Revue des Deux Mondes, *Paris, November 1992.*

---

* There is no anti-Americanism, of course, in what I am saying. I belong to the Marlborough Gallery in New York, where I think highly of a quantity of extremely talented creators. The trouble is, on both sides of the Atlantic, it is the least interesting artists who are taken up by the specialist press and the museums.

† The masterpiece is disparaged, when in truth only the masterpiece transcends time. An art magazine, alarmed at this state of affairs and giving a flawless definition of a masterpiece as 'That which has everyone's consensus', asked an eminent curator of contemporary art if the masterpieces for the next century existed already. 'Certainly,' replied our man, throwing across the pages of the magazine images utterly limited in outlook, a heap of trivialities that have as much chance of finding their way into the hearts of men as the headlines of the evening paper have of becoming permanent literature.

Raymond Mason,
The Latin Quarter,
1988–89

The Latin Quarter

THE SCENE OF THIS SCULPTURE, IN THE HEART OF THE Latin Quarter where the rue Soufflot comes down from the Panthéon to join the Boulevard St Michel, confronts me every day as I step outside my courtyard. For more than forty years I have witnessed the march and counter-march of students on the magical inclined plane of the Boul' Mich'. As wave after wave went by, I experienced the proximity of the nearest student to my gaze, then, tunnelled between each row, a distant glimpse of the opposite pavement. This tunnelling always seemed to be a sculptural possibility.

I breathe more deeply during these moments when commerce and traffic stop and the handsome architecture is graced solely by human forms. Moreover, however grave the nature of the demonstration, it is invariably accompanied by the exhilaration of sharing a common cause.

The rows fan inwards on a perspective cone to a vanishing point behind the main façade. To suggest the persuasion of exuberant youth, a second cone outwards is formed by their multiple gazes, each directed towards the spectator, its point to his eye. This all-important frontal dimension between sculpture and onlooker links him into the action.

Whilst it is not entirely based on the famous month of May 1968, I have retained that period of the year. The plane tree thus stands for the May tree and all it implies.

Paris Architecture

WHEN I ENTERED THE BIRMINGHAM COLLEGE OF Arts and Crafts in my early teens it was to follow the course of drawing and painting, but in my first year I often stood at the entrance of the architecture class with the idea in my mind that it was there that I would like to be. However, my family had no means and architectural studies were long and costly, thus the little dream was confused and quickly confounded. When I finally encountered sculpture, this mighty subject convinced me that all I had to say could be amply said therein.

I was always to be a city-dweller and have lived in Birmingham, Oxford, London and Paris, with lengthy periods of work in Rome and, later on, a more than passing acquaintance with its great modern counterpart, New York. Buildings have been the common background of my life, as they are to lives in general, and since the activity and aspect of my fellow beings have been the main nourishment for my art it is not surprising that the scene for such comedy, tragedy and sheer normality has been an architectural setting. (I had rendered my native city of Birmingham, when a painter, with particular love for the old red brick of pre-war days, feeling no irony that my name should be Mason, although years later there would be a grim smile when I was constructing the brick-built mine of *A Tragedy in the North*.)

However, the subject of this exhibition and thus this text is specifically Parisian architecture, which I encountered for the first time exactly fifty years ago. I don't remember being stunned by it at the outset as I was by the look and the life of its inhabitants, and my early, tumultuous contacts with the Parisian art world obliged its architecture to stand back and wait in its role as a decor, sometimes all the more dimly perceived at a time when the buildings were near-black. Shortly, however, to the passion of my early youth for the Midlands was added an admiration which has grown ever since for the sweep of the Paris scene. Now, general views of a city, if they are to be rendered with some degree of precision, seem to call initially for drawing and, in those past days when I was exclusively a pen-and-ink draughtsman and a sculptor in relief, the panorama and perspective of streets was my natural subject.

It was then that I began to appreciate a man much decried, Napoleon III's prefect and town planner Baron Haussmann, who was generally supposed to have wilfully destroyed great buildings and ancient abbeys and churches when drawing up his modern Paris. Of course, this was the price of modernity and there sprang into being well-lit boulevards and cafés, without which there would have been no Impressionist movement to record it. This wholesale demolition, carving broad thoroughfares through the still medieval city, was followed up with miraculous organization by instant, wholesale construction which, by and large, is the very Paris which confronts us today. Handsome stone façades lining boulevards, avenues and streets built to a great height, being in general to six or seven storeys, right to the gates of the city, so that, even after this last war, Paris was still the highest constructed city in the world. Yet this conformity is graced by subtle modulation and, from house to house, storeys and their balconies vary in height, and the corbelling, which supports the latter, differs in shape and importance.

Nonetheless, when Gilbert Lloyd felt that my long residency and deep involvement in Paris could well produce a watercolour exhibition of Paris architecture, the matter was not so cut-and-dried as one might imagine. Not views but architecture, its specifics and construction. A single building thus, but which of so many buildings would be my choice in a city whose architects of the seventeenth and eighteenth centuries were the best in Europe?

In the great summer of '95, in a quiet street not far from home, I happened across a fine mansion I already knew. The 'House of Hercules' it used to be called, and a strong sun dappled the late-seventeenth-century façade. Its vast attic had been for ten years the studio of Pablo Picasso, and it was there that he painted *Guernica* and spent the war years. The watercolour I at once undertook was nearing completion when a lady introduced herself as the concierge of the building and, liking what I was doing, suggested that I might care to visit the great man's studio (which has remained inexplicably empty). This was a good moment, since I had known Picasso in later life and it put me into the frame of mind to tackle the nearby Cour de Rohan, whose most secret courtyard shelters on a second floor the old studio of Balthus (he and Picasso were neighbours and close friends), and this place I knew well. Then obviously I had to continue further south to the back of Montparnasse, where still stands the home and workplace of Alberto Giacometti. But only just and, as such, it is a moving reminder of an erstwhile feature of Parisian architecture, the artist's studio. I portrayed all of the original building remaining from Giacometti's day and then corrected in pencil the recent additions.

The three artists I have mentioned had left these areas scores of years previously, and yet the local inhabitants knew at once why I was painting these particular spots. I was witness to a veritable cult of these artists and, even more important, of THE artist, underlining what I have always experienced when working in the streets of Paris – a total acceptance of the artist as a noble citizen, exercising an admired and envied profession. Hence a respectful distance, and, better still, if remarks are made they are normally completely to the point, discussing the quality of the paper or the make of the paints and often couched in artistic language, like the sullen-faced waiter, when I was working near the Opéra, who, looking at my watercolour on my third visit, brightened up to say: 'It's a nice state to be worked into'; which is exactly what my painting teacher used to tell me at Birmingham art school in the late 1930s. This is only natural one can say in a city which was the world art centre for a hundred and fifty years, and the strata run indeed deep.

The first watercolour the gallery received was a charmingly domed seventeenth-century edifice with a gateway of handsome figures which, in a narrow street a hundred yards down the Boulevard Saint-Michel, had always caught my eye. Now a part of the university, it had been the amphitheatre of the Barbers and Surgeons until the late nineteenth century. Then what did I learn? That the corpse of Marat, stabbed to death by Charlotte Corday a few houses down the same street, had been laid out beneath its dome, and it was there that the painter David had made the studies for his famous picture. My second watercolour was the façade of the Luxembourg Palace as seen from the gardens. Rubens had painted his Medici cycle for this palace, and it was there that Watteau learned the technique of his favourite artist. Being a friend of the guardian, Watteau often painted the view south over the gardens towards the hill of Montparnasse. One of his most beautiful works, prior, that is, to its being restored, called *Les Charmes de la vie* is the view from the palace loggia itself peopled with Watteauesque figures. This is in the Wallace

Collection and you will recognize the distinctive ringed Florentine columns both in the picture and in my watercolour because I am sitting, as do thousands of unwitting others in the Luxembourg Gardens, precisely in his view.

After the profound links between art and place in a city like Paris comes the total affinity between sculpture and architecture. I won't disguise the fact that very often a building assumes importance for me thanks to the sculpture adorning it. The Louvre, since its general renovation (buildings always look better cleaned, paintings worse) seizes my admiration by its richly peopled façades – caryatids, trophies, garlands, cherubs – and, above all, by the line-up of historical figures who grace the terrace of the first floor, each one shaping a significant attitude, every curl of hair, every pleat of clothing rhyming forcibly with the ornamentation of the great palace. They are mainly the works of little-known sculptors of the mid-nineteenth century and, indeed, the entire Louvre facing the Tuileries gardens is Napoleon III. I have mentioned the seventeenth and eighteenth centuries as the French highspot, yet in the nineteenth they could still build – and sculpt.

It will come as a surprise to my English reader that I class as an enemy of architectural study the humble tree. A tree is rarely alone, and in summer Parisian avenues, boulevards, quaysides and any space at all are bursting with foliage, hiding the façades, softening the vistas, veiling the charming theatre in its little square. London wisely confines this to its squares and parks, but my approval goes, of course, to the Italians – no trees anywhere to mask their mighty buildings and piazzas.

A final word. This is an exhibition devoted to Parisian buildings, not to myself. My general tendency carries me towards the outer world rather than insisting that it should all come to me. When one can find pleasure in every detail of one's subject, no distortion is possible – it would be to the detriment of the detail next door. All I have done here is to select that subject from the infinitely greater one of Paris and its architecture carrying me ever further afield, which is odd since, by its beauty, it arrests my every step.

Exhibition catalogue, Marlborough Fine Art, London, 1996.

Edgar Degas

ON 16 AUGUST 1996, FINDING MYSELF IN LONDON FOR the day, I felt an imperative need, once the work that had brought me over from Paris had been done, to visit the exhibition of Edgar Degas's late work, 'Degas beyond Impressionism', then in its final week at the National Gallery. I was rather surprised by this feeling of urgency, for a few years before I had not thought it necessary to cross the Seine to see the big Degas retrospective at the Grand Palais that all my friends, some of whom had come over from England for the show, had described to me as thrilling. To be truthful, I had never been thrilled by Degas's work, with its rather modest dimensions, its meticulous technique and impeccable draughtsmanship, all devoted to capturing the butterfly flutterings of ballet. Nevertheless, I had always laughed uproariously at his mordant remarks on the artists of the Salon of his day, and I take my hat off to the man who, to be kind to his doctor, said on his deathbed: 'Thank you, doctor. I die a cured man.'

Of this particular exhibition I hadn't heard the slightest echo, apart from my friend Georg Eisler who had remarked in passing: 'Oh, marvellous, of course.' I felt less a debt towards Degas than a conviction that the late work would certainly be more daring because of his failing vision and would perhaps be my best chance of getting to grips with this important artist at last.

This calm appraisal did not take place. To enter the very first room of the assembled ninety pastel drawings and charcoal drawings and one or two oils was to lose your footing in the enchanted world of great art. I was borne aloft, losing all my bearings with Degas's work as I had hitherto known it and with the ageing painter so often described, reduced to inactivity by poor eyesight, and increasingly solitary and taciturn. These twenty years prior to that final disability when he roamed the streets of Paris were, on the contrary, years of a titanic struggle to redefine and master his art. (It is quite certain that, without this total dedication, the modern artist cannot hope to equal the masters of the past, who were raised in an artistic culture sustained by religious faith and a great tradition.)

There is only one subject, the female figure, naked or dressed. One subject, one concentrated aim. The drawing gradually moves away from the defining of contours to linear shading of form in charcoal or pastel. Degas's cross-hatching of the human form is the best thing we have seen since Rembrandt, before whom there was Michelangelo, and it is the sculptor we should think of first. The repetition of drawings, traced endlessly one from the other, is no longer a precise search for form, but on the contrary an 'imprecision' allowing the form to bulge from a myriad of lines.

Ostensibly these works depict actual women performing their more intimate daily tasks: bathing, drying their bodies, brushing their hair, sometimes with the aid of a servant, or stretching their limbs if they are dancers. The interiors surrounding them are equally simple and authentic. In fact, of course, these works were drawn or painted from models in Degas' studio. The exhibition catalogue, edited by Richard Kendall, describes the woman in the magnificent *After the Bath, Woman Drying a Leg* of 1905 as 'exclusively occupied with drying and gently rubbing her leg' and, further on, remarks that 'the blurred pastel summarizes the woman's agitation'. Elsewhere, it speaks of the *Nude on the Edge of a Bath, Drying her Legs* as 'evoking tremendous energy', where in point of fact, to maintain these difficult poses, the models do not move at all but seal themselves in what were to become monumental statements of the human form. All these late pastels of dancers and naked women are magnificent expressions of form, of how to model it and how to colour it. Degas himself said to Paul Valéry: 'It's just a way of seeing form.' Those twenty years of utterly concentrated effort enabled Degas to attain to a purity of rendered form far superior to that of his contemporary Rodin, joining hands with the sculptors of ancient Greece, telling no story, expressing no sexuality and glorifying not the beauty of the human form as such but how to describe that beauty. Art.

The works on paper are far more sculptural than the bronzes, which because of their fragility *do* conjure up movement. Superb studies of arrested motion, the latter have never interested me as sculptures on account of their small size. Conversely, when consulting the catalogue I am constantly surprised by the actual size of the pastels, which appear larger and more voluminous. And while I am on the subject, I would like to know on what authority the sculptures are deemed more suitable for an artist of failing eyesight. These figures are not at all an effect of mass with surfaces that are simple to the touch, but exact replicas of the dancers in his pastels and drawings, each presented in a complicated pose that requires eyesight every bit as keen as that needed for the drawings and executed in the very difficult and delicate medium of wax. Above all, the resulting sculpture is made to be looked at and not caressed.

The exhibition at the National Gallery in London was well hung and superbly lit. There was none of the stupidity of the Musée d'Orsay in Paris, where Degas's late pastels are invisible in their crepuscular light. (It's paper that is spoiled by light, not the pure colour of pastel, and these Parisian pages are perfectly covered.)

The curator of the exhibition, Richard Kendall, makes the unforgivable mistake of treating Toulouse-Lautrec with condescension (as did Degas himself), describing him as having 'covered Paris in posters and music-hall programmes'. Lautrec was a major artist, and none of Degas's paintings transcends a Toulouse-Lautrec masterpiece like *At the Moulin Rouge* of the Chicago Art Institute.

In a lengthy description of Degas's followers, not enough mention is made of Maillol who, when you think about it, turns out to be an important descendant of Degas in his red-chalk drawings, and above all in his synthesis of the female figure in his sculptures. Nevertheless, we should all be grateful to Kendall as the moving spirit behind this very great exhibition.

The City

I HAVE ALWAYS BEEN A CITY-DWELLER. BORN IN BIRMINGHAM, England, I have lived in Oxford, London and, since the Second World War, in Paris, with long periods of foundry work in Rome, and both professional and family ties bringing me to its modern counterpart, New York. Buildings have thus accompanied my entire life, as they do lives in general, and the 'motion' and 'emotion' of my fellow men being the nourishment of my art, it is not surprising that their scene of comedy, tragedy and simple normality has taken place in an architectural setting.

To speak of the city is to evoke its streets full of people and possibilities. One can think, write, paint and sculpt elsewhere, but living in a big town necessarily implies the factor of a considerable number of people passing daily before your gaze. Their multitude has certainly fashioned the nature of my art, which seeks to unite by compositional devices the different elements of this great canvas of activity. I always think of the crowd which surrounds me as being myself multiplied, similar to all others, which is what I tried to suggest in the central head of my sculpture *The Crowd*.

A town is multiplication by its very nature, assembled on a geographic point, and I've always made the effort of climbing its heights to understand it better. The panorama of a big city is obviously incomplete, but it's just as well, further away would be too remote from the presence of human beings, its *raison d'être*. For Paris and Rome, you only need to mount the highest of their different hills, thus Montmartre for the former and Il Pincio for the second. I had begun drawing Paris in the 1950s, when the view from the dome of the Sacré Coeur revealed the historical city surrounded by the ordered lay-outs of Baron Haussmann and when, at its gates, the city stopped, the country began.

In those days, there was a guide to describe Paris to the visitors having ventured up to the vantage-point of the dome. Each time he passed by on his circular tour he examined the progress of my drawing and finally asked me the reason for this work. I explained that it was in order to make a sculpture in low relief. Perplexity. 'Yes, yes,' I said, 'because don't you see that, viewed from this height, the city stands up vertically?' It needed several other passages for him to be convinced on the matter until, coming around once again, I heard him declare: 'And here, ladies and gentleman, is the great view of Paris, and, as you can all see, the city stands up vertically.' Amazement of his group of foreigners and provincials, who quickly concluded that the man was the victim of sunstroke. Nonetheless, it was my little friendship with this guide which gave me access to the basilica's lantern, into which none save bats and pigeons had penetrated since before the war, and the drawing which led to the sculpture was done from there.

In the days when Balthus was director of the Académie Française at the Villa Medici in Rome, on the Pincio precisely, he accommodated me on more than one occasion in the handsome bedroom, ornamented with frescoes, overlooking all Rome and which had brought the Cardinal Ferdinand de Medici face to face with Saint Peter's and the Vatican. The drawing I did from here, and a larger one from the Turkish room above, produced the sculpture in relief. Only recently, but twenty-five years later, I returned to this same room in order to do a watercolour which would enable me to colour the relief. The view had not changed at all save the vegetation of different terraces. The Eternal City!

London, flattened on its estuary, and New York on its platform are fortunately not lacking in high-rises to dominate their extent. In London I had the privilege of access to the glass clerestory surmounting Millbank Tower, alongside the Tate Gallery and the river Thames, since, although designed by the architect for the ocular pleasure of Londoners, the different firms occupying its many floors had, from the start, refused the public any right of passage. I prided myself on being, thanks to the pull of Marlborough Fine Art, the first artist to have benefited from this superb point of view. But no, Richard Morphet of the Tate corrected me by sending the photograph of the painting done by Oskar Kokoschka from the same terrace, he at one end to give importance to the Thames, I at the other in order to concentrate on Whitehall.

My sculpture of downtown New York, the first of the series, was seen from the fifty-eighth floor of the Chrysler Building, in the office of my friend William. I was thus on Forty-Second Street, and it's Lexington Avenue which hurries to lower Broadway and its skyscrapers, the Chase Manhattan and World Trade Center. As for Hong Kong, I was standing with my easel amid hundreds of tourists and Chinese children, looking down from Victoria Peak on the breathtaking architecture climbing like so many organ pipes its steep slopes. One hears so much about the banks, the business and the nightlife of this mythical city but not enough about the fact that nature there is magnificent in its beauty and the water in the bay turquoise in colour.

Early this year, my old friendship with the sculptor Eduardo Paolozzi took me to Edinburgh, his native city, for the inaugural ceremony of his museum. I was about to return to London when my fibres reminded me that I am half-Scottish by my father, that decidedly I spend too little time in this fine land and that Edinburgh is a capital city which really looks the part. I took a top room in the biggest hotel with a six-a.m. call in order to catch a glimpse of sunlight on the Castle and the Royal Mile, facing northward, and my sculpture tries to seize this brief moment.

I am intoxicated, yes, by the amplitude of the city and attracted also by the challenge of representing it artistically. The cut-through of its streets invites drawing and already suggests the sculpted relief. My initial sentiment is nevertheless a surge of affection for the men, women and children who dwell therein. If I'm fond of the city, it stems from the warm proximity of its inhabitants, just as in art I am moved by a painting which is peopled, being nourished by the quattrocento, overwhelmed by Brueghel, thinking more of Michelangelo and his Sistine, perhaps, than the solitary marbles. Impossible for the citizen that I am not to admire two artists, metropolitan men, who have triumphed over the complexity of the great town, William Hogarth and his London of the eighteenth century and, today, the American Red Grooms, confronted with the mega-city, New York.

Preface, exhibition catalogue, Marlborough Gallery, New York, Nov.–Dec. 1999.

Honoré Daumier

DAUMIER, THEN. AT THE GRAND PALAIS, IN THE LAST few weeks of the twentieth century. And ending in the new century of a world whose technological organization will certainly exceed our wildest imaginings. What could be more removed, you may well ask, from the heart-rending *petit peuple* of Honoré Daumier?

However, an enthusiastic public – as the word gets round – is present in ever-increasing numbers, going slowly from room to room, nourishing itself, getting its colour back. This art is invigorating – 'We're still alive,' we say to ourselves, 'we're still human.' In the end, this distance between Daumier and ourselves is a good thing, for it enables us to see him for the momentous artist that he was.

For my own part, what convinced me of this was not the lithographs, for the most part well known, nor the paintings, albeit rich and convincing, nor even the marvellous sculptures, but the numerous works on paper in mixed media: watercolour, blackstone, pen and ink. Never before have I seen such finely detailed drawings, nor, as a result, the human soul so exactly scrutinized. Here we are a thousand miles from caricature – an exaggeration of the visible surface and superficial, therefore – prompting us to wonder if Honoré Daumier the cartoonist ever really existed.

The moment I entered the exhibition I was confronted by the thirty-six busts of parliamentarians, sketched in clay with lightning vivacity by the twenty-four-year-old artist. The caricature of these public figures is violent, but their characterization emerges so directly from reality that the conviction grows on us that they were indeed like that. Their vivacity is greatly augmented by the fact that they are coloured, making the group unique in its time and never equalled, or imitated even, since.

I had come across these extraordinarily attractive works some twenty years earlier when visiting an exhibition soberly entitled 'Daumier' in the little Galerie Sagot-Le-Garrec, in the rue du Four in Paris. The busts filled the central space of the gallery and, struck by their importance, I had asked the director of the gallery why in the devil's name they weren't in a museum. 'But, monsieur, I could ask for nothing better,' he replied. From what my fellow artist and friend the painter Avigdor Arikha told me, he had asked the same question when visiting the exhibition and received the same reply. At the time, Arikha was working as an assessor at the Louvre, and he had immediately gone back there to alert the director of the museum, Michel Laclotte, to the necessity of purchasing these busts by Daumier. He thus set in motion the acquisition process of this collection, which was initially displayed in the Louvre before crossing the Seine to take its rightful place in the temple of nineteenth-century art, the Musée d'Orsay. Here, I have always found their presentation unsatisfactory, being broken up into small groups in small display cabinets, like the fake jewellery in the corridors of the Ritz, and it was a real joy to see them reassembled once more at the Grand Palais, admirably lit, with a juicy commentary on each parliamentarian in turn.

That works of such striking novelty should have appeared so early on in the artist's life is little short of miraculous, but no less miraculous is their survival and presence among us today. These small sculptures are made of dried clay, which normally ensures a lifespan of two or three months before crumbling into dust. Only the film of paint with which they are coloured ensures their protection. We know that Daumier changed addresses several times, and these fragile, long-nosed, high-collared figures may well have been dragged over the rough paving stones of Paris in a hand-cart. Even being purchased by his publisher, Philipon, was no guarantee that they would be preserved, since they were used as models for the caricatures, which must have necessitated, it seems to me, a good deal of handling. Nearer our time, Sagot had moulds made from them in order to cast them in bronze! Let us pay our respects to the delicacy shown by that moulder. Now that these little clays have been saved – for ever, one hopes – are they really appreciated at their true worth? I have often read fervent tributes to the psychological realism of these busts of political figures, but there is seldom any mention of their polychrome painting, and in general it is the bronzes the writer has in mind.

Daumier's colour sense is revealed to us in his paintings, of course – muted it's true, but laid on in a rich impasto. They also furnish him with a large format at last, where his hand moves with force – witness his *Ecce Homo*. Nevertheless, even if his gifts as a draughtsman are primordial, his modelling of chiaroscuro gives a sculptural force to his forms that, following on from the refined drawing of the *Etudes de Moeurs*, reveals to us to our vast pleasure that Honoré Daumier, a simple, modest man, was a great, complete artist.

Raymond Mason, *Forward*, 1991, Centenary Square Birmingham. Cast in the Haligon studios, Paris

Picture Credits

3 Raymond Mason, *The Crowd*, 1969. Bronze.

7 Raymond Mason sketching. Photo © Henri Cartier-Bresson/Magnum.

25 Henry Moore, *Family Group*, 1949. Bronze, 152.5 (60). Collection of the Henry Moore Foundation.

49 left Alberto Giacometti, *The Palace at 4 a.m.*,1932–33. Wood, glass, string, wire, 63.5 x 71.8 x 40 (25 x 28 1/4 x 15 3/4). Museum of Modern Art, New York. © ADAGP, Paris and DACS, London 2003.

49 right Raymond Mason, *House of the Soul*, 1949. Painted wood, 60 x 47 x 39 (23 5/8 x 18 1/2 x 15 3/8). Courtesy Raymond Mason.

79 Balthus, *Le Passage du Commerce-Saint-André*, 1952–54. Oil on canvas, 294 x 330 (115 3/4 x 129 7/8). Private Collection. © ADAGP, Paris and DACS, London 2003.

108 Raymond Mason and the minister André Malraux before *The Crowd*, 1968. Photo © Martine Franck/Magnum.

125 Raymond Mason, *The Departure of Fruits and Vegetables from the Heart of Paris, 28 February 1969*. Epoxy resin and acrylic paint, 310 x 315 x 135 (122 x 124 x 53 1/8). Courtesy Raymond Mason.

149 Pablo Picasso painting *Guernica*, 1937. Photo Dora Maar. © ADAGP, Paris and DACS, London 2003.

167 Raymond Mason, *Barcelona*

Tram, 1953. Bronze, 47.5 x 125 x 24.5 (18 3/4 x 49 1/4 x 9 5/8). Courtesy Raymond Mason.

212 Alberto Giacometti, *Yanaihara I*, 1960. Bronze, 43.5 (17 1/8). Private Collection. © ADAGP, Paris and DACS, London 2003.

244 Raymond Mason, *The Latin Quarter*, 1988–89. Polyester resin and acrylic, 310 x 350 x 200, 122 x 137 3/4 x 78 3/4). Courtesy Raymond Mason.

258 Raymond Mason, *Forward*, 1991. Stratified polyester resin, polyeurethane paint, 505 x 933 x 366 (198 7/8 x 367 3/8 x 144 1/8). Courtesy Raymond Mason.

All drawings are courtesy Raymond Mason.

Index